CAMBRIDGE TEXTS IN THE
HISTORY OF POLITICAL THOUGHT

The English Levellers

CAMBRIDGE TEXTS IN THE HISTORY OF POLITICAL THOUGHT

Series editors

RAYMOND GEUSS

Lecturer in Philosophy, University of Cambridge

QUENTIN SKINNER

Regius Professor of Modern History in the University of Cambridge

Cambridge Texts in the History of Political Thought is now firmly established as the major student textbook series in political theory. It aims to make available to students all the most important texts in the history of Western political thought, from ancient Greece to the early twentieth century. All the familiar classic texts will be included but the series seeks at the same time to enlarge the conventional canon by incorporating an extensive range of less well-known works, many of them never before available in a modern English edition. Wherever possible, texts are published in complete and unabridged form, and translations are specially commissioned for the series. Each volume contains a critical introduction together with chronologies, biographical sketches, a guide to further reading and any necessary glossaries and textual apparatus. When completed, the series will aim to offer an outline of the entire evolution of Western political thought.

For a list of titles published in the series, please see end of book.

The English Levellers

EDITED BY

ANDREW SHARP

University of Auckland

CAMBRIDGE
UNIVERSITY PRESS

JN
193
.E54
1998

PUBLISHED BY THE PRESS SYNDICATE OF THE UNIVERSITY OF CAMBRIDGE
The Pitt Building, Trumpington Street, Cambridge CB2 IRP, United Kingdom

CAMBRIDGE UNIVERSITY PRESS
The Edinburgh Building, Cambridge, CB2 2RU, United Kingdom
40 West 20th Street, New York, NY 10011–4211, USA
10 Stamford Road, Oakleigh, Melbourne 3166, Australia

First published 1998

Printed in the United Kingdom at the University Press, Cambridge

Typeset in Ehrhardt 9.5/12 pt [wv]

A catalogue record for this book is available from the British Library

Library of Congress Cataloguing in Publication data

The English Levellers
The English Levellers: political works/edited by Andrew Sharp.
p.   cm. – (Cambridge texts in the history of political thought)
Includes bibliographical references and index.
ISBN 0 521 62402 9
1. Levellers.   2. Political science – Great Britain – Early works to
1800.   3. Great Britain – Politics and government – 1625–1649.
I. Sharp, Andrew.   1940–   .   II. Series.
UN193.E54 1998
193.320.53′12–dc21   97–18473 CIP

ISBN 0 521 62402 9 hardback
ISBN 0 521 62511 4 paperback

Contents

Leveller texts

Contents

Introduction: the English Levellers, 1645–1649

I am sure there was no man born marked of God above another;
for no man comes into the world with a saddle on his back, neither
any booted and spurred to ride him. *An old Leveller, Richard Rum-
bold, on the scaffold in 1685 for his part in Monmouth's rebellion*

I

The Leveller movement came together in London in 1645–6. It was
the product of the civil war breakdown of authority in the English
church-state. In 1642 the two houses of parliament and their king,
Charles I, had gone to war against each other. Each had claimed that
the other was subverting the ancient legal rights and properties of the
people and the ancient, legal balance of the English constitution of
king, Lords and Commons. Each had also claimed that the other was
bent on the destruction of the true Protestant religion – the king (with
the aid of Irish rebels and the French court) by returning it to papacy,
the parliament (courting the enemy Scots) threatening its unity by
encouraging a babel of separating sects. Each side had produced and
printed numerous 'remonstrances, declarations, votes, orders, ordinances, proclamations, petitions, messages and answers' to these effects,
collected and printed for parliament in an *Exact collection*, soon to be
much used by the Levellers in their propaganda (text 1). Charles had
deserted Westminster to recruit an army in the north. By 1643 the
Scots, whose king Charles also was, and whose invasions of England
(the first in 1637) had precipitated the crisis that led to civil war, had

joined the war on the side of parliament, bound to them by the terms of the Solemn League and Covenant. On 14 June 1645 they, together with parliament's newly constituted Puritan New Model Army, defeated the main royalist armies at Naseby, and by the middle of 1646 the last of the royalist resistance had petered out with the surrender of Oxford and the flight of the king to the Scots army at Newark. Parliament, urged on by the Presbyterian leadership of the City and clergy of London, by a kirk-and-king mob and by the commissioners of the Scots in Westminster, proceeded to conclude their Presbyterian reformation of the now-defunct episcopal church and set out to reach a settlement of the constitution with the defeated king.

The king had never been easy to deal with. Over-optimistic as to his chances of political success, and obstinate in his belief in his divine right to rule his state and his church with little interference from parliament, he had proved a man with whom treaty-making was difficult. In the end he was to die for it. Matters were made more difficult for the two Houses both because of the cost of their paying for the continued presence of the Scots army on English soil, and because, although it was financially desirable to pay them off, they knew that if the Scots were allowed to dictate a settlement it would be one that preserved their own Presbyterian church and extended it into England and Wales. It would be one which made of church government a clerisy: the black-coated ministers would rule without parliamentary control. Nor would a Scots settlement be one which preserved the English from the dangers of kingly prerogative rule – of 'arbitrary government'. The Scots were indifferent to parliament's desire to bridle their king. But still, parliament had to work with them and their City allies.

It was during the last phase of what we now know as the first civil war that pamphlets by the Levellers' emerging leaders – John Lilburne, Richard Overton and William Walwyn – began to echo and support each other in a way that suggests concerted action. Each with a previous history of disaffection with the religious and secular order of the realm, the three had been mutually acquainted from mid-1645 when the London sectarian congregations came together with the more radical urban politicians to defend themselves against the Presbyterian menace. And they were already among those who suspected the commitment of the more lukewarm parliamentary politicians to a victory that would bring the king to heel. It indicates a now-firm alliance among the three emerging leaders that Walwyn's *Toleration justified,* collected by George

Thomason the bookseller on 29 January 1646 (text 2) covers much the same ground as Overton's *Divine observations upon the London ministers' letter against toleration* collected by Thomason on 24 January. Both pamphlets defend religious non-conformity against the emerging leviathan of the new Presbyterian church. By June, Lilburne, in his *Freeman's freedom*, was beginning, in the midst of airing his personal grievances, to hint at a widespread network of friends joining against the tyranny of the Lords, and of anyone else who would not allow a commoner to be tried by his equals. In his remarkable *Postscript* too (text 3), he set out the principles of natural equality and government by consent which were to mark the Leveller movement from all other radical movements of the time. *A remonstrance of many thousand citizens* (7 July 1646, text 4), written mainly by Overton and Walwyn, clearly marries the concerns of all three as to tyranny in church and state, makes of Overton's and Lilburne's cases the case of all freeborn Englishmen, and appeals to Leveller principles.

The movement produced its first of many petitions to parliament in March 1647 (text 6). Soon after that it extended its rather loose organisation from its base among members of the London sectarian congregations and radical urban politicians to the officers and soldiers of the New Model Army. The victorious army was by then deeply disaffected with a parliament intent on demobbing many of the men and sending the rest to Ireland, where war had continued unabated since 1638. On 29 March, parliament, intent on reaching a Presbyterian church settlement and a traditionalist constitutional settlement which would stick with both the king and the Scots, had declared its 'dislike' of the Army's petitioning it on grievances as to its future composition and deployment, as to arrears of pay, and as to indemnity for acts carried out during war. By April, Lilburne and Edward Sexby were organising the election of 'agitators' by the New Model regiments of horse. Army dissatisfaction grew. In May the London militia was taken by parliament out of sectarian control and given into more conservative hands. The New Model officers until then had done their best to channel the dissatisfaction of their men to avoid the discussion of political and religious matters; but now they themselves were unhappy not only over military but also over political matters. Lieutenant-General Oliver Cromwell and his son-in-law Commissary-General Henry Ireton in particular were ready to enter the arena of high politics and join in negotiations with king, City, Scots and parliament.

In June the New Model seized the king from the Scots at Holdenby House in Northamptonshire and began a series of rendezvous, each nearer London and Westminster, and each carrying the threat of military force. As they manoeuvred, they put out a series of declarations as to their intentions, most famously in a declaration of 14 June: 'We were not a mere mercenary army, hired to serve any arbitrary power of state, but called forth and conjured by the several declarations of parliament to the defence of our own and the people's just rights and liberties. And so we took up arms in judgement and conscience to those ends, and have so continued them.' The officers needed the men, and in July the Army held its first General Council, in which officers and agitators (now elected from an increased number of regiments) discussed their common concerns. By August, with a march on London, the New Model brought to heel the more royalist and Presbyterian of the parliamentarians. The leading Presbyterian MPs went into exile. But the threat of counter-revolution, not least by the Presbyterians' opponents in parliament – the so-called 'Independents' – remained; and so therefore did the officers' need of their men. In this circumstance, the Leveller movement entered high politics, operating from organisational bases in the New Model as well as in London. 'New agents' of the Army, rather more Leveller and rather less simply disaffected soldiers than the more established 'agitators', were elected by five regiments; they met the London Levellers, and in October the combination of civilian and army Levellers produced *The case of the army truly stated*. The pamphlet was long and rambling, as bitter against the New Model officers for their prevarication and backsliding as against parliament, full of quotations of the New Model's declarations and engagements (cf. text 13) – all of them broken or twisted to the officers' corrupt interests. It nevertheless contained, along with its military complaints, the germ of *An agreement of the people* (text 7) which Cromwell and the officers, irritated as they were, showed themselves prepared to discuss in the General Council held at Putney from 28 October until 9 November (text 8).

Leveller influence was, however, already waning. Mutiny was breaking out, led, in Cromwell's view, 'by those not of the Army who drive at levelling and parity'. The mutinies were crushed, the officers ceased to listen, and the 'new agents' were heard no more. Leveller organisation nevertheless continued to flourish. Their newspaper, *The Moderate*, began publication in January 1648. They continued to petition and agitate in London and Westminster (text 9). But they were not again to be influential until the winter of 1648–9. Again the source of their leverage was – and could only be – the New Model. The Levellers co-operated with the Army in the second civil war of May to August 1648 against the king, the Scots and disaffected parliamentarians; and the play of politics from September to the end of January 1648–9 again made them necessary allies of the officers. But in the spring and summer of 1649 it was decided that the movement must be crushed. The officers, having carried out a revolution which began with their purging the Commons (in December 1648) and which continued with their abolishing kingship and the House of Lords (January to March 1649), were chary of going further. They were, moreover, now both angry and worried about Leveller mutiny in the ranks. In March of 1649, in the course of being questioned as to his authorship of seditious books, Lilburne heard Cromwell strike the Council table and cry 'I tell you, you have no other way to deal with these men but to break them in pieces.'

Cromwell succeeded in doing just that, and not simply because he had the military force to put down subsequent mutinies. In fact the movement was already coming apart at the seams. The sectarian congregations deserted it, wooed by the emerging régime with a promise of religious toleration. And the men of the New Model, who had always tended to dwell on the problems generated by their military and logistical problems rather than on the ills of the commonwealth, were now becoming more professionalised: becoming soldiers rather than citizens. Except for Lilburne, the Leveller leadership saw the writing on the wall. They could not continue to act without an organisation and without a popular constituency. *The remonstrance of many thousands of the free people of England* (September 1649), the 'death rattle of the party' according to Joseph Frank (see bibliographical note, p. xxxiii) claimed 98,000 signatures; Lilburne continued active and elicited support from the London crowd in treason trials of 1649 and 1653; Marchamont Nedham, the brilliant Commonwealth propagandist, still found it worthwhile to attack the Levellers in *The case of the commonwealth stated* in May 1650; the odd Leveller pamphlet appeared until the restoration of the monarchy in 1660; James Harrington disapproved of them on theoretical republican grounds later in the 1650s; old Levellers reappeared in the troubles of the 1680s; but the movement effectively died in a series of failed mutinies in 1649 (text 13). And, to exaggerate only slightly, it stayed dead in human memory until the 1880s when historians began to take an interest in them.

No historian has really believed that the Levellers ever stood a chance of success. Yet the curious thing is that they have been interested in them not so much as underdogs – as the voice of the inarticulate masses or of the emerging artisans, local merchants and small landholders of a pre-industrial society, doomed to defeat – though there is a bit of this. Much more often and much more emphatically they have been discussed as if they were in a way victorious: as men and women 'before their time' who 'anticipated' future developments in their writings, in their organisation and in their activity. In a word, they were 'democrats' – at least *some* kind of democrats. They have been called 'radical' democrats, 'liberal' democrats, 'social' democrats, 'constitutional' democrats, 'Christian' democrats, 'petty bourgeois' (and 'bourgeois') democrats. For English historians, they stand in line with the Wilkites of the 1760s, the radical reformers of the 1770s and 1780s and the 1820s, and with the Chartists. Historians from the USA, from Russia, central Europe, Italy and France have produced appropriately modified versions of where the Levellers stand in *their* democratic (and liberal, and constitutionalist, and republican, and socialist) traditions. And they take their place as minor figures in the canon of the history of western political thought as precursors of Locke. They may have been defeated at the time but their names and ideas live.

This interpretative situation can be explained as a function of the success of democratic ideas over the last hundred or so years. Defeat in 1649 began to look like success when democratic ideas became a touchstone for historians' interest and commendation. But more recently (in the 1980s and 1990s) our more fervent historicist sensibility has made the situation seem less clear. We can see why historians became interested in the Levellers. We can also, we think, further see that that interest has made the Levellers seem to us other than they were: *made* them seem democrats to us, when in historically located fact, they were not – at least not very straightforwardly. Thus David Wootton, their latest historian, having told the historiographical story and much more of the historical story than I have just related, and adding correctly that the Levellers were seldom called 'democrats' at the time, that the word 'democrat' had totally different connotations then, and that none of its modifiers as used by the historians existed, thinks that the description of the Levellers as democrats can be highly misleading. The best we can do is to call them 'Leveller' democrats, describe as best we can what they were like, and take care to distinguish their kind of democracy from all others.

My own view is that it is not all that misleading to describe them as liberal democrats. But they were such in conditions where to be one, for those with the temperament, was a standing temptation to rebellion and a mutiny. They exemplify the difficulties of being democratic in impossible circumstances.

II

Much Leveller activity occurred in print. The three leaders were all by 1646 veteran pamphleteers. They were soon to become experienced petitioners as well. And they were articulate speakers, with others like John Wildman and the agitators at Putney who faced the Army officers in debate on the form the English constitution should take. In these verbal modes they continually claimed that they sought to persuade others to their views, not to impose them through force of arms: their idea was, as famously put by Walwyn, to 'get victory on the understandings of men'. They set out to persuade their contemporaries of four things: that there must be a programme of reform in the church-state; that there should be a new constitution of authority designed to carry out and preserve those reforms; that the conditions were such that this new constitution should, could and must be instituted; and (finally) that the fundamental jural facts about being human justified the reforms, the constitution and its institution.

Their programme of reform varied somewhat over time (texts 6, 7, 9, 12). It always included reform of the legal system, both criminal and civil. The law should be put into English, simplified and changed. There should (for instance) be no imprisonment for debt; the prison system should be made more humane; punishments should fit crimes and capital punishment should be reserved for murder and treason. Procedure too should be reformed. Like the substantive law, it should be put into English; there should be no commitment without a warrant specifying the crime and nominating at least two witness-accusers; there should be no answers on interrogatories; cases should be heard by juries in the localities; the hearing of cases should be speeded up; the fees of judges, magistrates, lawyers and jailers should be limited and restrained. Most of the rest of their programme entailed changing the law, too: matters like the dissolution of the Merchant Adventurers and similar monopoly companies which acted in restraint of trade; the removal of legal immunities and privileges from groups and corporations (including the House of Lords and its members) based on 'tenure, grant, charter, patent, degree or birth'; freedom of religious speech and worship; the abolition of tithes; the provision of 'powerful means to keep men, women and children from begging and wickedness'. And there was a whole range of pressing but obviously more transient policies that would need reforming, again using legislative means: there should be no impressment into armed forces; there should be indemnity for soldiers' acts in the exigencies of war; there should be succour from the commonwealth for the widows and orphans of soldiers; there should be no liability for political actions during the wars; and so on.

But some reforms were so fundamental, and so contradictory to existing arrangements for law-making, that to understand their programme as one calling only for acts of legislation from an enlightened parliament, even without the king, was impossible. Theirs was rather a programme for massive constitutional reform. England had at this time a 'mixed monarchy' the crucial feature of which was that no statute could be made without the mutual consent of king, Lords and Commons. Parliament when at war with the king had invented the doctrine that the two Houses could in emergency make ordinances without the king; but when in 1646 and 1647 the Levellers proposed that the 'negative voices' of the king and Lords should be abolished and the Commons declared 'the supreme power', they were clearly leaving the realm of policy dispute and entering that of fundamental constitutional reform.

In what manner and through what channels could they operate to bring about these great changes? The traditional answer was humbly and by petition to parliament. The Levellers tried that in a campaign in 1647 only to see their petitions condemned and burned by the common hangman (text 6). Their problem was partly that they chose to petition the Commons as the 'supreme authority' and refused to recognise the Lords. Neither House could stomach that insult to the ancient constitution and to the individual rights of the Lords which were sustained by it. It was also that the Levellers seemed to be *demanding* unpalatable policy changes from a body that felt itself to be the repository of traditional authority, and knew that authority did not bow to demands. It was, after all, a convention mainly of well-to-do country gentlemen, together with lesser numbers of prosperous international merchants, courtiers and professional men; and it felt little but contempt mixed with fear for those of the lower ranks: the apprentices, tradesmen, tub-preachers and the odd not-so-distinguished gentleman who made up the Leveller 'riots'. So in the spring of 1647, the Levellers began to argue that if parliament would not act for the people, then the New Model should.

The change in allegiance had this to commend it: the New Model was 'no mere mercenary Army'. Authority was not extinct in England; it had merely migrated. The many Army declarations had shown it to be not only authorised by parliament but to be intent on acting according to parliament's own declarations which ('in the days of its virginity') had called Englishmen to oppose their king. The Levellers, like almost all other Englishmen, were eager to depict themselves as authorised in what they did by a superior power. That is why they had at first appealed to the Commons, and that is why, when they were rejected by the Commons, they proceeded to search for allies in the New Model.

Having found those allies, it soon emerged (to their allies' dismay) that not only would they have particular reforms, together with a reform of the constitution. They would also reconstitute authority anew in England by means of an 'agreement of the people', and not rely on the authority of the New Model any more than on that of parliament. At the *Agreement*'s heart would be a single, supreme legislative body, a 'representative of the people'. When the Army leaders first heard of their proposals (texts 7 and 8), the Levellers claimed that every adult male should have a vote in electing 'the Representative' and be eligible for membership of it; and they insisted that the constituencies be made more evenly relative to population size. At Putney, Cromwell, chairing a famous General Council attended by civilian as well as military Levellers in October 1647, was told by Colonel Thomas Rainborough:

> really I think that the poorest he that is in England hath a life to live as the greatest he; and therefore truly, sir, I think it's clear that every man that is to live under a government ought first by his own consent to put himself under that government; and I do think that the poorest man in England is not at all bound in a strict sense to that government that he hath not had a voice to put himself under.

They were indeed to modify this programme of universal male suffrage and not all Levellers may have espoused it anyway, but whatever its modifications from earlier on (texts 9, 12, 13) their proposal for a supreme Representative of the People still meant that the franchise would be vastly extended, that there would be no (or a weakened) king and no House of Lords, and that men would be eligible to be legislators who previously had not even been allowed the vote.

This was clearly a programme that was democratic in the sense of expanding the universe of those who might make important decisions – especially taken together with the proposals that justice should be done in the localities (much of it by juries), and that magistrates like JPs should be locally elected. It was also a liberal programme, for the *Agreement* insisted that certain powers should be 'reserved' to 'the people' as matters for individual and not governmental decision. The Representative would not be empowered to proceed against anyone if there was no law forbidding them doing what the proceeding concerned; it might not grant trading monopolies; it might not raise money by excise and customs. Most importantly perhaps, the Representative might not allow tithes for the maintenance of a state church, and it might not enforce forms and expressions of religious worship.

It was in one sense less important that they had to insist, against false accusations, that they were not Levellers: 'it shall not be in the power of any representative in any wise to . . . level men's estates, destroy propriety or make all things common' (texts 9, 11, 12). But underlying the accusation to which they were forced to reply in this way was the fundamental fact that their formula of governing authority was democratic. Legitimate authority, they held, could be created and sustained only by 'the people'. It was not inherent in law or customary social and political arrangements; no man or institution could govern without the people's original and continuous agreement. This was precisely the point of having an 'agreement of the people'; and the point of their liberal-democratic arrangements was both to capture what they took to be what the people would currently agree to, and to protect that agreement against its undermining by self-interested rulers.

Cromwell, whose closest adviser, his son-in-law Commissary-General Henry Ireton, was to produce a rather similar *Agreement of the people* in early 1649 (see footnotes on pp. 141–5), put his finger on the problem. It was not so much the programme that was the problem for the officers: they were in fact still dealing, together with opposition, 'independent' MPs and lords, with Charles; and they were contemplating in some *Heads of proposals* biennial parliaments, a reformed distribution of seats, a cropping of the Lords' powers, the removal of monopolies and excise, even control of the king's veto in a number of areas. It was rather the authority of the Levellers to *make* the proposals which was at issue:

> How do we know that if whilst we are disputing these things another company of men shall gather together and they shall put out a paper as plausible perhaps as this? I do not know why it might not be done by that time you have agreed on this – or got hands to it if that be the way. And not only another, and another, but many of this kind. And if so, what do you think the consequence would be. Would it not be confusion? Would it not be utter confusion?

It *would*, according to Cromwell, be confusion. According to him (no less than to the Levellers themselves over much of their careers) there must be a constituted authority to decide what the settlement should be; but also, according to him (and here the Levellers could not agree), 'the people' had no authority in themselves to change the settled modes of proceeding. Only constituted powers could do that. The people could only petition them and abide by their decisions. This is why he supported parliament as long as he could; this is why he stood by while it was purged rather than dissolved; this is why he supported all attempts to clothe the successive interregnum regimes in the cloak of traditional authority. He 'very much cared', he said, that there should be king, Lords and Commons, and would only move against them if he saw God's clearly manifested providence pronouncing against them.

It emerged that neither he nor the senior officers nor the bulk of the Army would adopt the Levellers' platform, at least not at the Levellers' instigation. The General Council was dissolved. Cromwell and Ireton continued to work to reach a settlement for as long as they could with parliament – and worse (though the Levellers from time to time were monarchists) – the king. Mutiny at Ware followed on 15 November 1647 and the Leveller movement had its first martyr, Richard Arnold. Leveller propaganda now held the officers in turn to be 'vile apostates', who had, like parliament, 'betrayed their trusts' and broken those solemn engagements, which, taken with the common soldiers and promulgated to the people, constituted the only bonds of political authority that existed once the kingdom had been deserted by king and parliament. Lilburne now held that 'all magistracy in England was broke by the Army, who . . . by their swords reduced us into the original state of chaos and confusion wherein every man's lusts become his law, and his depraved will and forcible power his judge and controller'. In *The bloody project* of August 1648, even the mild-mannered and silken-tongued Walwyn is to be observed appealing to the 'soldiers and the people' against 'king, parliament, great men in the City and Army' – those who 'have made you the stairs by which they have mounted to honour, wealth and power. . . But the people's safety is the supreme law; and if a people may not be left without a means to preserve itself against the king, by the same rule they may preserve themselves against the parliament and Army too.'

The Levellers were to work with the officers again, and they were to moderate their claim that England was now reduced to a state of nature. But in 1649, after the Army had finally decided it could not work with the king and an unpurged parliament – after it had executed the king and set up a commonwealth on the basis that 'the people are, under God, the original of all just power' – Lilburne told the judge at his trial for treason in 1649 that there was 'no magistracy in England either upon principles of law or reason'. He was asking of Cromwell what Cromwell had asked of them in 1647: what gave a few men the right to constitute authority in England? It certainly could not be simply that they had swords in their hands, though subsequent Leveller activity and doctrine (text 13), while it denied that proposition in so far as the New Model officers held the sword, did not deny its use to an armed common soldiery.

At this point we must ask who the Levellers thought had the right not only to speak about and complain about the organisation of magistracy, but also to constitute, to be members of, to oversee, even to overpower governments, and why. Their answer throughout their careers was clear enough but in no way capable of being institutionalised. They believed that God ordained, and God's creation – nature – displayed, the existential equality of authority among human beings, their natural right to sustain and defend themselves and their natural duty to defend and succour others. Such creatures were duty-bound to God, and through God to others, to erect and sustain political society. The only way they could constitute authority was by their consent; and the only proper authority – the only authority which they could constitute and subsequently obey – would be one which they in fact continually consented to and which acted as the trustee of each and every one of them for the purpose of attaining the common weal. The men who held magistracy could be only those committed to those ends. This is a highly abstract summary of what appears throughout their pamphlets, most notably in the Postscript to Lilburne's *Freeman's freedom* (text 2) and in the first pages of Overton's *Arrow against all tyrants* (text 5). As for Walwyn, his writings breathe the doctrine not only of toleration but of practical Christianity demanded by God's love: 'love makes you no longer your own but God's servants'. One has a duty to defend the 'truth' – which is the monopoly of no man or set of men – and a duty to defend one's 'brother and neighbour from oppression and tyranny'. One's right – and the Levellers' right – to speak as one did, derived from one's Christian duty to seek and speak God's truth. One's individual right to act derived from one's individual duty to God, and through him to all one's fellow creatures. (As Milton put it in *Areopagitica* (1644), some duties to God were simply not 'dividual'.) The constitution of magistracy and the policies of magistracy must express those rights.

III

But no-one was capable of putting these ideals into practice. 'I did not dream', wrote one of the MPs who had in fact begun parliament's practice of appealing to 'the people' in 1640, 'that we should remonstrate downwards, tell stories to the people'. And at the restoration of kingship in 1660, Harrington, author of *Oceana* (1656) and other republican writings, was under threat of his life because of 'some . . . saying that I, being a private man, had been so mad as to meddle with politics', and asking 'what a private man had to do with government?' It had indeed emerged in 1640 that 'private men' could speak: from then onwards, pamphlets and newsbooks poured from the presses in unprecedented numbers. But it was impossible that 'the people' should exert significant political, let alone constitutive power. It was not that there was not a 'people': the English knew who they were and the geographical boundaries of their realm. It was rather that too few believed like the Levellers in a God-ordained equality which had political implications. Most, and not just royalists, believed in inequality. (Not even the Levellers, among whose number there were very active women, could imagine women with political rights of any kind.) Too few believed that God's law, natural law or equity intimated any other arrangements than the traditional legal arrangements which defined and sustained not only the constitution of authority, but the liberties and properties of the people. In a time of civil war and unsettlement too, the ideal of a permanent, unchallengeable order was displayed by all sorts. By 1647, and with stronger reason in 1649, the country was predominantly restorationist. Those who held out against a restoration of kingship and the traditional ways did so largely on the negative grounds that they could not trust Charles to keep his word and not reintroduce prerogative rule. So the fact was that it would have been impossible to base a settlement on an Agreement of the People.

The whole social order in the church-state – imitated throughout the counties, towns, boroughs and hamlets, as at the political centre at Westminster – was buttressed by belief in a divinely ordained series of gradations between all things that existed: from God through the ranks of angels, humans, animate and inanimate creation. Anglican cate-chismal teaching had reminded the congregations of the parishes of England that the Fifth Commandment, 'honour thy father and thy mother', provided ('honour' being translated into 'obey' at the appro-priate points) a pattern of subordination throughout society. It com-manded subordination not only to parents, but to social superiors in general: to teachers, ministers, elders – and above all to ruling magis-trates. Romans 13, 'Obey the powers that be, for they that resist shall bring unto themselves damnation', was a prescribed Anglican text for times of trouble. And the Presbyterian successor to the old episcopal church thought no differently. 'What', asked the *Larger catechism*, put out by the Westminster Assembly of Divines in 1648 as part of a refor-mation of church government ordered by parliament, 'is the honour inferiors owe to superiors?'

> ANSWER. The honour which inferiors owe to their superiors is all due reverence in heart, word, and behaviour; prayer and thanksgiv-ing for them; imitation of their virtues and graces; willing obed-ience to their lawful commands and counsels; fidelity to [and] defence and maintenance of their persons and authority according to their several ranks and the nature of their places; bearing with their infirmities, and covering them with love; that so they may be an honour to them and their government.
>
> QUESTION. What are the sins of inferiors against their superiors?
>
> ANSWER. The sins of inferiors against their superiors are all neg-lect of duties toward them; envying at, contempt of, and rebellion

against their persons and places and their lawful counsels, commands and corrections; cursing, mocking, and all such refractory
and scandalous carriage as proves a shame and dishonour to them
and their government.

It was this set of injunctions, expressing so eloquently the practical
beliefs of all but a few pockets of dissidents, that the Levellers challenged. Of England's five million or so people, perhaps only $2\frac{1}{2}$ per cent
were members of families among the directive minority. The rest were
born to be ruled. To attack the existing powers was to be an anarchist.

As to the traditional constitution of authority and rights, both royalist and parliamentarian had similarly claimed to be fighting for it.
Before the first civil war, parliament's *Protestation* of May 1641 had
required an oath not only to 'maintain and defend, as far as I lawfully
may with my life, power and estate . . . the true reformed Protestant
religion expressed in the doctrine of the Church of England against all
popery and popish innovation within this realm', but also to 'maintain
and defend his majesty's royal person and estate, as also the power of
and privilege of parliaments [and] the lawful rights and liberties of the
subjects'. Charles's *Answer to the nineteen propositions* (June 1642) was
uncontradicted by the parliamentarians in speaking of the constitution
as 'ancient, equal, happy, well-poised', one in which the separate and
shared powers of king, Lords and Commons, were balanced in such a
way as to protect the subjects' liberty and property. The Solemn
League and Covenant bound the parliamentarians and the Scots to fight
not only for a 'reformed Protestant religion', but 'to preserve the rights
and privileges of parliaments, and the liberties of the kingdoms, and to
preserve and defend the king's majesty's person and authority'. And
the Long Parliament – 'long' because it had first met in November
1640 and was not to finally be dissolved until 1660 – was to keep saying
the same thing, even during the second war, when it fought now not
only against Charles and old royalists, but against its old allies the
Scots, and against many of the directive minority in the deeply disaffected counties. On 28 April 1648 the parliament roundly declared that
it would not alter 'the fundamental government of the kingdom by
king, Lords and Commons'.

It was for challenging this God-ordained order, worked out in its
legal detail in long tradition, that the Levellers were given their name –
according to Lilburne, at Putney by Henry Ireton. Ireton's idea in

'christening' them 'Levellers' (an idea also fathered on Cromwell and on Charles I) was doubtless to call up images of Watt Tyler and Jack Cade, of a peasantry that would destroy enclosures. They would level everything. There would be no government, no property, no family. All would be held in common. Though it was an unfair description, the name stuck, and the tendency of the insults was anyway not new. They had been reviled, like Paul and Silas in Acts 17, as among those who 'have turned the world upside down'. They were compared with the 'false teachers' of 2 Timothy 3: 'lovers of their own selves, covetous, boasters, proud, blasphemers, disobedient to parents, unthankful . . . without natural affection, trucebreakers, false accusers, incontinent, fierce, despisers of those that are good, traitors, heady, highminded'. They were men who led the congregations full of 'itching ears' away from 'sound doctrine'.

They could not reply by calling themselves democrats any more than they could call themselves Levellers: to call themselves that would be to join in insulting themselves. The vocabulary was available but the connotations – anarchy and liberty – would not have helped them. *We* are, it has recently been said, 'all democrats now'. *They* had no series of shibboleths to which to appeal and had to content themselves with making specific proposals and calling themselves such names as 'the Godly', the 'well-affected', 'many thousands earnestly desiring the glory of God, the freedom of the commonwealth and the peace of all men', 'ingenuous well-minded people', 'divers well-effected citizens', the 'honest non-substantive soldiers' and so on. They could not call themselves democrats, and they could not call up that strength of public opinion necessary to constitute an armed force.

So when will democracy not work, if the Levellers' fate is an example to us? Leaving aside cases where it is doubtful whether a 'people' exists at all, democracy will not work when, if it is to be a viable option, it requires a breakdown of traditional, unequal, authority; and when that option (as it will be) is so foreign to the imaginations of the political community at large that it will be rejected out of hand. We in the West might well take the fate of the Levellers as seriously as we have taken their shining example.

Chronological table

1625 Charles I succeeds to the throne
1628 The Petition of Right
1629–40 Charles rules without parliaments
1635 Ship-money levy extended to all counties
1637–40 Imposition of English prayer book on Scotland unites the Scots in two Bishops' wars against their neighbour

1630 Lilburne apprenticed in London

1638 Lilburne tried, whipped and imprisoned by Star Chamber. He begins to publish anti-episcopal tracts describing his sufferings

1640–2 A period of reform and drift to civil war
1640 The Short Parliament (April–May)
1640 The Long Parliament called (November)
1640–1 Impeachment and attainder of Stafford
1641 *The protestation* (May); Acts against dissolving the Long Parliament; for the Abolition of Star Chamber, High Commission, ship-money and other prerogative taxes; against

1640–1 Attacks on bishops and the established church

1641 The 'paper war' between king and parliament begins in December. Religious controversy continues. Walwyn's first (and tolerationist) tract: *A new petition for papists* (1641)

ecclesiastical innovations (May–September). *The Grand remonstrance* (December)

1642 King's attempted arrest of 5 MPs and a lord (Jan.); bishops removed from Lords (Feb.). The Militia Ordinance (March) makes possible the calling of a parliamentary army

1642 A controversy as to control of the militias of England and Wales widens into a royalist parliamentarian controversy as to the location and nature of a subject's obedience. Edward Coke's *Second part of the institutes of the laws of England* published

June 1642 Henry Parker, *Observations upon some of his majesties late answers and expresses*

July 1642 Parliament votes to raise an army

August 1642–6 First civil war
August 1642 Charles raises his war standard at Nottingham
October 1642 Edgehill. The first pitched battle

March 1643 Husband's *Exact collection of all remonstrances* published. (Parliament's *Book of declarations*)

1643 The Westminster Assembly of Divines meets (July); The Solemn League and Covenant (September). The English and Scots allied
1644 Parliamentary victory at Marston Moor (July) not pushed home politically or militarily. Cromwell quarrels with earl of Manchester. Emergence of Independents and Presbyterians in parliament
1645 The Self-denying Ordinance (April). Military command and membership of parliament to be incompatible. The New Model takes the field (May). New Model victory at Naseby (June)

August 1645 Lilburne, *'On the 150th page'*

November 1645 Presbyterian alliance among Westminster Assembly, City clergy and municipal government

1646–8 A period of negotiation between Charles, the Army, parliament and City

January 1646 Walwyn, *Toleration justified*

March 1646 London independents and sectaries begin an alliance

June 1646 Charles surrenders Oxford and proceeds to surrender to the Scots at Newark

June 1646 Lilburne, *Freeman's freedom*

July 1646 Overton and Walwyn, *A remonstrance of many thousand citizens.*

December 1646 London returns a Presbyterian Common Council

January 1647 The Scots depart from English soil, leaving the king in parliament's hands

March 1647 Parliament begins to move to reduce the size of the New Model and to send men to Ireland

10–14 March 1647 The levellers' *Large petition* subscribed

26 March Army petitions come to the eyes of parliament

29 March 1647 Parliament's 'Declaration of dislike' of the New Model's proceedings

April 1647 Lilburne and Sexby co-operating in election of agitators in the New Model regiments.

April–May A series of declarations from agitators

May 1647 London given control of its own militia

June 1647 Army begins series of rendezvous, ever nearer London

June 1647 Cornet Joyce removes Charles from parliament's hands at Holdenby House, and brings him near the Army, to Hampton Court

5 June The Army's *Solemn Engagement* not to disband

14 June The Army's *Declaration* charges 11 Presbyterian MPs and London

treasurers. Lilburne and
Overton attack army officers
16–28 July 1647 First General
Council of the Army

July–August 1647 The New
Model threatens London and
parliament. Fairfax made
Commander-in-Chief of all
armies; trained bands removed
from corporation control;
counter-revolutionary petitions
and violence in London and
Westminster; parliament
resolves to bring king to London
and restore trained bands to the
municipality. 27 July Speaker of
Lords, together with 57 MPs
and 8 Lords, seeks refuge with
the New Model at Bedford.
Army marches on London,
enters at Southwark on 4
August. Restores MPs. 11 MPs
withdraw from parliament

September–October 1647
Cromwell makes overtures to
Lilburne in the Tower. New
agents of the Army meet
levellers at the Mouth
(Aldersgate) and the Windmill
(Coleman Street); Wildman and
Petty emerge as intermediaries
between the agents and the
London Levellers. The meetings
continue throughout November
21 October 1647 *Case of the
army* is brought to the General
Council at Putney
23 October Robert Lilburne's
regiment refuses to march to

Newcastle and proceeds by degrees to march to Ware under Capt. Lieutenant William Bray
28 October 1647 *An agreement of the people*
28 October–9 November General Council of the Army meets at Putney
15 November 1647 Mutiny suppressed at Corkbush Field near Ware
25 November 1647 A Leveller petition of the same day results in 5 Levellers being imprisoned. In the Commons Cromwell attacks those 'not of the Army' who 'drive at levelling and parity'
15 December *Rapprochement* between Army grandees and agents. Approaches to the king by the grandees will cease. But Walwyn publishes *Putney projects* later on 30 December, attacking Cromwell and Ireton

January–April 1648 Parliament's 'vote of no addresses' to the king. Royalist rioting in London and the provinces. New Model reduced from 44,000 to 24,000 men. Independents attempt to negotiate with Charles
25 April 1648 In the midst of London unrest, stirrings in Wales and Essex, and hearing that Scots are about to raise an army, the officers of the New Model resolve to bring Charles Stuart, 'that man of blood', to account

1648 January–February Leveller London organisation flourishes – outliers in Bucks., Oxford, Cambs. and Rutland. *The Moderate*, a Leveller newspaper, begins publication

May–August 1648 Second civil war

July–August Polarisation between war and peace parties in London. Scots defeated at Preston 17 August. Colchester falls to Fairfax 27 August

1648–9 The Army settles a Commonwealth

September Radical petitioning against a personal treaty with the king

November Parliament refuses to debate Army's *Remonstrance*

6 December Pride's Purge. Rule of the Rump Parliament begins

26 December 1648 Commons begin to discuss whether Charles should be tried

4 January Parliament declares: 'the people are, under God, the original of all just power'

Levellers co-operate with Army during second civil war

11 September 1648 Leveller *Humble petition of divers well-affected persons*. Signed by 40,000 October–December 1648. At least 17 petitions to Fairfax supporting petition of 11 September

29 October 1648 Thomas Rainborough assassinated

16 November Ireton's Army *Remonstrance* calling for justice on the king, supporting *Agreement* and *Petition* of 11 September

November–December 1648 Negotiations among Levellers, City Independents, army officers and 'gentleman Independents' at the Nag's Head (London), at Windsor, and in early December at Whitehall

Mid-December Walwyn withdraws from Leveller activity, though he will write defences of himself until June or July 1649, and will join in the *Agreement* of May. London Leveller organisation in disarray

8–11 January 1649 Freedom of conscience debated in General Council at Whitehall. Lilburne and Wildman present, until a disgusted Lilburne leaves for Durham

20 January 1649 The 'officers agreement' presented to parliament. Never discussed

20–27 January 1649 Trial of Charles I. Executed 30 January

1649–53 The Commonwealth

6 February 1649 House of Lords voted 'useless and dangerous'

February Lilburne returns to London from Durham

29 February Lilburne, *England's new chains discovered*

3–6 March Eight troopers tried for petitioning; made to ride the wooden horse in the Palace Yard. Now the Levellers' military friends begin to desert them

28 March Arrest of Lilburne, Overton, Prince and Walwyn for *The second part of England's new chains discovered*. Levellers deserted by independent congregations, notably the Baptists. Cromwell swears he will 'break them'

14 April Lilburne, Overton, Prince and Walwyn, *A manifestation*

Late April–May Army unrest and mutiny in London. Robert Lockyer executed. Unrest in provinces, especially around Bristol and between Banbury and Oxford

1 May *An agreement of the free people of England*

14–15 May Mutiny crushed at Burford

7 June 1649 Day of thanksgiving for Leveller defeat. Levellers' sea-green colours are no longer radical chic

July 1649 Overton's last known publication: *A picture of the Council of State*
29 August *The young men's and apprentices' outcry*
21 September *The remonstrance of many thousands of free people of England* claims 98,000 signatures
24–28 October Lilburne's first trial for treason
8 November Lilburne, Overton, Prince and Walwyn released. Walwyn returns to his trade as a merchant and takes no more part in Leveller activity
December 1651 Walwyn, *Juries justified*
January 1652 Lilburne banished
May 1652 Walwyn argues free trade to the Committee for Trade and Foreign Affairs

April 1653 Rump Parliament dissolved by Cromwell. 'Barebone's' parliament

May–August 1653 Lilburne returns, condemned for treason, imprisoned (27 August) on the Isle of Jersey and later at Dover

1654–8 The Protectorates of Oliver Cromwell and his son, Richard

1650s Walwyn's interests turn to medicine
1655 Lilburne becomes a quietist Quaker
1657 Lilburne dies

1660 Restoration of monarchy

1681 Walwyn dies

Bibliographical note

1 Introductory reading

The Levellers' many writings were not systematic treatises on politics; they were very much reactions to, and interventions in, the highly complex politics of the time; and they combined arguments from many sources. This means that an approach to the study of Leveller 'political thought' is not easy, because often what it is *about*, and its tone and approach vary with the times. But good summaries of the Levellers' writings and careers, which take into account the events and attitudes of the time, and attempt to make their ideas seem coherent in the light of them, are David Wootton, 'Leveller democracy' in J. H. Burns and Mark Goldie (eds), *The Cambridge history of political thought, 1450–1700* (Cambridge, 1991); and chapters in John Sanderson, *'But the people's creatures': the philosophical basis of the English civil war* (Manchester and New York, 1989) and Perez Zagorin, *A history of political thought in the English revolution* (London 1954, repr. 1965). An interesting recent attempt to make Leveller thought seem coherent is Alan Craig Houston, 'A way of settlement': the Levellers, monopolies and the public interest', *History of Political Thought*, 9 (1993), pp. 381–419.

2 Commentaries on particular themes

Despite the eclecticism and occasionalism of Leveller writings, there are in them certain recurrent moves in argument and expressions of opinion, and there are commentaries which deal with these (not always easily separable) moves and expressions:

Appeals to the traditional positive law and custom

Andrew Sharp, 'John Lilburne and the Long Parliament's *Book of declarations*: a radical's exploitation of the words of authorities', *History of Political Thought*, 9 (1988), pp. 19–44; Andrew Sharp, 'John Lilburne's discourse of law', *Political Science*, 40, 1 (1988), pp. 18–33.

Appeals to equity, reason and the stain of the Norman Conquest against traditional law and custom

J. C. Davis, 'The Levellers and Christianity' in Brian Manning, (ed.) *Politics, religion and the English civil war* (London, 1973); Christopher Hill, 'The Norman yoke' in his *Puritanism and revolution* (London, 1958, 1962); Richard A. Gleissner, 'The levellers and natural law: the Putney debates of 1647', *Journal of British Studies*, 20 (1980), pp. 74–89; J. G. A. Pocock, *The ancient constitution and the fundamental law* (Cambridge, 1987); R. B. Seaberg, 'The Norman Conquest and the common law: the Levellers and the argument from continuity', *Historical Journal*, 24 (1981), pp. 791–806; Ann Hughes, 'Gender politics in Leveller literature', in Susan D. Amussen and Mark A. Kishlansky (eds.), *Political culture and cultural politics in early modern Europe* (Manchester, 1995).

Appeals in the name of and in the interest of 'the people' over and against settled institutions

Iain Hampsher-Monk, 'The political theory of the Levellers: Putney, property and Professor Macpherson', *Political Studies*, 24 (1976), pp. 397–422; C. J. Davis, 'The Levellers and democracy', in Charles Webster (ed.), *The intellectual revolution of the eighteenth century* (London, 1974); C. B. Macpherson, *The political theory of possessive individualism* (Oxford, 1962); A. L. Morton, 'Leveller democracy – fact or myth?' in his *The world of the ranters: religious radicalism in the English revolution* (London, 1979); Keith Thomas, 'The Levellers and the franchise' in G. E. Aylmer (ed.), *The interregnum: the quest for settlement 1646–1660* (London, 1972).

An insistence on liberty of conscience against any kind of enforced church conformity

A. S. P Woodhouse (ed)., *Puritanism and liberty: being the Army debates (1647–49)* (reprinted with a Preface by Ivan Roots, London, 1974).

3 The milieu of political practice

The politics of parliament, London and the New Model Army provide the environment of Leveller activity. The most useful writings which cover those politics and the Leveller place in them are: Ian J. Gentles, *The New Model Army in England, Ireland and Scotland, 1645–1653* (Oxford, 1992); Ian J. Gentles, 'The struggle for London in the second civil war', *Historical Journal*, 26, 2 (1983), pp. 277–305; William Haller, *Liberty and reformation in the Puritan revolution* (New York, 1955); J. S. Morrill, *The nature of the English revolution: essays by John Morrill* (London and New York, 1993); Murray Tolmie, *The triumph of the saints: the separate churches of London 1616–1649* (Cambridge and New York, 1977); Valerie Pearl, 'London's counter-revolution' in Aylmer, *The interregnum: the quest for a settlement*; and Austin Woolrych, *Soldiers and statesmen: the General Council of the Army and its debates 1647–1648* (Oxford, 1987).

4 Book-length studies of Levellers as individuals or as a group

These include Maurice Ashley, *John Wildman, plotter and postmaster* (London, 1947); H. N. Brailsford, *The Levellers and the English revolution* (ed. Christopher Hill, London, 1976); Joseph Frank, *The Levellers* (Cambridge, Mass., 1955); M. A. Gibb, *John Lilburne the Leveller, a Christian democrat* (London, 1947); Marie Gimmelfarb-Brack, *Liberté, égalité, fraternité, justice. La Vie et l'oeuvre de Richard Overton, niveleur* (Peter Lang, Berne, Frankfurt/M, Las Vegas, 1979); Pauline Gregg, *Free-born John* (London, 1961); and Theodore Calvin Pease, *The leveller movement* (Gloucester, Mass., 1916, 1965).

5 Collections of Leveller writings

There are a number of collections of various Leveller writings: G. E. Aylmer, *The Levellers in the English revolution* (London, 1975); William

Haller (ed.), *Tracts on liberty in the Puritan revolution* (3 vols., New York, 1933–4); William Haller and Godfrey Davies (eds), *The Leveller tracts 1647–1653* (New York, 1944); Jack R. McMichael and Barbara Taft (eds), *The writings of William Walwyn* (Athens, Ga. and London, 1989); ed. A. L. Morton, *Freedom in arms: a collection of Leveller writings* (London, 1975); Howard Shaw, *The Levellers* (London, 1978); Don M. Wolfe (ed.), *Leveller manifestos of the Puritan revolution* (New York, 1944).

Notes on the texts

Except for the extract from the Putney debates, and the body (as opposed to the appendix) of *Freeman's freedom*, all the texts are printed in full. I have silently modernised the spelling, punctuation and printing formats, and often I have silently corrected words and confusing number headings. Until 1752, with the replacement of the Julian by the Gregorian calendar, the new year was usually but not always taken to begin on 25 March. The 'popish' Gregorian calendar was also ten days ahead. I correct for the year but not for the day throughout. I have not changed the short titles of books and pamphlets referred to in the footnotes for ease of finding in catalogues – though in the interests of consistent modernisation I have changed the name of some the texts thus, e.g.: *Tolleration justified* into *Toleration justified*; *Englands new chains* into *England's new chains*. Where I have changed wording and where something might hang on it, this is indicated in the footnotes.

Except for the extract from the Putney debates and the *Young men's and apprentices' outcry*, all the texts are taken from editions in the Thomason Tracts in the British Library, all readily available on microfilm. The extract from the Putney debates is taken from Woodhouse's edition in *Puritanism and liberty*, with reference to C. H. Firth's edition in *The Clarke Papers* (Camden Society, London, vol. I, 1891). *The young men's and apprentices' outcry* is taken from the Bodleian Library edition printed at Oxford (which is exactly the same as the Thomason Tract edition printed in London, except for the title: the London edition is called *The Outcrys of the Young men and apprentices*).

Leveller texts

I

John Lilburne, 'On the 150th page': an untitled broadsheet of August 1645

In the 150th page of the book called *An exact collection of the parliament's remonstrances, declarations, etc.*[1] (published by special order of the House of Commons, 24 March, 1642)[2] we find there a question answered fit for all men to take notice of in these times.[3]

> QUESTION. Now in our extreme distractions – when foreign forces threaten, and probably are invited, and a malignant and popish party at home offended – the devil has cast a bone and raised a contestation between the king and parliament touching the militia. His majesty claims the disposing of it to be in him by the right of law; the parliament saith, *rebus sic stantibus*, and *nolenti Rege*: the ordering of it is in them.
>
> ANSWER. Which question may receive its solution by this distinction: that there is in laws an equitable, and a literal, sense. His majesty (let it be granted) is entrusted by law with the militia,[4] but it's for the good and preservation of the republic against foreign invasions or domestic rebellions. For it cannot be supposed that the parliament would ever by law entrust the king with the militia against themselves, or the commonwealth that entrusts *them*, to provide for their weal,[5] not for their woe. So that when there is certain appearance or grounded suspicion that the letter of the law shall be improved[6] against the equity of it (that is, the public good,

---

[1] The long title of the book, usually catalogued under the name of Edward Husbands, parliament's stationer, begins: *An exact collection of all the remonstrances, declarations, votes, orders, ordinances, proclamations, petitions, messages, answers, and other remarkable passages betweene the kings most excellent majesty, and his high court of parliament beginning at his majesties return from Scotland, being in December 1641, and continued untill March the 21, 1643*. It was much quoted by the Levellers, especially Lilburne.

[2] 1643 in New Style.

[3] The quoted section is the totality of an anonymous broadsheet called *A question answered: how laws are to be understood and obedience yeelded?*, which King Charles condemned on 22 April 1642 as containing 'seditious distinctions', and affirming 'that human laws do not bind the conscience'. See *Exact collection*, pp. 150–1. The broadsheet was probably by Henry Parker, parliament's most gifted propagandist.

[4] As he certainly was.

[5] weal = good, or wellbeing.

[6] improved = found condemnable.

3

whether of the body real or representative[7]) then the commander going against its equity, gives liberty to the commanded to refuse obedience to the letter. For the law, taken abstract from its original reason and end, is made a shell without a kernel, a shadow without a substance, and a body without a soul. It is the execution of laws according to their equity and reason which (as I may say) is the spirit that gives life to authority. The letter kills.

Nor need this equity be expressed in the law, being so naturally implied and supposed in all laws that are not merely imperial, from that analogy which all bodies politic hold with the natural – whence all government and governors borrow a proportionable respect. And therefore when the militia or an army is committed to the general, it is not with any express condition that he shall not turn the mouths of his cannons against his own soldiers. For that is so naturally and necessarily implied that it's needless to be expressed; insomuch as if he did attempt or command such a thing against the nature of his trust and place, it did *ipso facto* estate[8] the army in a right of disobedience – except we think that obedience binds men to cut their own throats, or at least their companions'.[9]

And indeed if this distinction be not allowed, then the legal and mixed monarchy[10] is the greatest tyranny. For if laws invest the king in an absolute power and the letter be not controlled by the equity, then, whereas other kings that are absolute monarchs and rule by will and not by law are tyrants *perforce*, those that rule by law and not by will have hereby a tyranny conferred upon them *legally*, and so the very end of laws, which is to give bounds and limits to the exorbitant wills of princes, is by the laws themselves disappointed: for they hereby give corroboration and much more

[7] The idea here is that the 'real' commonwealth consists of the people who make it up, and the representative commonwealth is constituted by those institutions entrusted by the real commonwealth to act for them.

[8] estate = instate.

[9] This image was to reappear in *A declaration from Sir Thomas Fairfax and the Army* of 14 June 1647 (mainly by Ireton) justifying the New Model's not disbanding until political and military grievances were satisfied: 'And accordingly the parliament hath declared it no resistance of magistracy to side with the just principles of law, nature, and nations, being that law upon which we have assisted you, and that the soldiery may lawfully hold the hands of the general who will turn his cannon against the army on purpose to destroy them, the seamen the hands of the pilot who wilfully runs his ship upon the rock (as our brethren of Scotland argued).'

[10] England was widely held to have a legal and mixed monarchy as opposed to an arbitrary and absolute one. The monarch's legislative powers, it was held, were mixed (in law) with those of the Commons and the Lords, or alternatively, with those of the 'three estates' of lay lords, bishops and commons.

4

justification to an arbitrary tyranny, by making it legal, not assumed – which laws are ordained to cross, not countenance. And therefore is the letter (where it seems absolute) always to receive qualification from the equity, else the foresaid absurdity must follow.

It is confessed by all rational men that the parliament has a power to annul a law, and to make a new law, and to declare a law; but known laws in force, and unrepealed by them, are a rule as long as they so remain for all the commons of England whereby to walk; and upon rational grounds are conceived to be binding to the very parliament themselves as well as others. And though by their legislative power they have authority to make new laws, yet no freeman of England is to take notice (or *can* he) of what they intend till they declare it; neither can they – as is conceived – justly punish any man for walking closely to the known and declared law, though it cross some pretended privilege of theirs, remaining only in their own breasts.

For where there is no law declared, there can be no transgression.[11] Therefore it is very requisite that the parliament would declare their privileges to the whole commons of England, that so no man may through ignorance (by the parliament's default) run causelessly into the hazard of the loss of their lives, liberties, or estates. For here it is acknowledged by themselves that their power is limited by those that betrust them, and that they are not to do what they list[12] but what they ought, namely, to provide for the people's weal and not for their woe: so that unknown privileges are as dangerous as unlimited prerogatives – being both of them secret snares, especially for the best-affected people.

It is the greatest hazard and danger that can be run unto, to desert the only known and declared rule, the laying aside whereof brings in nothing but will and power, lust and strength, and so the strongest to carry all away. For it is the known, established, declared and unrepealed law that tells all the freemen of England that the knights and burgesses chosen according to law and sent to make up the parliament, are those that all the commons of England (who send and choose them) are to obey.

But take away this declared law, and where will you find the rule of obedience? And if there be no rule of obedience, then it must necessarily follow that if a greater and stronger number come to a parliament sitting, and tell them that they are more and

---

[11] Romans 4: 15: 'for where no law is, there is no transgression'.
[12] what they list = whatever they please.

stronger than themselves – and therefore they shall not make laws
for them, but they will rather make laws for them – must they not
needs give place? Undoubtedly they must.

Yea, take away the declared, unrepealed law, and then where is
meum et tuum[13] and liberty, and property? But (you will say) the
law declared binds the people but is no rule for a parliament sitting
who are not to walk by a known law. It is answered: it cannot be
imagined that ever the people would be so sottish[14] as to give such
a power to those whom they choose for their servants. For this
were to give them a power to provide for their woe but not for their
weal, which is contrary to their own foregoing maxim. Therefore
doubtless that man is upon the most solid and firm ground that
has both the letter and equity of a known, declared and unrepealed
law on his side, though his practice do cross some pretended privilege of parliament.

And whereas by an act made this present parliament, Anno 17
Caroli Regis[15] (entitled *An act for regulating of the Privy Council,
and for taking away the court commonly called the Star Chamber*) it
is there declared that 'the proceedings, censures, and decrees' of
the Star Chamber 'have by experience been found to be an intolerable burden to the subject and the means to introduce an arbitrary
power and government', and that the Council Table 'have adventured to determine of the estates, and liberties of the subject, contrary to the law of the land and the rights and privileges of the
subject'. Which laws are there recited, as first, *Magna Carta*,[16] and
the 5 Ed. III cap. 9 and 25 Ed. III cap. 4 and 28 Ed. III cap. 3[17] –
the last of which saith that 'it is accorded, assented and established,
that none shall be taken by petition or suggestion made to the king
or his council, unless it be by indictment, or presentment of good
and lawful people of the same neighbourhood where such deeds be
done, in due manner, or by process made by writ original at the
common law, and that none be put out of his franchise or freehold,
unless he be duly brought in to answer and forejudged of the same
by the course of the law'. And by another statute made in the 42
Ed. III cap. 3, it is there enacted that 'no man be put to answer

---

[13] *meum et tuum* = mine and yours.
[14] sottish = foolish.
[15] The regnal year anno 17 *Caroli Regis*, is the seventeenth year of the reign of Charles I,
i.e. 1642, because he reigned from 1625.
[16] 9 H[enry] III. cap. 29.
[17] Acts of parliament were conventionally indicated first by the regnal year of the king
(e.g. 5 Ed[ward] III), then by the chapter number given to them in the printed statutes.

without presentment before justices, or matter of record, or by due process and writ original according to the old law of the land'.

Therefore for the subjects' good and welfare in future time, it is enacted: 'that from henceforth no court, council, or place of judicature shall be erected, ordained, constituted, or appointed within this realm of England, or dominion of Wales, which shall have, use, or exercise the same, or the like jurisdiction, as is, or has been used, practised, or exercised in the said Court of Star Chamber'.

From the equity and letter of which law, it is desired that our learned lawyers would answer these ensuing queries.

First, whether the letter and equity of this law do not bind the very parliament themselves during the time of their sitting, in the like cases here expressed, to the same rules here laid down?

Which, if it should be denied, then secondly: whether the parliament itself, when it is sitting, be not bound to the observation of the letter and equity of this law, when they have to do with freemen that in all their actions and expressions have declared faithfulness to the commonwealth?

And, if this be denied, then thirdly: whether ever God made any man lawless? Or whether ever the commonwealth when they choose the parliament, gives them a lawless unlimited power, and at their pleasure to walk contrary to their own laws and ordinances before they have repealed them?

Fourthly, whether it be according to law, justice or equity, for the parliament to imprison or punish a man for doing what they command him, and by oath enjoin him?

Fifthly, whether it be legal, just or equal, that when free men do endeavour according to their duty, oath and Protestation[18] to give in information to the parliament of treason acted and done by Sir John Lenthall against the state and kingdom[19] – and long since communi-

---

[18] Lilburne is referring to *The protestation* of 3 May 1641. Lilburne's reference is to the part of an oath in which the oathtaker swears to 'oppose, and by all good ways and means endeavour to bring to condign punishment all such as shall by force, practice, counsels, plots, conspiracies or otherwise do anything contrary to the present *Protestation*'.

[19] On 19 July 1645, Lilburne had met some City friends and Walwyn (probably for the first time). It emerged that they had gone to Westminster Hall to give evidence against Lenthall, the Keeper of the Marshalsea Prison (and brother of Sir William Lenthall, Speaker of the House of Commons) for correspondence with royalists and for sending

cated to several members of the House of Commons, but by them concealed and smothered, and now by God's providence brought upon the stage again – and during the time that inquisition is made of it before the Committee of Examinations, before any legal charge be fixed upon Sir John Lenthall, or he required to make any answer or defence, that he shall be present to out-face, discourage and abuse the informers and witnesses in the face of the committee, without any check or control from them? And sometimes, while they are sitting about the examination of his treason, that he shall sit down beside them with his hat on, as if he were one of them, and that he shall enjoy from the committee ten times more favour and respect than the just, honest, and legal informers against him, who by some of the committee themselves while they are sitting, are threatened, jeered, nicknamed and otherways most shamefully abused?

Yea, and the friends of the informers for the state are kept without doors and the friends of the accused admitted to come in always without control; and during the examination of the information, that the committee shall refuse to remove the informers out of Sir John Lenthall's custody of King's Bench[20] to another prison, although they have been truly informed that he has set instruments on work to murder them, and also importuned to remove them?

Sixthly, whether it be not most agreeable to law, justice and equity, that seeing Sir John Lenthall having so many friends in the house concerned in the business, that he should not rather be tried by the same Council of War in London where Sir John Hotham and his son were,[21] than at the parliament – his principal crime being against the law martial, as theirs was.

London, 30 August 1645[22]

money to the king. Lilburne joined the City men's cause, was imprisoned for it and wrote this broadsheet from prison.

[20] Marshalsea was the prison of the Court of King's Bench.

[21] Sir John Hotham had been parliamentary governor of Hull from January 1642. In April he refused to let the king enter the town – a great blow to the royalist cause. But he and his son John defected to the royalists at the lowest ebb of parliament's military fortunes, in March 1643. They were captured in June by parliament, court-martialled, and condemned to death. They were finally executed in January 1645.

[22] The date is in the hand of George Thomason, the collector of civil war writings.

2
Toleration justified and persecution condemned

In an answer or examination of the London ministers'
letter, whereof many of them are of the Synod and yet
framed this letter at Sion College to be sent, among others,
to themselves at the Assembly: in behalf of reformation
and church government

2 Corinthians 11: 14–15: 'And no marvail, for Sathan himself is
transformed into an Angell of Light. Therefore it is no great thing,
though his Ministers transform themselves, as though they were
the ministers of righteousnesse; whose end shall be according to
their works.'[1]
London. Printed in the Year, 1646

―――――――――――――――――――――――――― [2]

The letter of the London ministers to the Assembly of Divines at Westminster
against toleration,[3] mildly examined, and the mistakes thereof friendly
discovered, as well for the sakes of the Independent and Separation,[4] as for
the good of the commonwealth.

When I call to mind the general oppression before the parliament exercised upon good people conscientious in the practice of their religion,
and that the presbyters did not only suffer as much as any therein but
exclaimed and laboured as much as any thereagainst, it is a wonder to
me – now that yoke is removed and a blessed opportunity offered by
Almighty God to the people and their parliament to make every honest
heart glad by allowing a just and contentful freedom to serve God
without hypocrisy and according to the persuasion of conscience – that

―――――――――

[1] These verses come from the Geneva Bible of 1560, the language and spelling of which
would have seemed archaic in 1645. At almost all other times the Levellers used the
Bible of 1611, authorised by King James I.
[2] End of title page.
[3] *A letter of the ministers of the City of London, presented the first of Jan. 1645* (1 January
1646).
[4] 'Independent' and 'Separation' were the names given to the membership of the Independent and Separating churches. The distinction between the two was unclear in
conception and in practice; but, roughly, Independent churches (and Independents)
claimed the right to meet separately from the parochial congregations of the established
church (at first episcopal, then Presbyterian) while remaining willing that their members
should attend them. Separatists (sometimes also called Sectaries) resisted any dealings
at all with the established church.

one sect amongst us, that is the presbyters that have been yoke-fellows with us, should not rest satisfied with being free as their brethren but become restless in their contrivances and endeavours till they become lords over us. The wonder is the same as it would have been had the Israelites after the Egyptian bondage[5] become task-masters in the Land of Canaan one to another; but it is more in them who have been instructed by our Saviour in that blessed rule of doing unto others what they would have others do unto themselves.[6]

To discover the several policies the presbyters have used to get into the chair they have jostled the bishops out of, whose example they have followed in many particulars, as especially in the politic and gradual obtaining the Ordinance for Licensing[7] upon a pretence of stopping the king's writings, but intentionally obtained and violently made use of against the Independents, Separation, and commonwealthsmen, who either see more than, or something contrary to the designs of the licenser. To signify to the people how the presbyters have laboured to twist their interest with the parliament's, as the bishops did theirs with the king, how daily and burdensomely importunate they are with the parliament to establish their government (which they are pleased to call Christ's)[8] and back it with authority and a compulsive power (which by that very particular appears not to be His). To lay open their private juntos and counsels, their framing petitions for the easy and ignorant people, their urging them upon the Common Council, and obtruding them upon the choosers of common councilmen at the wardmote elections, even after the parliament had signified their dislike thereof.[9] To sum up their bitter invectives in pulpits and strange liberty they take

---

[5] On the Egyptian bondage see Genesis 45 to Exodus 25.

[6] This 'golden rule' was much favoured by Walwyn, Overton and Lilburne. Its classic formulation by Christ is at Matthew 7: 12: 'Therefore all things whatsoever ye would that men should do unto you, do ye even so unto them: for this is the law and the prophets.'

[7] By ordinances of June and July 1643 licences for printing were established and the licensed texts were ordered to be entered on the register of the Stationers' Company. Unlicensed printing presses, or presses printing unlicensed texts, were to be destroyed; those implicated in producing unlicensed books were to be arrested and taken to parliament's Committee of Examinations for appropriate punishment.

[8] They claimed that their form of church government was *jure divino*, by right according to God's law indicated in the practice of church government followed by the apostles.

[9] The Presbyterian clergy of London were strongly opposed to the parliament's policy of accommodating 'tender consciences' (n. 43 below). They were behind citizen's petitions for Presbyterianism and non-toleration addressed to parliament from September 1645 onwards.

as well there as in their writings to make the Separation and Independents odious by scandals and untrue reports of them, in confidence of
having the press in their own hands, by which means no man without
hazard shall answer them. To lay open the manner and depth of these
proceedings is not the intention of this work.

I only thought good to mention these particulars that the presbyters
may see they walk in a net[10] – know 'tis no cloud that covers them –
and that they may fear that in time they may be discerned as well by
the whole people as they are already by a very great part thereof.

The London ministers' letter, contrived in the conclave of Sion College is one of the numerous projects of the clergy not made for the
information of the Synod[11] but the misinformation of the people, to
prevent which is my business at this time. I will only take so much of
it as is to the point in hand, to wit, toleration.

Letter: 'It is true, by reason of different lights and different sights
among brethren, there may be dissenting in opinion; yet why should
there be any separating from church communion?'

Why? Because the difference in opinion is in matters that *concern*
church communion. You may as well put the question why men play
not the hypocrites – as they must needs do if they should communicate
in that church society their mind cannot approve of. The question had
been well put if you had said: 'by reason of different lights and different
sights, there may be dissenting in opinion, yet why should our hearts
be divided one from another? Why should our love from hence, and
our affections grow cold and dead one towards another? Why should
we not peaceably bear one with another till our sights grow better, and
our light increase?' *These* would have been questions, I think, that
would have puzzled a truly conscientious man to have found an answer
for.

That which next follows, to wit, 'the church's coat may be of divers
colours,[12] yet why should there be any rent in it?' is but an old jingle[13]

---

[10] Psalm 9: 15: 'The heathen are sunk down in the pit that they made: in the net which
they hid is their own foot taken.'

[11] Synod = (here) the Westminster Assembly of Divines, which, authorised by parliament,
met in the Jerusalem Chapel of Westminster Abbey from 1643–8 to settle the form and
discipline of a new church government to replace episcopacy. Sion House was the
Cripplegate Street meeting place – virtually the club – of the London Presbyterian
divines who, allied with Scots ministers seconded to the Assembly, agitated for a strict
Presbyterian settlement.

[12] Genesis 37: 3, 23, 32.

[13] 'jing' in the original.

of the bishops, spoken by them formerly in reference to the presbyters, and now mentioned to make that which went before – which has no weight in itself – to sound the better.

Letter: 'Have we not a touchstone of truth: the good word of God? And when all things are examined by the word, then that which is best may be held fast; but first it must be known, and then examined afterward.'

I shall easily concur with them thus far: that the word of God is the touchstone that all opinions are to be examined by that and that the best is to be held fast. But now 'who shall be the examiners'? must needs be the question. If the presbyter examine the Independent and Separation they are like to find the same censure the presbyters have already found (being examined by the bishops) and the bishops found from the pope. Adversaries certainly are not competent judges. Again, in matters disputable and controverted, every man must examine for himself – and so every man does, or else he must be conscious to himself that he sees with other men's eyes and has taken up an opinion not because it consents[14] with his understanding but for that it is the safest and least troublesome as the world goes, or because such a man is of that opinion (whom he reverences) and verily believes would not have been so, had it not been truth. I may be helped in my examination by other men, but no man or sort of men are to examine for me, insomuch that before an opinion can properly be said to be *mine* it must concord with my understanding. Now here is the fallacy – and you shall find it in all papists, bishops, presbyters or whatsoever other sort of men who have or would have in their hands the power of persecuting – that they always suppose themselves to be competent examiners and judges of other men differing in judgement from them. And upon this weak supposition (by no means to be allowed) most of the reasons and arguments of the men forementioned are supported.

They proceed to charge much upon the independents for not producing their model of church-government. For answer hereunto, I refer the reader to the reasons printed by the independents and given into the House in their own justification,[15] which the ministers might have taken notice of.

---

[14] consents = agrees.

[15] Thomas Goodwin, Jeremiah Burroughs etc., *A copy of a remonstrance lately delivered to the Assembly ... declaring the grounds and reasons of their declining to bring into the Assembly their model of church government* (1645). The authors were Independent ministers.

I proceed to the supposed reasons urged by the ministers against the toleration of independency in the church.

I

1. Their first reason is, 'because the desires and endeavours of Independents for a toleration are at this time extremely unseasonable and preposterous', for 'the reformation of religion is not yet perfected and settled amongst us according to our Covenant.[16] And why may not the reformation be raised up at last to such purity and perfection that truly tender consciences may receive abundant satisfaction for ought that yet appears?'

I would to God the people – their own friends especially – would but take notice of the fallacy of the reason. They would have reformation perfected according to the Covenant before the independents move to be tolerated. Now, reformation is not perfected according to the Covenant, 'till schism and heresy is extirpated' – which in the sequel of this letter,[17] they judge independency to be. Their charity thinks it, then, most seasonable to move that independency should be tolerated *after* it is extirpated. Their reason and affection in this are a like sound to the Independents. Their drift in this indeed is but too evident. They would have the Independents silent till they get power in their hands – and then let them talk if they dare. Certainly, the most seasonable time to move for toleration is while the parliament are in

---

[16] I.e. *The Solemn League and Covenant for the reformation and defence of religion, the honour and happiness of the king, and the peace and safety of the three kingdoms of England, Scotland and Ireland.* It was taken by members of the House of Commons on 25 September 1643 as the price for gaining the Scots as allies against Charles I. Presbyterians believed the Solemn League required a Presbyterian church reformation, but Independents and Sectaries exploited an ambiguity of wording lodged in the document at the time of its negotiation with the Scots. The first article called for 'the preservation of the church of Scotland, in doctrine, worship, discipline and government', together with the 'reformation of religion in the kingdoms of England and Ireland, in doctrine, worship, discipline and government, according to the word of God and the example of the best reformed churches'. But what, the opponents of Presbyterianism asked, *were* the 'best reformed churches'?

[17] sequel = (here) later on in the *Letter*. There (p. 3), Independents are argued to be in schism because they depart from 'our churches, being true churches'; they seduce others into following them; they 'erect separate congregations under separate and undiscovered government'; they refuse communion in the sacraments with 'our churches'; their ministers will not preach 'amongst us as officers; and their members, when they do join 'with us' in hearing the word and praying, 'yet they do it not as with the ministerial word and prayer, nor as acts of church communion'. And schism is not to be tolerated: 1 Corinthians 1: 10, 10: 3, 12: 25; Romans 16: 17; Galatians 5: 20.

debate about church government; since if stay be made till a church government be settled, all motions that may but seem to derogate from that – how just soever in themselves, how good soever for the commonwealth – must needs be hardly obtained.

And whereas they say: 'Why may not reformation be raised up at last to such purity and perfection that truly tender consciences may receive abundant satisfaction, for ought that yet appears?' Observe that these very ministers, in the sequel of their letter, impute it as levity in the independents that they are not at a stay,[18] but in expectation of 'new lights' and 'reserves' (as they say) so that a man would think *they themselves* were at a certainty. But 'tis no new thing for one sort of men to object that as a crime against others which they are guilty of themselves – though indeed but that the presbyters use any weapons against the Independents is no crime at all. Yea, 'tis excellency in any man or woman not to be pertinacious or obstinate in any opinion but to have an open ear for reason and argument against whatsoever he holds, and to embrace or reject whatsoever upon further search he finds to be agreeable to, or dissonant from, God's holy word. It doth appear from the practices of the presbyters and from this letter and other petitions expressly against toleration, that unless the Independents and Separation will submit their judgements to theirs, they shall never be tolerated if *they* can hinder it.

2. Their second reason is that it 'is not yet known what the government of the Independent is; neither would they ever let the world know what they hold in that point, though some of their party have been too forward to challenge the London petitioners as led with blind obedience and pinning their souls upon their priest's sleeve for desiring an establishment of the government of Christ before there was any model of it extant.'[19]

3. Their third reason is much to the same purpose.

I answer, that the ministers know that the independent government *for the general* is resolved upon by the Independents, though they have not yet modelised every *particular* – which is a work of time, as the

---

[18] not at stay = not at rest.

[19] The City petition of November 1645 *To the right honourable Lords and Commons*, had asked parliament 'to make all possible haste to establish, by your civil sanction, that government and discipline amongst us, which Christ hath left his church (a model whereof the reverend Assembly of Divines, according to the wisdom given unto them, have framed, and – as we understand – already presented unto your honours)'. This elicited the response of their being ignorant of the model proposed.

framing of the Presbyterian government was. The Independents, however, have divers reasons for dissenting from the Presbyterian way, which they have given in already. And though they have not concluded every particular of their own but are still upon the search and enquiry, yet it is seasonable however to move for toleration. For that the ground of moving is not because they are *Independents* but because *every man* ought to be free in the worship and service of God – compulsion being the way to increase, not the number of converts, but of hypocrites. Whereas it is another case for people to move for establishing of a government they understand not, having never seen it, as the London petitioners did. That is most evidently a giving up of the understanding to other men. Sure the presbyters themselves cannot think it otherwise, nor yet the people upon the least consideration of it. Besides, the London petitioners did not only desire (as here the ministers cunningly say) an establishment of the government of Christ, but an establishment of the government of Christ 'a model whereof the reverend Assembly of Divines have framed'[20] – which they never saw! So that herein the people were abused by the divines by being put upon a petition wherein they suppose that government which they never saw to be Christ's government. If this be not sufficient to discover to our Presbyterian lay-brethren the divines' confidence of their ability to work them by the smoothnesses of phrase and language to what they please, and of their own easiness and flexibility to be so led, I know not what is.

II

Secondly, the ministers urge 'that the desires and endeavours of the Independents for toleration are unreasonable and unequal in divers regards'.

1. 'Partly because no such toleration has hitherto been established (so far as we know) in any Christian state, by the civil magistrate.'

But that the ministers have been used to speak what they please for a reason in their pulpits without contradiction, they would never sure have let so slight a one as this have passed from them. It seems by this reason, that *if in any* Christian state a toleration by the magistrate had been allowed, it would not have been unreasonable for *our* state to allow it – the practice of states being here supposed to be the rule of what's

---

[20] See previous note.

reasonable. Whereas *I* had thought that the practice of Christian states is to be judged by the rule of reason and God's word, and not reason by them. That which is just and reasonable is constant and perpetually so; the practice of states, though Christian, is variable we see – different one from another and changing according to the prevalency of particular parties – and therefore a most uncertain rule of what is reasonable. Besides, the state of *Holland* doth tolerate; and therefore the ministers' argument, even in that part where it seems to be most strong for them, makes against them. Again, if the practice of a Christian state be a sufficient argument of the reasonableness of a toleration, *our* state may justly tolerate because Christian, and because they are free to do whatever any other state might formerly have done. But I stay too long upon so weak an argument.

2. 'Partly because some of them have solemnly professed that they cannot suffer presbytery, and answerable hereunto is their practice in those places where independency prevails.'

(1) 'Tis unreasonable it seems to tolerate Independents because Independents would not (if they had the power) suffer presbyters. A very Christianly argument, and taken out of Matthew 5: 44. 'Love your enemies, bless them that curse you, do good to them that hate you, and pray for them which hurt you, and persecute you.' What, were all our London ministers forgetful of their Saviour's instructions? Does their fury so far blind their understanding and exceed their piety? (Which seems to be but pretended now, since in their practice they would become Jews and cry out 'an eye for an eye, and a tooth for a tooth'.[21]) Whosoever meddles with them it seems shall have as good as they bring. Was ever so strange a reason urged by a sect of men that say they are ministers – Christ's ministers, reformers too, that would make the world believe they are about to reduce all matters Christian to the original and primitive excellency of Christ and the apostles – and yet who[22] speak and publish to the world a spleenish reason so expressly contrary to the precepts and the practices of Christ and his followers? To Christ I say, that bids us love our enemies,[23] that we may be the

---

[21] Matthew 5: 38–9: 'Ye have heard that it hath been said, An eye for an eye, and a tooth for a tooth: But I say unto you, That ye resist not evil: but whosoever shall smite thee on thy right cheek, turn to him the other also.' (The Jewish versions: Exodus 21: 42; Leviticus 24: 20; Deuteronomy 19: 21.)

[22] 'to' in the original.

[23] Matthew 5: 44; Luke 6: 27, 35.

children of our Father which is in heaven, who makes the sun to shine on the evil and the good, and sends rain on the just and on the unjust.[24] The ministers should be like the Master. What a disproportion is here? As if the title were taken up for some other end. We know the Apostle[25] speaks of ministers that could transform themselves as though they were the ministers of righteousness. I pray God *our* ministers do not so. I would willingly suppress those fears and suspicions, which, do what I can, arise in me from their words and practice. Sure they had approved themselves better Christians if upon the discovery of so bad a spirit in any of the Independents as to persecute had they power (though I believe there are not any such) – I say it had been more Christ-like in our ministers to have dissuaded them from so unmanly, so much more *unchristianly* a vice, than to have it made an argument for practice in themselves. They might by the same rule be Jews to the Jew or Turk to the Turk, oppressors to the oppressor, or do any evil to other that others would do to them if other men's doing of it be an argument of the reasonableness thereof. But I hope our ministers will be so ingenuous, as, where they see their weaknesses, to forsake them. It will be both more comfortable to all other sorts of men and in the end more happy for themselves.

(2) Again, I suppose your suggestion to be very false: namely, that the Independents, if they had power, would persecute the presbyters. Though let me tell you, of all sects of men, those deserve least countenance of a state that would be persecutors, not because of their consciences in the practice and exercise of their religion (wherein the ground of freedom consists) but because a persecuting spirit is the greatest enemy to human society, the dissolver of love and brotherly affection, the cause of envyings, heart-burnings, divisions, yea, and of war itself. Whosoever shall cast an impartial eye upon times past and examine the true cause and reason of the subversion and devastation of states and countries, will, I am confident, attribute it to no other than the tyranny of princes and persecution of priests. So that all states, minding their true interests – namely the good and welfare of the people – ought by all means to suppress in every sect or degree of men (whether papists,[26] episcopals,[27] presbyters, Independents,

---

[24] Matthew 5: 25.
[25] I.e. St Paul. See the quotation from 2 Corinthians on the title page of this pamphlet.
[26] The rude, and most common, word in England for Roman Catholics.
[27] The supporters of an English episcopalian church, i.e. one with bishops.

Anabaptists,[28] etc.) *the spirit of domination and persecution*, the disquieter and disturber of mankind, the offspring of Satan. God being all love, and having so communicated himself unto us, gave us commands to be like him: merciful, as he our heavenly Father is merciful,[29] to bear with one another's infirmities.[30] Neither does reason and true wisdom dictate any other to us than that we should do unto others as we would be done unto ourselves. That spirit therefore which is contrary to God, to reason, to the well being of states – as the spirit of persecution evidently is – is most especially to be watched and warily to be circumscribed and tied up by the wisdom of the supreme power in commonwealths. I speak not this to the disgrace of presbyters as *presbyters*. For as such I suppose they are not persecutors, forasmuch as I know some (and I hope there are many more of them) that are zealous and conscientious for that form of government[31] and yet enemies to a compulsive power in matters of religion. But I speak for this end only: namely to beget a just and Christian dislike in all sorts of men, as well presbyters as others, of forcing all to one way of worship, though disagreeable to their minds – which cannot be done without the assistance of this fury and pestilent enemy to mankind, persecution.

III

I proceed to the ministers' third reason: 'And partly to grant to them, and not to other sectaries who are free-born as well as they and have

---

[28] English Baptists were often called Anabaptists to identify them with the horrors of the regime of John of Leyden in Münster and of German peasant revolts, and with the doctrine that all human power and magistracy was rooted in sin. In fact it was their theology that distinguished them from other sects. They believed in baptism only when a person had reached adulthood and could make a reasonable choice. 'Particular' Baptists (like Lilburne before and during his Leveller phase) were Calvinists and believed that only the elect, preordained as such by God, should be baptised; 'General' Baptists did not believe in predestination but (like Overton and many other military and civilian Levellers) in the 'free grace' of God which made it possible for individual people by their own belief and action to attain (or reject) salvation: so baptism was not to be limited. Walwyn himself believed in free grace, does not seem to have cared much about the forms and ceremonies of worship, and attended his parochial Anglican church as well as many other sectarian ones.

[29] Luke 6: 36.

[30] Romans 15: 1.

[31] Presbyterian church government (unlike episcopalian, which was governed by clerics) was mixed among clerics (the presbyters or ministers) and laymen. Again, where bishops and archbishops were chosen by the king and governed their dioceses, each Presbyterian congregation (within limits) chose its own minister and (lay) elders; these in turn sent

done as good service as they to the public (as they use to plead) will be counted injustice, and great partiality. But to grant it to all, will scarce be cleared from impiety.'

To the former part of this argument I gladly consent, that sectaries have as good claims to freedom as any sorts of men whatsoever: because free-born, because well-affected and very assistant to their country in its necessities. The latter part of the argument is only an affirmation without proof. The ministers think sure it will be taken for truth because they said it – for such a presumption it seems they are arrived to. In the meantime, what must they suppose the people to *be* that do imagine their bare affirmations sufficient ground for the people's belief? I would the people would learn from hence to be their own men and make use of their own understandings in the search and belief of things. Let their ministers be never so seemingly learned or judicious, God has not given them understandings for nothing. The submission of the mind is the most ignoble slavery, which being in our own powers to keep free, the subjection thereof argues in us the greater baseness.

But to the assertion that it will be impiety to grant it to all sectaries, I answer that the word 'sectary' is communicable both to presbyters and Independents, whether it be taken in the good sense for the followers of Christ – for such, all presbyters, Independents, Brownists,[32] Anabaptists and all else suppose and profess themselves to be – or, in the common sense, for followers of some few men more eminent in their parts and abilities than others. And hereof the Independents and presbyters are as guilty as the separation, and so are as well sectaries. Now all sectaries (whether presbyters, Independents, Brownists, Antinomians,[33] Anabaptists, etc.) have a like title and right to freedom or a toleration, the title thereof being not any particular of the opinion, but the equity of every man's being free in the state he lives in and is obedient to – matters of opinion being not properly to be taken into cognisance any further than they break out into some disturbance or disquiet to the state. But you will say that by such a toleration,

representatives to Classes, which sent representatives to Provinces, which sent representatives to a national Assembly.

[32] Here used as a generic word for strict Separatist congregations gathered on a covenanting principle. They were named after Robert Browne, the Elizabethan churchman (1550?–1633?).

[33] Those who believed that they were freed from the Mosaic law of the Old Testament by Christ's living, redeeming grace. They tended to be anti-scripturalist and anti-clerical, and to sin purposefully to show that they were free in Christ.

blasphemy will be broached, and such strange and horrid opinions as would make the ears of every godly and Christian man to tingle. What, must *this* also be tolerated? I answer, it cannot be just to set bounds or limitations to toleration any further than the safety of the people requires. The more horrid and blasphemous the opinion is the easier suppressed by reason and argument, because it must necessarily be that the weaker the arguments are on one side the stronger they are on the other; the grosser the error is the more advantage has truth over it, the less colour likewise and pretence there is for imposing it upon the people. I am confident that there is much more danger in a small but speciously formed error that has a likeness and similitude to truth than in a gross and palpable untruth.

Besides, can it in reason be judged the meetest[34] way to draw a man out of his error by imprisonment, bonds or other punishment? You may as well be angry and molest a man that has an imperfection or dimness in his eyes and think by stripes or bonds to recover his sight. How preposterous would this be? Your proper and meet way, surely, is to supply things pertinent to his cure. And so likewise to a man whose understanding is clouded, whose inward sight is dim and imperfect, whose mind is so far misinformed as to deny a deity or the scriptures – for we'll instance in the worst of errors. Can Bedlam or the Fleet reduce such a one?[35] No certainly. It was ever found by all experience that such rough courses did confirm the error, not remove it. Nothing can do that but the efficacy and convincing power of sound reason and argument, which, 'tis to be doubted, they are scarce furnished withal that use other weapons. Hence have I observed that the most weak and passionate men, the most unable to defend truth or their own opinions, are the most violent for persecution. Whereas those whose minds are established and whose opinions are built upon firm and demonstrable grounds care not what winds blow, fear not to grapple with any error, because they are confident they can overthrow it.

IV

'Independency is a schism, and therefore not to be tolerated.' The principal argument brought to prove it is this: because they depart from

---

[34] meetest = most appropriate.
[35] Notoriously the most unpleasant prisons in London.

the presbyter churches, which are 'true churches', and so confessed to be by the Independents.

I answer that this argument only concerns the Independents, because they only acknowledge them to be true churches. Whether they are still of that opinion or no, I know not; 'tis to be doubted they are not,[36] especially since they have discerned the spirit of enforcement and compulsion to reign in that church – the truest mark of a *false* church. I believe the Independents have changed their mind, especially those of them whose pastors receive their office and ministry from the election of the people or congregation and are not engaged to allow so much to the presbyters because of their own[37] interest as deriving their calling from the bishops and pope for the making up a supposed succession from the apostles, who for their own sakes are enforced to acknowledge the presbyter for a true church, as the presbyters are necessitated to allow the episcopal and papist church true or valid for the substance – as they confess in the Ordinance for Ordination[38] – because they have received their ministry therefrom, without which absurdity they cannot maintain their succession from the apostles.

But that the Independents are not a schism, they have and will, I believe, upon all occasions sufficiently justify. I shall not therefore – since it concerns them in particular – insist thereupon, but proceed to the supposed mischiefs which the ministers say will inevitably follow upon this toleration, both to the church and commonwealth.

V(i)
First to the Church

1. 'Causeless and unjust revolts from our ministry and congregations.' To this I say that it argues an abundance of distrust the ministers have in their own abilities and the doctrines they preach to suppose their auditors will forsake them if other men have liberty to speak. 'Tis *authority* it seems must fill their churches, and not the truth and efficacy of their doctrines. I judge it for my part a sufficient ground to suspect that for gold that can't abide a trial.[39] It seems our ministers'

---

[36] 'tis to be doubted they are not = they are probably not.
[37] I.e. the presbyters' interest.
[38] 4 October 1644.
[39] A reference to Revelation 3: 18–19, a favoured quotation of Walwyn's to be used as the title of *Gold tried in the fire* (1647) printed below. The church at Laodicea is 'neither hot nor cold'; it is rich; the prophet reports God as saying 'I counsel thee to buy of me

doctrines and religion are like Dagon of the Philistines that will fall to pieces at the appearance of the ark.[40] Truth sure would be more confident, in hope to appear more glorious, being set off by falsehood. And therefore I do adjure the ministers, from that loveliness and potency that necessarily must be in truth and righteousness – if they think they do profess it – that they would procure the opening of every man's mouth, in confidence that truth, in whomsoever she is, will prove victorious, and like the sun's glorious lustre, darken all errors and vain imaginations of man's heart. But I fear the *consequence* sticks more in their stomachs – the emptying of their churches being the eclipsing of their reputations and the diminishing of their profits. If it be otherwise, let it appear by an equal allowing of that to others which they have laboured so much for to be allowed to themselves.

2. 'Our people's minds will be troubled and in danger to be subverted, Acts 15: 24.'

Answer. The place of scripture may concern themselves and may as well be urged upon them by the Separation or Independents as it is urged by them upon the Separation and Independents: namely that they trouble the people's minds and lay injunctions upon them they were never commanded to lay. And 'tis very observable, the most of those scriptures they urge against the separation do most properly belong unto themselves.

3. 'Bitter heart-burnings among brethren, will be fomented[41] and perpetuated to all posterity.'

I answer. Not *by*, but for *want* of a toleration, because the state is not equal in its protection but allows one sort of men to trample upon another. From hence must necessarily arise heart-burnings, which, as they have ever been so they will ever be perpetuated to posterity, unless the state wisely prevent them by taking away the distinction that foments them – namely the particular indulgence to one party and neglect of the other – by a just and equal toleration. In that family, strife and heart-burnings are commonly multiplied where one son is more cockered[42] and indulged than another, the way to foster love and

gold tried in the fire, that thou mayest be rich', because salvation is through trial: 'As many as I love, I rebuke and chasten: be zealous therefore, and repent.'

[40] 1 Samuel 5.
[41] fomented = stimulated.
[42] cockered = pampered.

amity as well in a family as in a state being an equal respect from those that are in authority.

4. They say the 'godly, painful, and orthodox ministers will be discouraged and despised'.

Answer. Upon how slight foundation is their reputation supported that fear being despised unless authority forces all to church to them? Since they have confidence to vouch themselves godly, painful and orthodox, methinks they should not doubt an audience. The apostles would empty the churches and Jewish synagogues and by the prevalency of their doctrine convert 3,000 at a sermon. And do our ministers fear, that have the opportunity of a church and the advantage of speaking an hour together without interruption, that they cannot keep those auditors they have, but that they shall be withdrawn from them by men of meaner lights (in their esteem) by the illiterate and under-valued lay preachers that are (as the ministers suppose) under the cloud of error and false doctrine? Surely they suspect their own tenets or their abilities to maintain them? They esteem it a discouragement to be opposed and fear they shall be despised if disputed withal.

5. They say 'the life and power of godliness will be eaten out by frivolous disputes and vain janglings.'

Answer. Frivolous disputes and vain janglings are as unjustifiable in the people as in the ministry; but mild and gentle reasonings (which authority are only to countenance) make much to the finding out of truth, which doth most advance the life and power of godliness. Besides, a toleration being allowed, and every sect labouring to make it appear that they are in the truth – whereof a good life, or the power of godliness being the best badge or symptom – hence will necessarily follow a noble contestation in all sorts of men to exceed in godliness, to the great improvement of virtue and piety amongst us. From whence it will be concluded too, that that sect will be supposed to have least truth in them that are least virtuous and godlike in their lives and conversations.

6. They urge that 'the whole course of religion in private families will be interrupted and undermined'.

Answer. As if the Independents and Separation were not as religious in their private families as the presbyters.

7. 'Reciprocal duties between persons of nearest and dearest relations will be extremely violated.'

Answer. A needless fear, grounded upon a supposition that difference in judgement must needs occasion coldness of affection – which indeed proceeds from the different countenance and protection which states have hitherto afforded to men of different judgements. Hence was it that in the most persecuting times, when it was almost as bad in the vulgar esteem to be an Anabaptist as a murderer, it occasioned disinheritings and many effects of want of affection in people of nearest relations. But since the common odium and vilification is in great measure taken off by the wise and just permission of all sects of men by the parliament,[43] man and wife, father and son, friend and friend, though of different opinions, can agree well together and love one another – which shows that such difference in affection is not properly the effect of difference in judgement but of persecution and of the distinct respect and different countenance that authority has formerly shown towards men not conforming.

8. They say that 'the whole work of reformation, especially in discipline and government, will be retarded, disturbed, and in danger of being utterly frustrate and void'.

It matters not, since they mean in the *Presbyterian* discipline and government, accompanied with persecution. Nay, it will be abundantly happy for the people and exceedingly conducing to a lasting peace (to which persecution is the greatest enemy) if such a government so qualified be never settled. The presbyters I hope will fall short in their aims. (1) 'Tis not certain that the parliament mean to settle the Presbyterian government, since they have not declared that government to be agreeable to God's word – although the presbyters are pleased, in their expressions, frequently to call their government, 'Christ's government'. Howsoever, their determination (which may well be supposed to be built upon their interest) is not binding. They are called to *advise* withal, not to *control*.[44] (2) In case the parliament should approve of

---

[43] On 13 September 1644, the Assembly had been subject to the Accommodation Order of the Commons to 'take into consideration the differences of opinion of the members of the Assembly in point of church government and to endeavour a union if it be possible; and, in case it cannot be done, to endeavour the finding out some ways how far tender consciences who cannot in all things submit to a common rule which shall be established, may be born with, according to the Word and as may stand with the public peace'.

[44] The Assembly had been ordered to 'consult with' and 'advise' parliament on 'a government . . . in the church as shall be most agreeable to God's holy word, and most apt to procure the peace of the church at home and nearer agreement with the church of Scotland and other reformed churches abroad'. Parliament was not amenable to the

that government in the main, yet the prelatical and persecuting power of it we may well presume (since they themselves may smart under it as well as the rest of the people) they will never establish.

9. 'All other sects and heresies in the kingdom will be encouraged to endeavour the like toleration.'

Sects and heresies! We must take leave to tell them that those are terms imposed *ad placitum*,[45] and may be retorted with the like confidence upon themselves. How *prove* they Separation to be sects and heresies? Because they differ and separate from them? That's no argument, unless they can first prove themselves to be in the truth – a matter with much presumption supposed but never yet made good. And yet upon this groundless presumption the whole fabric of their function – their claim to the churches, their pre-eminence in determining matters of religion, their eager pursuit after a power to persecute, is mainly supported. If the Separation are sects and heresies because the presbyters (supposing themselves to have the countenance of authority and some esteem with the people) judge them so, the presbyters by the same rule were so because the *bishops* – once in authority and in greater countenance with the people – did so judge *them* to be.

And whereas they say that sects and heresies will be 'encouraged to endeavour the like toleration' with the independents, I answer that 'tis their right, their due as justly as their clothes or food; and if they endeavour not for their liberty they are in a measure guilty of their own bondage. How monstrous a matter the ministers would make it to be for men to labour to be free from persecution. They think they are in the saddle already, but will never I hope have the reins in their hands.

10. Their tenth fear for the church is the same. They say 'the whole Church of England' (they mean *their* whole Church of England) 'in short time will be swallowed up with distraction and confusion'.

These things are but said, not proved. Were it not that the divines blew the coals of dissension and exasperated one man's spirit against another, I am confidently persuaded we might differ in opinion and yet love one another very well. As for any distraction or confusion that might entrench upon that civil peace, the laws might provide against

ideas that the form of church government was laid down in detail in God's law or (because of that) that it was immune from the control of the secular power. It took the so-called Erastian line that the secular power ought to control the church.

[45] *ad placitum* = at their own pleasure, without constraint of rule, or of reason.

it – which is the earnest desires both of the Independents and Separation.

V(ii)

They say toleration will bring divers mischiefs upon the commonwealth. For:

1. 'All these mischiefs in the church will have their proportionable influence upon the commonwealth.'

This is but a slight supposition and mentions no evil that is like[46] to befall the commonwealth.

2. They urge 'that the kingdom will be woefully weakened by scandals and divisions, so that the enemies both domestic and foreign will be encouraged to plot and practice against it'. I answer that the contrary hereunto is much more likely, for two reasons. (1) There is like to be a concurrence and joint assistance in the protection of the commonwealth which affords a joint protection and encouragement to the people. (2) There can be no greater argument to the people to venture their estates and lives in defence of their country and that government under which they enjoy not only a liberty of estate and person but a freedom likewise of serving God according to their consciences, which religious men account the greatest blessing upon earth. I might mention notable instances of late actions of service in Independents and Separatists, which, arising but from hopes of such a freedom, can yet scarce be paralleled by any age or story.

3. They say 'it is much to be doubted lest[47] the power of the magistrate should not only be weakened but even utterly overthrown – considering the principles and practices of independents, together with their compliance with other sectaries, sufficiently known to be antimagistratical'.

An injurious but common scandal this, whereof much use has been made to the misleading the people into false apprehensions of their brethren the separatists, to the great increase of enmity and disaffection amongst us – whereof the ministers are most especially guilty.[48] Let

---

[46] like = likely.
[47] much to be doubted lest = very likely that.
[48] The most famous exercise in this respect was to be Thomas Edwards' *Gangraena: or a catalogue and discovery of many of the errors, heresies, blasphemies and pernicious practices of the Sectaries*, which was published in three parts in 1646, beginning in February. But there were already other books attacking Independents and Sectaries, by authors like William Prynne and John Bastwick (puritan 'martyrs' who had had their ears clipped in 1639 by the bishops) and by Robert Baillie, a Scots commissioner in London.

any impartial man examine the principles and search into the practices of the Separation, and he must needs conclude that *they* are not the men that trouble England, but those rather that lay it to their charge. The Separation indeed and Independents are enemies to tyranny – none more – and oppression, from whence I believe has arisen the fore-mentioned scandal of them. But to just government and magistracy, none are more subject and obedient; and therefore the ministers may do well to lay aside such obloquies, which will otherwise, by time and other discovery, turn to their own disgrace.

VI

In the last place they say 'tis opposite to the Covenant, (1) because opposite to the reformation of religion, 'according to the word of God, and example of the best reformed churches'.[49]

I answer that the example of the best reformed churches is not binding further than they agree with the word of God, so that the word of God indeed is the only rule. Now the word of God is express for toleration, as appears by the parable of the tares growing with the wheat,[50] and by those two express and positive[51] rules: (i) every man should be fully persuaded of the truth of that way wherein he serves the Lord, and (ii) that whatsoever is not of faith is sin;[52] and (iii) by that rule of reason and pure nature cited by our blessed Saviour: namely, whatsoever ye would that men should do unto you, that do you unto them.[53]

2. They say it 'is destructive to the three kingdoms'[54] nearest conjunction and uniformity in religion and government'.

I answer that the same toleration may be allowed in the three kingdoms, together with the same religion and government – whether it

---

[49] See note 16 above.

[50] Matthew 13: 3–23.

[51] Positive rules were those rules in the Bible directly commanded by God or by Jesus.

[52] See Romans 14, a letter in which the apostle Paul enjoins toleration of differences in observance among Christians, and argues that no-one should undertake an observance (e.g. either eating meat or not, or worshipping on one particular day of the week and not another) if they do not believe that observance to be commanded. It concludes (v. 23) 'And he that eateth is damned if he eat, because he eateth not of faith: for whatsoever is not of faith is sin'.

[53] Matthew 7: 12.

[54] 1. England and Wales; 2. Scotland; 3. Ireland.

shall be Presbyterian or Independent or Anabaptistical. Besides that, I suppose which is principally intended by this part of the Covenant, 'tis the union of the three kingdoms, and making them each defensive and helpful to the other – which a toleration will be a means to further because of the encouragement that every man will have to maintain his so excellent freedom, which he cannot better do than by maintaining them all, because of the interdependency[55] they will have one upon the other.

3. 'Tis expressly 'contrary to the extirpation of schism, and whatsoever shall be found contrary to sound doctrine, and the power of godliness'.

I answer that when it is certainly determined by judges that cannot err, who are the schismatics, there may be some seeming pretence to extirpate them – though then also no power or force is to be used, but lawful means only, as the wise men have interpreted it. That is, schism and heresy (when they appear to be such) are to be rooted out by reason and debate: the sword of the spirit, not of the flesh; arguments, not blows – unto which men betake themselves upon distrust of their own foundations and consciousness of their own inability. Besides, as the presbyters judge others to be a schism from them, so others judge them to be a schism from the truth, in which sense only the Covenant can be taken.

4. 'Hereby we shall be involved in the guilt of other men's sins, and thereby be endangered to receive of their plagues.'

I answer that compulsion must necessarily occasion both much cruelty and much hypocrisy: whereof the divines, labouring so much for the cause – which is persecution – cannot be guiltless.

5. 'It seems utterly impossible (if such a toleration should be granted) that the Lord should be one, and His name one in the three kingdoms.'

I suppose they mean by that phrase, it is impossible that our judgements and profession should be one. So I believe it is whether there be a toleration or no. But certainly the likeliest way – if there be any thereunto – is by finding out one truth, which most probably will be by giving liberty to every man to speak his mind and produce his reasons and arguments, and not by hearing one sect only. That, if it does produce a forced unity, it may be more probably in error than in truth – the ministers being not so likely to deal clearly in the search thereof because of their interests as the laity, who live not thereupon,

---

[55] 'independency' in original.

but enquire for truth for truth's sake and the satisfaction of their own minds.

And thus I have done with the argumentative part of the letter. I shall only desire that what I have said may be without prejudice considered, and that the people would look upon all sorts of men and writings as they are in themselves and not as they are represented by others or forestalled by a deceitful rumour or opinion.

In this controversy concerning toleration, I make no question but the parliament will judge justly between the two parties – who have both the greatest opportunity and abilities to discern between the integrity of the one side and the interest of the other: that the one party pleads for toleration for the comfort and tranquillity of their lives and the peaceable serving of God according to their consciences, in which they desire no man's disturbance; and that the other that plead against it, may (I would I could say only *probably*) be swayed by interest and self-respects, their means and pre-eminence. I make no question but the parliament, before they proceed to a determination of matters concerning religion, will as they have heard one party – the divines – so likewise reserve one ear for all other sorts of men, knowing that they that give sentence, all parties being not heard, though the sentence be just (which then likely will not be) yet they are unjust. Besides the parliament themselves are much concerned in this controversy, since upon their dissolution they must mix with the people and then either enjoy the sweets of freedom or suffer under the most irksome yoke of priestly bondage. And therefore since they are concerned in a double respect: first, as chosen by the people to provide for their safety and freedom, whereof liberty of conscience is the principal branch, and so engaged by duty; secondly, as members of the commonwealth, and so obliged to establish freedom out of love to themselves and their posterity.

I shall only add one word more concerning this letter, which is this: that 'tis worth the observation that the same men are part of the contrivers of it, and part of those to whom 'twas sent – Mr Walker being President of Sion College, Mr Seaman one of the Deans (observe that word) and Mr Roborough, one of the Assistants.[56] All three, members

---

[56] George Walker (1581?–1651), Henry Roborough (*fl.* 1642–51), and Lazarus Seaman (d. 1675). The problem with Seaman being a Dean was probably that the word was not

of the Synod, who with the rest framing it seasonably and purposely to meet with the letter from Scotland concerning church government, may well remove the wonder and admiration that seemed to possess one of the Scotch grand divines in the synod, at the concurrence of providence in these two letters[57] – of the politic and confederated ordering whereof he could not be ignorant.

FINIS

---

biblical, and that 'deans and chapters' had been abolished as part of the ongoing church reform.

[57] Overton, *Divine observations upon the London ministers' letter* (21 January 1646) explains (p. 3) that on 1 January a letter from the General Assembly of the Church of Scotland against the toleration of Independency was read in the Westminster Assembly, and has Alexander Henderson, the Scots divine and member of the Assembly, exclaiming: 'Doubtless no other but God was the father of two such blessed twins! That at one instant of time, so many godly, learned and orthodox of the two kingdoms should so happily concourse and meet with their desires and advice for this general uniformity.'

3
The freeman's freedom vindicated
A postscript, containing a general proposition

God, the absolute sovereign lord and king of all things in heaven and earth, the original fountain and cause of all causes; who is circumscribed, governed, and limited by no rules, but doth all things merely and only by His sovereign will and unlimited good pleasure; who made the world and all things therein for His own glory; and who by His own will and pleasure, gave him, His mere creature, the sovereignty (under Himself) over all the rest of His creatures (Genesis 1: 26, 28–9) and endued him with a rational soul, or understanding, and thereby created him after His own image (Genesis 1: 26–7; 9: 6). The first of which was Adam, a male, or man, made out of the dust or clay; out of whose side was taken a rib, which by the sovereign and absolute mighty creating power of God was made a female or woman called Eve: which two are the earthly, original fountain, as begetters and bringers-forth of all and every particular and individual man and woman that ever breathed in the world since; who are, and were by nature all equal and alike in power, dignity, authority, and majesty – none of them having (by nature) any authority, dominion or magisterial power, one over or above another. Neither have they or can they exercise any but merely by institution or donation, that is to say by mutual agreement or consent – given, derived, or assumed by mutual consent and agreement – for the good benefit and comfort each of other, and not for the mischief, hurt, or damage of any: it being unnatural, irrational, sinful, wicked and unjust for any man or men whatsoever to part with so much of their power as shall enable any of their parliament-men, commissioners, trustees, deputies, viceroys, ministers, officers or servants to destroy and undo them therewith. And unnatural, irrational, sinful, wicked, unjust, devilish, and tyrannical it is, for any man whatsoever – spiritual or temporal, clergyman or layman – to appropriate and assume unto himself a power, authority and jurisdiction to rule, govern or reign over any sort of men in the world without their free consent; and whosoever doth it – whether clergyman or any other whatsoever – do thereby as much as in them lies endeavour to appropriate and assume unto themselves the office and sovereignty of God (who alone doth, and is to rule by His will and pleasure), and to be like their creator, which was the sin of the devils', who, not being content with their first station but would be like God; for which sin they were thrown down into hell, reserved in everlasting chains, under darkness, unto the judgement of the great day (Jude verse 6). And Adam's sin it was, which brought the curse upon him and all his posterity, that he was not content with the station and condition that God created him in, but did aspire unto a better and more excellent – namely to be like his creator – which proved his ruin. Yea, and indeed had been the everlasting ruin and destruction of him and all his, had not God been the more merciful unto him in the promised Messiah (Genesis 3).

From my cock-loft in the Press Yard, Newgate[1]

19 June 1646. *Per me*[2] John Lilburne

---

[1] Lilburne was in prison for scandalling Lords whom he regarded as not having prosecuted the war against the king with sufficient vigour.

[2] *Per* me = by me.

4

A remonstrance of many thousand citizens and other freeborn people of England to their own House of Commons, occasioned through the illegal and barbarous imprisonment of that famous and worthy sufferer for his country's freedoms, Lieutenant-Colonel John Lilburne. Wherein their just demands in behalf of themselves and the whole kingdom concerning their public safety, peace and freedom, is expressed, calling these their commissioners in parliament to an account: how they (since the beginning of their session to this present) have discharged their duties to the universality of the people, their sovereign lord, from whom their power and strength is derived, and by whom (ad bene placitum)[1] it is continued

Printed in the year 1646

---
[2]

A remonstrance of many thousand citizens and other freeborn people of England to their own House of Commons

We are well assured ye cannot forget that the cause of our choosing you to be parliament-men was to deliver us from all kind of bondage and to preserve the commonwealth in peace and happiness. For effecting whereof we possessed you with the same power that was in ourselves to have done the same; for we might justly have done it ourselves without you if we had thought it convenient, choosing you (as persons whom we thought fitly qualified, and faithful) for avoiding some inconveniences.

But ye are to remember this was only of us but a power of trust – which is ever revocable, and cannot be otherwise – and to be employed to no other end than our own well-being. Nor did we choose you to continue our trusts longer than the known, established constitution of this commonwealth will justly permit. And that could be but for one year at the most: for by our law, a parliament is to be called once every

---

[1] *ad bene placitum* = by their good pleasure.
[2] End of title page.

33

year, and oftener if need be – as ye well know.[3] We are your principals, and you our agents; it is a truth which you cannot but acknowledge. For if you or any other shall assume or exercise any power that is not derived from our trust and choice thereunto, that power is no less than usurpation and an oppression from which we expect to be freed, in whomsoever we find it – it being altogether inconsistent with the nature of just freedom, which ye also very well understand.

The history of our forefathers since they were conquered by the Normans does manifest that this nation has been held in bondage all along ever since by the policies and force of the officers of trust in the commonwealth, amongst whom we always esteemed kings the chiefest. And what in much of the former time was done by war and by impoverishing of the people to make them slaves and to hold them in bondage, our latter princes have endeavoured to effect by giving ease and wealth unto the people; but withal corrupting their understanding by infusing false principles concerning kings and governments and parliaments and freedoms, and also using all means to corrupt and vitiate the manners of the youth, and the strongest prop and support of the people, the gentry.

It is wonderful[4] that the failings of former kings to bring our forefathers into bondage (together with the trouble and danger that some of them drew upon themselves and their posterity by those their unjust endeavours) had not wrought in our latter kings a resolution to rely on and trust only to justice and square dealing with the people, especially considering the unaptness of the nation to bear much, especially from those that pretend to love them and unto whom they expressed so much hearty affection (as any people in the world ever did) as in the quiet admission of King James from Scotland[5] – sufficient (if any obligation would work kings to reason) to have endeared both him and his

---

[3] The Triennial Act of February 1641 laid down procedures for calling a new parliament if there had been no session of parliament for three years. But it had a preamble which began: 'Whereas by the laws and statutes of this realm the parliament ought to be holden at least once every year for the redress of grievances', because it followed much debate in which two statutes to this effect (4 Ed III.cap.14; 36 Ed III.cap. 10) were quoted against the king's prerogative of calling and dissolving parliaments at will. Lilburne and other reformers had already begun to concentrate on the preamble and its suggestion of more frequent parliaments. Overton follows their lead.

[4] wonderful = a matter of puzzlement.

[5] James VI of Scotland became also James I of England on Queen Elizabeth's death in 1604, despite having a title that could have been seriously disputed. He moved to England unopposed.

son King Charles to an inviolable love and hearty affection to the English nation. But it would not do.

They chose rather to trust unto their policies and court arts – to king-waste and delusion – than to justice and plain dealing, and did effect many things tending to our enslaving (as in your first remonstrance you show skill enough to manifest the same to all the world).[6] And this nation, having been by their delusive arts and a long-continued peace much softened and debased in judgement and spirit, did bear far beyond its usual temper or any example of our forefathers, which (to our shame), we acknowledge.

But in conclusion: longer they would not bear; and then ye were chosen to work our deliverance and to estate[7] us in natural and just liberty agreeable to reason and common equity. For whatever our forefathers were, or whatever they did or suffered or were enforced to yield unto, we are the men of the present age and ought to be absolutely free from all kinds of exorbitances, molestations or arbitrary power; and you we chose to free us from all, without exception or limitation either in respect of persons, officers, degrees, or things; and we were full of confidence that ye also would have dealt impartially on our behalf and made us the most absolute free people in the world.

But how ye have dealt with us we shall now let you know; and let the righteous God judge between you and us. The continual oppressors of the nation have been kings, which is so evident that you cannot deny it. Yourselves have told the king (whom yet you own) that his whole sixteen years' reign was one continued act of the breach of the law. You showed him that you understood his under-working with Ireland, his endeavour to enforce the parliament by the army raised against Scotland.[8] Ye were eye-witnesses of his violent attempt about the five members;[9] ye saw evidently his purpose of raising war; ye have seen him engaged, and with obstinate violence persisting in the most bloody war that ever this nation knew – to the wasting and destruction of multitudes of honest and religious people. Ye have experience that none

---

[6] Parliament's *Grand Remonstrance* of 1 December 1641 had listed nearly 200 grievances in the narrative it gave of Charles's government.

[7] estate = instate.

[8] The parliamentary claim was that the king had wished to use Irish and Scots armies to reduce his parliament to obedience in late 1641.

[9] In January 1642 the king had tried to arrest five MPs and one lord, against whom he had prepared charges of treason. Soon after, he left Westminster to find armed supporters.

but a king could do so great intolerable mischiefs – the very name of 'king' proving a sufficient charm to delude many of our brethren in Wales, Ireland, England, and Scotland too, so far as to fight against their own liberties, which you know no man under heaven could ever have done. And yet – as if you were of counsel with him and were resolved to hold up his reputation, thereby to enable him to go on in mischief – you maintained 'the king can do no wrong', and applied all his oppressions to 'evil counsellors', begging and entreating him in such submissive language to return to his kingly office and parliament as if you were resolved to make us believe he were a god without whose presence all must fall to ruin, or as if it were impossible for any nation to be happy without a king.

You cannot fight for our liberties, but it must be in the name of king and parliament; he that speaks of his cruelties must be thrust out of your House and society; your preachers must pray for him – as if he had not deserved to be excommunicated by all Christian society, or as if ye or they thought God were a respecter of the persons[10] of kings in judgement.

By this and other your like dealings – your frequent treating and tampering to maintain his honour – we that have trusted you to deliver us from his oppressions and to preserve us from his cruelties are wasted and consumed in multitudes to manifold miseries, whilst you lie ready with open arms to receive him and to make him a great and glorious king.

Have you shook this nation like an earthquake to produce no more than this for us? Is it for this that ye have made so free use and been so bold both with our persons and estates? And do you (because of our readiness to comply with your desires in all things) conceive us so sottish[11] as to be contented with such unworthy returns of our trust and love? No. It is high time we be plain with you. We are not, nor shall not be so contented. We do expect according to reason that ye should in the first place declare and set forth King Charles his wickedness openly before the world, and withal to show the intolerable inconveniences of having a kingly government from the constant evil practices of those of this nation – and so to declare King Charles an enemy, and to publish your resolution never to have any more to do with him,

---

[10] Acts 10: 34. 'Then Peter opened his mouth, and said, Of truth I perceive that God is no respecter of persons.'
[11] sottish = foolish.

but to acquit us of so great a charge and trouble forever and to convert the great revenue of the crown to the public treasure to make good the injuries and injustices done heretofore, and of late, by those that have possessed the same. And this we expected long since at your hand; and until this be done we shall not think ourselves well dealt withal in this original of all oppressions – to wit kings.

Ye must also deal better with us concerning the Lords than you have done. Ye only are chosen by us the people; and therefore in you only is the power of binding the whole nation by making, altering, or abolishing of laws. Ye have therefore prejudiced us in acting so as if ye could not make a law without both the royal assent of the king (so ye are pleased to express yourselves) and the assent of the Lords; yet when either king or Lords assent not to what you approve ye have so much sense of your own power as to assent what ye think good by an order of your own House.[12]

What is this but to blind our eyes, that we should not know where our power is lodged, nor to whom to apply ourselves for the use thereof? But if we want a law, we must await till the king and Lords assent; if an ordinance, then we must wait till the Lords assent. Yet ye, knowing their assent to be merely formal (as having no root in the choice of the people, from whom the power that is just must be derived),[13] do frequently importune their assent, which implies a most gross absurdity. For where their assent is necessary and essential, they must be as free as you to assent or dissent as their understandings and consciences should guide them and might as justly importune you as ye them.

Ye ought in conscience to reduce this case also to a certainty, and not to waste time, and open your counsels, and be liable to so many obstructions as ye have been. Ye ought to prevail with them – enjoying their honours and possessions – to be liable and stand to be chosen for knights and burgesses by the people as other the gentry and free men of this nation do, which will be an obligation upon them as having one and the same interest; then also they would be distinguished by their

---

[12] From 1642–9 there were no ordinances made without the Lords, but severe pressure was often put on them.

[13] Contemporary peers were created by a royal patent installing them in one of the various degrees of peerage or by a king's writ calling them to parliament as peers of a certain degree. However created, the degrees, titles and the rights to sit in the House of Lords thenceforth descended by primogeniture to the eldest son, and so were the result of an act of royal prerogative uncontrolled by parliament.

virtues and love to the commonwealth, whereas now they act and vote in our affairs but as intruders or as thrust upon us by kings to make good their interests, which to this day have been to bring us into a slavish subjection to their wills.

Nor is there any reason that they should in any measure be less liable to any law than the gentry are. Why should any of them assault, strike, or beat any, and not be liable to the law as other men are? Why should not they be as liable to their debts as other men?[14] There is no reason. Yet have ye stood still and seen many of us – and some of yourselves – violently abused without reparation.

We desire you to free us from these abuses *and* their negative voices, or else tell us that it is reasonable we should be slaves – this being a perpetual prejudice in our government neither consulting with freedom nor safety. With freedom it cannot: for in this way of voting in all affairs of the commonwealth, being not chosen thereunto by the people they are therein masters and lords of the people – which necessarily implies the people to be their servants and vassals. And they have used many of us accordingly, by committing divers to prison upon their own authority – namely William Larner, Lieutenant-Colonel John Lilburne, and other worthy sufferers – who upon appeal unto you have not been relieved.[15]

We must therefore pray you to make a law against all kinds of arbitrary government as the highest capital offence against the commonwealth, and to reduce all conditions of men to a certainty, that none hence forward may presume or plead anything in way of excuse, and that ye will have no favour or scruple of tyrannical power over us in any whatsoever.

Time has revealed hidden things unto us – things covered over thick and threefold with pretences of the true reformed religion – when as we see apparently that this nation and that of Scotland are joined together in a most bloody and consuming war by the waste and policy

---

[14] All members of parliament and their servants were immune from civil actions (for instance, actions for debt) during parliamentary sessions, but it was a common legal opinion that peers, their families, and those protected by them were *never* liable.

[15] On Larner, see p. 206. He had been arrested in March 1646 for publishing an unlicensed book defending religious toleration and in April was brought before the Lords, where he had refused to answer them on grounds of their incompetence to try commoners, and was imprisoned. Lilburne had suffered the same fate in June. A Leveller campaign against the Lords ensued – Overton and Walwyn prominent in it – and Overton himself was to be imprisoned by the Lords in August.

of a sort of lords in each nation that were malcontents and vexed that the king had advanced others, and not themselves, to the managing of state affairs.[16] Which they suffered till the king, increasing his oppressions in both nations, gave them opportunity to reveal themselves; and then they resolve to bring the king to their bow and regulation, and to exclude all those from managing state-affairs that he had advanced thereunto, and who were grown so insolent and presumptuous as these discontented ones were liable to continual molestations from them, either by practices at Council Table, High Commission, or Star Chamber. So as their work was to subvert the monarchical lords and clergy, and therewithal to abate the power of the king, and to order him.

But this was a mighty work and they were nowise able to effect it of themselves. 'Therefore' (say they) 'the generality of the people must be engaged; and how must this be done'? 'Why' (say they) 'we must associate with that part of the clergy that are now made underlings and others of them that have been oppressed, and with the most zealous religious non-conformists; and by the help of these we will lay before the generality of the people all the popish innovations in religion, all the oppressions of the bishops and High Commission, all the exorbitances of the Council Board and Star Chamber, all the injustice of the Chancery and courts of justice, all the illegal taxations (as ship-money, patents and projects) whereby we shall be sure to get into our party the generality of the city of London and all the considerable substantial people of both nations – by whose cry and importunity we shall have a parliament, which we shall by our manifold ways, allies, dependants, and relations soon work to our purposes.'[17]

'But' (say some) 'this will never be affected without a war; for the king will have a strong party and he will never submit to us.'

''Tis not expected otherwise' (say they); 'and great and vast sums of money must be raised, and soldiers and ammunition must be had,

---

[16] In England such peers as Lord Saye and Seal, and Lord Brooke; in Scotland the 'covenanting Lords'. Overton is describing splits in the ruling classes of the two nations who shared the same king.

[17] A very reasonable catalogue of parliament's case against the king. In 1641 the Star Chamber, the Council Board (the Privy Council acting in a judicial capacity) and High Commission were abolished, and ship money (a tax without the consent of parliament) was declared illegal. In February 1642 clerics, including bishops, were forbidden to exercise secular powers, though episcopacy was not actually abolished (and provision made for selling church lands) until October 1646.

whereof we shall not need to fear any want. For what will not an oppressed, rich, and religious people do to be delivered from all kinds of oppression, both spiritual and temporal, and to be restored to purity and freedom in religion, and to the just liberty of their persons and estates? All our care must be to hold all at our command and disposing. For if this people thus stirred up by us should make an end too soon with the king and his party, it is not much to be doubted they would place the supreme power in the House of Commons, unto whom only of right it belongs – they only being chosen by the people, which is so presently discerned that as we have a care the king and his lords must not prevail, so more especially we must be careful the supreme power fall not into the people's hands, or House of Commons'.'

'Therefore we must so act as not to make an end with the king and his party, till, by expense of time and treasure, a long, bloody and consuming war, decay of trade, and multitudes of the highest impositions, the people by degrees are tired and wearied, so as they shall not be able to contest or dispute with us either about supreme or inferior power. But we will be able, afore they are aware, to give them both law and religion.'[18]

'In Scotland it will be easy to establish the presbyterial government in the church. And that being once effected, it will not be very difficult in England – upon a pretence of uniformity in both nations and the like – unto which there will be found a clergy as willing as we, it giving them as absolute a ministry over the consciences of the people, over their persons and purses, as we ourselves aim at, or desire. And if any shall presume or oppose either us or them, we shall be easily able by the help of the clergy, by our party in the House of Commons, and by their and our influence in all parts of both nations, easily to crush and suppress them.'

'Well', (say some) 'all this may be done, but we, without abundance of travail[19] to ourselves and wounding our own consciences – for we

---

[18] It was the tension between 'peace' 'middle' and the 'war' groups in parliament which underlay a famous quarrel between Cromwell and the earl of Manchester, in which Lilburne took Cromwell's side, for which Lilburne was imprisoned, and which brought Lilburne and Walwyn together. Cromwell, who was to be in the forefront of the attempt in 1644 to reorganise the parliamentary armies for a more vigorous prosecution of the war, was told by Manchester – the paradigmatic peace-group member – 'We may beat the king ninety and nine times, and yet he will be king still. But if the king beat us once, we shall be hanged.'

[19] travail = painful labour.

must grossly dissemble before God, and all the world will see it in time – we can never do all this that ye aim at but by the very same oppressions as were practised by the king, the bishops, and all those his tyrannical instruments both in religion and civil government. And it will never last or continue long. The people will see it and hate you for it – more than ever they hated the former tyrants and oppressors. Were it not better and safer for us to be just, and *really* to do that for the people which we pretend and for which we shall so freely spend their lives and estates: and so have their love, and enjoy the peace of quiet consciences?'

'No' (say others). 'Are not we a lord, a peer of the kingdom? Have you your lordship or peerage, or those honours and privileges that belong thereunto from the love and election of the people? Your interest is as different from theirs and as inconsistent with their freedoms as those lords' and clergy's are whom we strive to supplant. And therefore rather than satisfy the people's expectations in what concerns their freedoms, it were much better to continue as we are and never disturb the king in his prerogatives nor his lords and prelates in their privileges. And therefore let us be as one; and when we talk of conscience, let us make conscience to make good unto *ourselves* and our *posterities* those dignities, honours and pre-eminencies conveyed unto us by our noble progenitors by all the means we can, not making questions for conscience' sake, or any other things. And if we be united in our endeavours, and work wisely, observing when to advance and when to give ground, we cannot fail of success, which will be an honour to our names for ever.'

These are the strong delusions that have been amongst us; and the mystery of iniquity[20] has wrought most vehemently in all our affairs. Hence it was that Strafford was so long in trial and that he had no greater heads to bear his company.[21] Hence it was that the king was

---

[20] 2 Thessalonians 2: 7–8: 'For the mystery of iniquity doth already work: only he who now letteth will let, until he be taken out of the way. And then shall that Wicked be revealed, whom the Lord shall consume with the spirit of his mouth, and shall destroy with the brightness of his coming.' The 'mystery of iniquity' was widely held to be the (variously identified) conjunction of the forces of evil (popish or English episcopal mostly) which would be overthrown in the Last Days preceding Christ's return to earth and the Last Judgement.

[21] Thomas Wentworth, first earl of Strafford, was the first of the two of Charles's 'evil councillors' to be executed by parliament for his service to the king before the war. He was condemned to death by Act of Attainder in May 1641. The other 'evil counsellor' to be executed was William Laud, archbishop of Canterbury, in January 1645.

not called to an account for his oppressive government and that the treachery of those that would have enforced you was not severely punished. Hence it was that the king gained time to raise an army, and the queen to furnish ammunition, and that our first and second armies were so ill-formed, and as ill-managed. Sherborne, Brentford, Exeter, the slender use of the Associate Counties, the slight guarding of the sea, Oxford, Dennington, the west defeat, did all proceed from (and upon) the mystery of iniquity.[22]

The king and his party had been nothing in your hands had not some of you been engaged, and some of you ensnared, and the rest of you overborne with this mystery, which you may now easily perceive if you have a mind thereunto. That ye were put upon the continuation of this parliament during the pleasure of both houses[23] was from this mystery, because in time these politicians had hopes to work and pervert you to forsake the common interest of those that chose and trusted you, to promote their unjust design to enslave us – wherein they have prevailed too, too, much.

For we must deal plainly with you. Ye have long time acted more like the house of peers[24] than the House of Commons. We can scarcely approach your door with a request or motion, though by way of petition, but ye hold long debates whether we break not your privileges. The king's or the Lords' pretended prerogatives never made a greater noise nor was made more dreadful than the name of privilege of the House of Commons.

Your members, in all impositions, must not be taxed in the places where they live, like other men. Your servants have their privileges too. To accuse or prosecute any of you is become dangerous to the prosecutors. Ye have imprisonments as frequent for either witnesses or prosecutors as ever the Star Chamber had: and ye are furnished with new-devised arguments to prove that ye only may justly do these gross injustices which the Star Chamber, High Commission, and Council Board might not do – and for doing whereof (whilst ye were untainted) ye abolished them. But ye now frequently commit men's persons to

---

[22] These sieges and battles were lost at the low point in parliament's fortunes in 1643 and 1644. Associations of separate county armies were thought to be a solution by the 'war' party.

[23] By *An Act to prevent inconveniences which may happen by the untimely adjourning, proroguing, or dissolving this present parliament* (10 May 1641), the Long Parliament (as it was now set to become) could not be dissolved except by statute.

[24] peers = lords.

prison without showing cause; ye examine men upon interrogatories and questions against themselves and imprison them for refusing to answer; and ye have officious servile men that write and publish sophistical arguments to justify your so doing – for which they are rewarded and countenanced, as the Star Chamber and High Commission beagles lately were – whilst those that ventured their lives for your establishment are many of them vexed and molested and impoverished by them. Ye have entertained to be your committees' servants those very prowling varlets that were employed by those unjust courts who took pleasure to torment honest conscionable people; ye vex and molest honest men for matters of religion and difference with you and your Synod in judgement, and take upon you to determine of doctrine and discipline – approving this, and reproaching that, just like unto former ignorant politic and superstitious parliaments and convocations[25] – and thereby have divided honest people amongst themselves by countenancing only those of the presbytery and discountenancing all the Separation, Anabaptists and Independents.

And though it rests in you to acquiet[26] all differences in affection (though not in judgement) by permitting everyone to be fully persuaded in their own minds, commanding all reproach to cease, yet as ye also had admitted Machiavel's[27] maxim '*Divide et impera*, divide and prevail', ye countenance only one, open the printing press only unto one, and that to the presbytery, and suffer them to rail and abuse and domineer over all the rest – as if also ye had discovered and digested that without a powerful, compulsive, presbytery in the church, a compulsive mastership or aristocratical government over the people in the state could never long be maintained.

Whereas truly we are well assured, neither you nor none else can have any power at all to conclude the people in matters that concern the worship of God. For therein every one of us ought to be fully assured in our own minds and to be sure to worship Him according to our consciences. Ye may *propose* what form ye conceive best and most available for information and well-being of the nation, and may per-

---

[25] National convocations, made up of two houses of clergy (an upper house of bishops), were called at the king's command – most recently in 1604, 1606 and 1640. They claimed, with the king's consent (perhaps parliament's too), to make canon law to govern the church. The convocation of 1640 had been extremely subservient to the king.

[26] acquiet = make quiet.

[27] Machiavelli's.

suade and invite thereunto; but *compel*, ye cannot justly. For ye have no power from us so to do, nor could you have. For we could not confer a power that was not in ourselves, there being none of us that can without wilful sin bind ourselves to worship God after any other way than what (to a tittle) in our own particular understandings we approve to be just. And therefore we could not refer ourselves to you in things of this nature. And surely if we could not confer this power upon you ye cannot have it, and so not exercise it justly. Nay, as we ought not to revile or reproach any man for his differing with us in judgement more than we would be reviled or reproached for ours, even so ye ought not to countenance any reproachers or revilers or molesters for matters of conscience but to protect and defend all that live peaceably in the commonwealth, of what judgement or way of worship whatsoever.

And if ye would bend your minds thereunto and leave yourselves open to give ear and to consider such things as would be presented unto you, a just way would be discovered for the peace and quiet of the land in general and of every well-minded person in particular. But if you lock up yourselves from hearing all voices, how is it possible you should 'try all things'?[28] It is not for you to assume a power to control and force religion or a way of church government upon the people because former parliaments have so done. Ye are first to prove that ye *could have* such a power justly entrusted unto you by the people that trusted you – which you see you have not.

We may haply be answered that the king's writ that summons a parliament and directs the people to choose knights and burgesses implies the establishment of religion.[29] To which we answer that if kings would prove themselves lawful magistrates they must prove themselves to be so by a lawful derivation of their authority, which

---

[28] 1 John 4: 1. 'Beloved, believe not every spirit, but try the spirits whether they are of God: because many false prophets are gone out in the world.'

[29] In the writ sheriffs were told that the king proposed to hold a parliament 'for certain difficult and urgent businesses concerning us [the king], the state and defence of England and the English church', and that knights from the shires and burgesses from the boroughs should be caused by the sheriff in question to be elected so as 'to have conference and to treat with the prelates, great men and peers' and be delegated sufficient power to 'perform and consent to those things' which would happen in parliament. The king – and then the parliament without him, obviously with more difficulty – argued against the *jure divino* claims of their established churches (anglican and Presbyterian respectively) that they (king or parliament, without the church) had the power to settle religion.

must be from the voluntary trust of the people; and then the case is the same with them as between the people and you – they (as you) being possessed of no more power than what is *in* the people justly to entrust. And then all implications in the writs of the establishment of religion show that in that particular, as many other, we remain under the Norman yoke of an unlawful power, from which we ought to free ourselves, and which ye ought not to maintain upon us, but to abrogate.

But ye have listened to any counsels rather than to the voice of us that trusted you. Why is it that you have stopped the press but that you would have nothing but pleasing, flattering, discourses and go on to make yourselves partakers of the lordship over us, without hearing anything to the contrary?

Yea, your lords and clergy long to have us in the same condition with our deluded brethren, the commons of Scotland, where their understandings are so captivated with a reverend opinion of their presbytery that they really believe them to be by divine authority, and are as zealous therein as ever the poor deceived papists were. As much they live in fear of their thunder-bolts of excommunication – and good cause they have, poor souls, for those excommunications are so followed with the civil sanctions, or secular power – that they are able to crush any opposer or dissenter to dust, to undo or ruin any man. So absolute a power has their new clergy already gained over the poor people there, and earnestly labour to bring us into the same condition, because if we should live in greater freedom in this nation it would (they know) in time be observed by *their* people, whose understandings would be thereby informed, and then they would grow impatient of their thraldom and shake off their yoke.

They are also in no less bondage in things civil. The lords and great men over-rule all as they please; the people are scarce free in anything.

Friends, these are known truths.

And hence it is that in their counsels here they adhere to those that maintain their own greatness and usurped rule over us, lest if we should dare possess greater liberty than their vassals, the people in Scotland, they might in short time observe the same and discharge themselves of their oppressions.

It is from the mystery of iniquity that ye have never made that use of the people of this nation in your war as you might have done, but have chosen rather to hazard *their* coming in than to arm your own native undoubted friends: by which means they are possessed of too

45

many considerable strengths of this nation, and speak such language in their late published papers as if they were not paid for their – slow – assistance. Whereas ye might have ended the war long ere this, if by sea or land you had showed yourselves resolved to make us a free people. But it is evident a change of our bondage is the uttermost is intended us, and that, too, for a worse, and longer – if we shall be so contented.

But it is strange you should imagine that. For the truth is we find none are so much hated by you as those you think do discern those your purposes, or that apply themselves unto you with motions tending to divert you from proceeding therein. For some years now, no condition of men can prevail with you to amend anything that is amiss in the commonwealth.

The exorbitances in the city's government and the strivings about prerogatives in the mayor and aldermen against the freedoms of the commons (and to their extreme prejudice) are returned to the same point they were at in Garway's time[30] – which you observe, and move not, nor assist the commons. Nay, worse than in his time, they are justified by the mayor in a book published and sent by him to every Common Councilman.[31]

The oppression of the Turkey Company and the Adventurers' Company, and all other infringements of our native liberties of the same nature and which in the beginnings of the parliament ye seemed to abominate, are now by you complied withal and licensed to go on in their oppressions.[32]

Ye know the laws of this nation are unworthy a free people and deserve from first to last to be considered and seriously debated, and reduced to an agreement with common equity and right reason, which ought to be the form and life of every government – Magna Carta itself being but a beggarly thing containing many marks of intolerable

[30] Sir Henry Garway was Lord Mayor in 1639–40. Active in collecting ship money and severe on anti-episcopal demonstrators, he attempted to stop the Common Council petitioning the king about city grievances. He became a royalist.

[31] The Mayor was Thomas Adams (1586–1688), a political Presbyterian and neo-royalist.

[32] Overton refers mainly to the Merchant Adventurers' Company and the Levant Company, who had monopolies on overseas trade, notably in the Low Countries and Germany, and in the Mediterranean. Industrial monopolies, granted by crown patent to individuals and companies, had long been unpopular. Many were abolished in 1624, and the Long Parliament undertook a revision of the system. But the trading monopolies had been less of a kingly than a traders' convenience, and they survived.

bondage; and the laws that have been made since by parliaments have in very many particulars made our government much more oppressive and intolerable.

The Norman way for ending of controversies was much more abusive than the English way; yet the Conqueror, contrary to his oath, introduced the Norman laws and his litigious and vexatious way amongst us. The like he did also for punishment of malefactors – controversies of all natures having *before* a quick and final dispatch[33] in every hundred. He erected a trade of judges and lawyers to sell justice and injustice at his own unconscionable rate and in what time he pleased, the corruption whereof is yet remaining upon us to our continual impoverishing and molestation from which we thought you should have delivered us.

Ye know also imprisonment for debt is not from the beginning. Yet ye think not of these many thousand persons and families that are destroyed thereby. Ye are rich and abound in goods and have need of nothing; but the afflictions of the poor – your hunger-starved brethren – ye have no compassion of.[34] Your zeal makes a noise as far as Argiere to deliver those captived Christians at the charge of others,[35] but those whom your own unjust laws hold captive in your own prisons – these are too near you to think of. Nay, ye suffer poor Christians, for whom Christ died, to kneel before you in the streets – aged, sick, and crippled – begging your half-penny charities, and ye rustle by them in your coaches and silks daily, without regard or taking any course for their constant relief. Their sight would melt the heart of any Christian and yet it moves not you nor your clergy.

We entreat you to consider what difference there is between binding a man to an oar as a galley-slave in Turkey or Argiere, and pressing of men to serve in your war. To surprise a man on the sudden, force him from his calling where he lived comfortably from a good trade, from his dear parents, wife or children, against inclination and disposition to

---

[33] dispatch = speedy settlement.

[34] Small producers and merchants might have been expected to react very favourably to this proposal. As extenders of credit, they needed machinery for recovery of debts – and a man in prison could not be forced to pay, indeed might even go there (where the living was comfortable enough if they had money to buy provisions and to bribe the jailers) to avoid it. And when they were debtors themselves, they needed to stay out of prison to trade their way into a position to pay.

[35] Argiere = Algiers. A continuing problem was that Moorish and Turkish pirates captured and imprisoned English merchants there for ransom.

fight for a cause he understands not and in company of such as he has
no comfort to be withal, for pay that will scarce give him sustenance –
and if he live, to return to a lost trade, or beggary, or not much better:
if any tyranny or cruelty exceed this, it must be worse than that of a
Turkish galley-slave.[36]

But ye are apt to say, 'what remedy? Men we must have.' To which
we answer in behalf of ourselves and our too-much-injured brethren
that are pressed: that the Hollanders, our provident neighbours, have
no such cruelties, esteeming nothing more unjust or unreasonable; yet
they want no men. And if ye would take care that all sorts of men
might find comfort and contentment in your government ye would not
need to enforce men to serve your wars. And if ye would in many
things follow their good example and make this nation a state free from
the oppression of kings and the corruptions of the court and show love
to the people in the constitutions of your government, the affection of
the people would satisfy all common and public occasions. And in many
particulars we can show you a remedy for this and all other inconveniences – if we could find you inclinable to hear us.

Ye are extremely altered in demeanour towards us. In the beginning
ye seemed to know what freedom was, made a distinction of honest
men, whether rich or poor. All were welcome to you and ye would mix
yourselves with us in a loving familiar way, void of courtly observance
or behaviour. Ye kept your committee doors open. All might hear and
judge of your dealings. Hardly ye would permit men to stand bareheaded before you, some of you telling them ye more regarded their
health, and that they should not deem[37] of you as of other domineering
courts. Ye and they were one, all commons of England. And the like
ingenious carriage by which ye won our affections to that height that
ye no sooner demanded anything but it was effected. Ye did well then.
Who did hinder you? The mystery of iniquity: that was it that per-
verted your course.

---

[36] The New Model had great difficulty in pressing infantry ('scum', said an officer) and
dragoons ('middling sorts'). The horse, volunteering themselves and equipment,
remained fairly stable from the spring of 1645 to the summer of 1646 (5,000 to 6,500)
but the foot and dragoons varied from 6,500 to 18,000. Only one of every two pressed
men arrived at the front. Perhaps 40,000 men were recruited during the period to keep
the army's strength at the low 20,000 mark. Desertion was endemic, especially after
victory and the chance to escape with loot. The core of the faithful was maybe 11,000.

[37] deem = judge.

What a multitude of precious lives has been lost? What a mass of monies has been raised? What one way was proposed to advance monies that was refused by you, though never so prejudical to the people? (Allowing your committees to force men to pay or lend or else to swear that they were not worth so or so – the most destructive course to tradesmen that could be devised: fifty entire subsidies to be lent throughout London, if not procured, yet authorised by you?)[38] Never the like heard of.

And the excise, that being once settled, all other assessments should cease. Notwithstanding, in few months comes forth ordinance upon ordinance for more monies.[39] And for the customs. They were thought an oppression in the beginning, and being so high, an hindrance to trade and extremely prejudicial to the nation; nevertheless they are now confirmed with many augmentations, insomuch as men of inferior trading find great trouble to provide monies for customs and have so many officers to please that it is a very slavery to have anything to do with them; and no remedy – the first commissioners being more harsh and ingenious than the late farmers, and the last worse then the former. Truly it is a sad thing but too true: a plain quiet-minded man in any place in England is just like a harmless sheep in a thicket – can hardly move or stir but he shall be stretched and lose his wool – such committees have ye made in all cities and counties, and none are so ill-used as honest godly men.

Ye have now sat full five years, which is four years longer than we intended; for we could choose you but for (at most) one year. And now

[38] War finance was always a problem for the parliament, and the measures taken were in fact objected to by the municipality of London and its Presbyterian supporters as much as by the now emerging Leveller movement. Enforcement was difficult. Loans were required, and those who had property and moveables worth more than £100 p.a. were required to pay weekly (later monthly) assessments. Tax avoiders were assessed at one-twentieth of their real estate and one-fifth of their personal possessions. A parliamentary committee was set up at Haberdashers' Hall to administer these and other extraordinary taxes throughout the nation; a sub-committee at Weavers' Hall spawned at least 110 collectors and overseers throughout London, its outparishes and surrounding villages. Outside London, county committees were responsible for the assessment and collection of taxes.

[39] Excise, a tax on manufactured goods before they went to sale, had first been imposed in 1643. It covered an expanding range of essential goods, like beer and meat (though not bread). It spawned a horde of excise officers, the hope being it would finance the war. But by 1645 assessments, fines on delinquents' estates and sale of crown-fee farm rents overtook it.

we wish ye would publish to all the world the good that you have done for us, the liberty ye have brought us unto. If ye could excuse yourselves as ye used to do by saying it has been a time of war, that will not do. For when the war might in the beginning have been prevented if ye had drawn a little more blood from the right vein, and might often (ere this) have been ended, occasion has been given away and treated away. And now, when through the faithfulness of the New Model[40] ye have almost forced an end and have no great part to effect, now again at the instigation of those that love their kings more than all this nation and their own, his 'sacred' or 'holy' majesty must again be treated with – their national and Solemn League and Covenant with their God binding them to be respecters of persons in judgement and to preserve his person in the defence of the true, Protestant religion and liberty of the people[41] – that has constantly against all persuasion and obligation done whatever he could to subvert both. If this be not the height of the mystery of iniquity, what is higher?

But let not these be deceived, nor thus under zealous expressions deceive you. We wish your souls may no further enter into their secret; for God will not be mocked nor suffer such gross hypocrisy to pass without exemplary punishment.[42] And if ye believe there is a God, ye *must* believe it; and if ye *do* believe it, and consider the ways ye have trod and truly repent, *show* it by walking contrary to what ye have done or purposed to do and let us quickly and speedily partake thereof. For God is a God that takes vengeance[43] and will not suffer you to go on to our ruin.

We have some hopes ye will; for amongst you there have been always faithful and worthy men whose abundant grief it has been to observe

---

[40] The formation of the New Model Army in the first three months of 1645 was part of a process in which three southern armies under aristocratic and incompetent army commanders (the earls of Essex and Manchester among them) were replaced by a single army under Sir Thomas Fairfax. It was this army that took parliament to victory.

[41] Article III of the *Solemn League and Covenant*: 'We shall with the same sincerity, reality and constancy, in our several vocations endeavour with our estates and lives mutually to preserve the rights and privileges of the parliaments, and the liberties of the kingdoms, and to preserve and defend the king's majesty's person and authority in the preservation of the true religion and liberties of the kingdoms, that the world may bear witness with our consciences of our loyalty, and that we have no thoughts or intentions to diminish his majesty's just power and greatness.'

[42] Galatians 6: 7. 'Be not deceived; God is not mocked; for whatsoever a man soweth, that shall he also reap.'

[43] E.g. Psalms 94: 1; Nahum 1: 2; 2 Thessalonians 1: 8.

the strange progress of the chosen men of the commonwealth, and have strove exceedingly on all occasions to produce better effects, and some Christians of late produced to their praise.

Others there are that have been only misled by the policies and stratagems of politic men; and these, after this our serious advice, will make you more seriously study the common interest of this nation. Others there are – and those a great number – that are newly chosen into your House,[44] and we trust are such as will exceedingly strengthen the good part that hitherto has been too weak to steer an even course amidst so many oppositions and cross waves, but henceforth joined all in one will be able to do and carry on whatsoever is just and good for the commonwealth: the more just and good, the more easily effected; for such things are easily to be made evident to all men and can never fail of the uttermost assistance of all well-minded people. And therefore we would not have you to be discouraged in attempting whatsoever is evidently just. For we will therein assist you to the last drop of our blood. Fear neither the Anakims nor the sons of the giants: for the Lord our God He will stand by you in all things that are just and will bless and prosper you therein.[45]

Forsake and utterly renounce all crafty and subtle intentions; hide not your thoughts from us and give us encouragement to be open-breasted unto you. Proclaim aforehand what ye determine to do in establishing anything for continuance; and hear all things that can be spoken with or against the same; and to that intent, let the imprisoned presses at liberty that all men's understandings may be more conveniently informed and convinced as fair as is possible by the equity of your proceedings.

---

[44] 'Recruiters', new men, were elected to the House of Commons, mainly in 1645 and 1646, to replace royalist defectors. Before the parliamentarian victory in the first civil war they tended to be what historians call 'Political Independents' (i.e. eager to win the war and force the king to a settlement; more likely to be somewhat tolerant in religion, even if some were 'Religious Presbyterians'); after the victory they tended to be 'Political Presbyterians' (i.e. willing to settle for minimum constitutional change, but insisting on a Presbyterian church settlement, often not so much because they believed that that was the form of church ordained in scripture, but for the sake of social order and control. Not all of them were against toleration, but their city and clerical allies were.)

[45] The Anakims were the gigantic descendants of Arba, founder of Hebron and the despair of Israel. Though they were to be conquered and contained by Moab and Joshua, the Israelites regarded themselves as 'grasshoppers' compared with this gigantic race (Numbers 13: 28, 33). A common saying was 'Who shall stand before the sons of Anakim?' (Deuteronomy 9: 2).

We cannot but expect to be delivered from the Norman bondage whereof we now as well as our predecessors have felt the smart by these bloody wars, and from all unreasonable laws made ever since that unhappy conquest. As we have encouragement, we shall inform you further, and guide you as we observe your doings.

The work, ye must note, is ours and not your own, though ye are to be partakers with us in the well or ill-doing thereof. And therefore ye must expect to hear more frequently from us then ye have done; nor will it be your wisdom to take these admonitions and cautions in evil part. If ye consider well ye may wonder we are no tarter. Ye may perceive we have not yet left our true English confidence, but are willing that both you and all our neighbour nations should know that we both see and know all stratagems and policies that are laid in wait to entrap – and so to enslave – us, and that we bid defiance to their worst our enemies can do. We know we have store of friends in our neighbour countries.

Our head is not yet so intoxicated with this new mystery of iniquity but that a reasonable cordial administered by your hand will set us fast in our seat.

Ye are not to reckon that ye have any longer time to effect the great work we have entrusted unto you; for we must not lose our free choice of a parliament once every year, fresh and fresh for a continual parliament. For so, if a present parliament be mistaken in their understandings and do things prejudicial, we may so long remain under these prejudices that the commonwealth may be endangered thereby. Nor do we value a triennial parliament. Before three years come to an end grievances and mischiefs may be past remedy. And therefore our advice is that ye order a meeting of the chosen of parliament-men to be expressly upon one certain day in November yearly throughout the land in the places accustomed and to be by you expressed, there to make choice of whom they think good, according to law – and all men that have a right to be there, not to fail upon a great penalty, but no summons to be expected. And if any person without exception shall write letters or use any endeavours to incline the choosers to choose any man, or use any means to disturb or pervert them from a free choice, then that all such sinister dealing be made punishable or a most heinous crime. And that a parliament so chosen in November, succeeding year by year, may come in stead of the preceding parliament, and proceed with the affairs of the commonwealth. Nor would we have it in the power of our parliament to receive any member from his place or service of the House without the consent had of those counties, cities and boroughs respectively that choose him – great inconveniences depending thereon, whereof we have seen and felt too much.

Now, if ye shall conscionably[46] perform your trust the year ensuing and order the parliaments to succeed as aforesaid, then we shall not doubt to be made absolute freemen in time, and become a just, plenteous and powerful nation. All that is past will be forgotten and we shall yet have cause to rejoice in your wisdom and fidelity.

Postscript

Moreover as for me, God forbid that I should sin against the Lord in ceasing to pray for you: but I will teach you the good and the right way: Only fear the Lord, and serve him in truth and with all your heart: for consider how great things he has done for you. But if ye shall still do wickedly, ye shall be consumed, both ye and your king. 1 Samuel 12: 23–25.[47]

---

[46] conscionably = in good conscience.
[47] The original says verse 22.

53

5

*An arrow against all tyrants and tyranny, shot from the
prison of Newgate into the prerogative bowels of the
arbitrary House of Lords and all other usurpers and
tyrants whatsoever. Wherein the original, rise, extent, and
end of magisterial power, the natural and national rights,
freedoms and properties of mankind are discovered and
undeniably maintained; the late oppressions and
encroachments of the Lords over the commons legally (by
the fundamental laws and statutes of this realm, as also by
a memorable extract out of the records of the Tower of
London) condemned; the late Presbyterian ordinance
(invented and contrived by the diviners, and by the motion
of Mr Bacon and Mr Tate read in the House of
Commons) examined, refuted, and exploded, as most
inhumane, tyrannical and barbarous*

By Richard Overton

*Prerogative archer to the arbitrary House of Lords, their prisoner in
Newgate, for the just and legal properties, rights and freedoms of the commons of England. Sent by way of a letter from him, to Mr Henry Marten,[1]
a member of the House of Commons*

*Imprimatur
Rectat Justitia*

*Printed at the backside of the Cyclopian Mountains, by Martin Claw-
Clergy, printer to the reverend Assembly of Divines, and are to be sold
at the sign of the Subject's Liberty, right opposite to Persecuting Court.
1646*

---

[2]

*An arrow against all tyrants and tyranny, shot from the prison of Newgate
into the prerogative bowels of the arbitrary House of Lords, and all other
usurpers and tyrants whatsoever*

---

[1] Marten. See biographies below, pp. 207–8.
[2] End of title page.

Sir,

To every individual in nature is given an individual property by nature not to be invaded or usurped by any. For every one, as he is himself, so he has a self-propriety, else could he not *be* himself; and of this no second may presume to deprive any of without manifest violation and affront to the very principles of nature and of the rules of equity and justice between man and man. Mine and thine cannot be, except this be. No man has power over my rights and liberties, and I over no man's. I may be but an individual, enjoy my self and my self-propriety and may right myself no more than my self, or presume any further; if I do, I am an encroacher and an invader upon another man's right – to which I have no right. For by natural birth all men are equally and alike born to like propriety, liberty and freedom; and as we are delivered of God by the hand of nature into this world, every one with a natural, innate freedom and propriety – as it were writ in the table of every man's heart, never to be obliterated – even so are we to live, everyone equally and alike to enjoy his birthright and privilege; even all whereof God by nature has made him free.

And this by nature everyone's desire aims at and requires; for no man naturally would be befooled of his liberty by his neighbour's craft or enslaved by his neighbour's might. For it is nature's instinct to preserve itself from all things hurtful and obnoxious; and this in nature is granted of all to be most reasonable, equal and just: not to be rooted out of the kind, even of equal duration with the creature. And from this fountain or root all just human powers take their original – not immediately from God (as kings usually plead their prerogative) but mediately by the hand of nature, as from the represented to the representers. For originally God has implanted them in the creature, and from the creature those powers immediately proceed and no further. And no more may be communicated than stands for the better being, weal, or safety thereof. And this is man's prerogative and no further; so much and no more may be given or received thereof: even so much as is conducent to a better being, more safety and freedom, and no more. He that gives more, sins against his own flesh; and he that takes more is thief and robber to his kind – every man by nature being a king, priest and prophet in his own natural circuit and compass, whereof no second may partake but by deputation, commission, and free consent from him whose natural right and freedom it is.

And thus sir and no otherwise are you instated into your sovereign capacity for the free people of this nation. For their better being, discipline, government, propriety and safety have each of them communicated so much unto you (their chosen ones) of their natural rights and powers, that you might thereby become their absolute commissioners and lawful deputies. But no more: that by contraction of those their several individual communications conferred upon and united in you, you alone might become their own natural, proper, sovereign power, therewith singly and only empowered for their several weals, safeties and freedoms, and no otherwise. For as by nature no man may abuse, beat, torment, or afflict himself, so by nature no man may give that power to another, seeing he may not do it himself; for no more can be communicated from the general than is included in the particulars whereof the general is compounded.

So that such, so deputed, are to the general no otherwise than as a school-master to a particular – to this or that man's family. For as such an one's mastership, ordering and regulating power is but by deputation – and that *ad bene placitum*[3] and may be removed at the parents' or headmaster's pleasure upon neglect or abuse thereof, and be conferred upon another (no parents ever giving such an absolute unlimited power to such over their children as to do to them as they list, and not to be retracted, controlled, or restrained in their exorbitances) – even so and no otherwise is it with you our deputies in respect of the general. It is in vain for you to think you have power over us to save us or destroy us at your pleasure, to do with us as you list, be it for our weal or be it for our woe, and not be enjoined in mercy to the one or questioned in justice for the other. For the edge of your own arguments against the king in this kind may be turned upon yourselves. For if for the safety of the people he might in equity be opposed by you in his tyrannies, oppressions and cruelties, even so may you by the same rule of right reason be opposed by the people in general in the like cases of destruction and ruin by you upon them; for the safety of the people is the sovereign law,[4] to which all must become subject, and for the which all powers human are ordained by them; for tyranny, oppression and cruelty whatsoever, and in whomsoever, is in itself unnatural, illegal,

---

[3] *ad bene placitum* = during the good pleasure (of the deputer).
[4] *salus populi suprema lex* was a phrase especially prominent in the writings of Parker, with which Overton and Lilburne were very familiar. Compare text 1.

yea absolutely anti-magisterial; for it is even destructive to all human civil society, and therefore resistible.

Now sir, the commons of this nation, having empowered their body representative (whereof you are one) with their own absolute sovereignty, thereby authoritatively and legally to remove from amongst them all oppressions and tyrannies, oppressors and tyrants – how great soever in name, place, or dignity – and to protect, safeguard and defend them from all such unnatural monsters, vipers and pests, bred of corruption or which are intruded amongst them; and as much as in them lies to prevent all such for the future. And to that end you have been assisted with our lives and fortunes most liberally and freely with most victorious and happy success, whereby your arms are strengthened with our might, that now you may make us all happy within the confines of this nation if you please. And therefore sir, in reason, equity and justice we deserve no less at your hands.

And (sir) let it not seem strange unto you that we are thus bold with you for our own. For by nature we are the sons of Adam, and from him have legitimately derived a natural propriety, right and freedom, which only we require. And how in equity you can deny us we cannot see. It is but the just rights and prerogative of mankind (whereunto the people of England are heirs apparent as well as other nations) which we desire; and sure you will not deny it us, that we may be men and live like men. If you do, it will be as little safe for yourselves and posterity as for us and our posterity. For sir, look: what bondage, thraldom, or tyranny soever you settle upon us, you certainly, or your posterity will taste of the dregs. If by your present policy and (abused) might, you chance to ward it from yourselves in particular, yet your posterity – do what you can – will be liable to the hazard thereof.

And therefore sir we desire your help for your own sakes as well as for ourselves, chiefly for the removal of two most insufferable evils daily encroaching and increasing upon us, portending and threatening inevitable destruction and confusion of yourselves, of us, and of all our posterities: namely the encroachments and usurpations of the House of Lords over the commons' liberties and freedoms, together with the barbarous, inhuman, blood-thirsty desires and endeavours of the Presbyterian clergy.

For the first, namely the exorbitances of the Lords: they are to such an height aspired, that contrary to all precedents, the free commoners of England are imprisoned, fined and condemned by them (their incompetent, illegal, unequal, improper judges) against the express letter of Magna Carta chapter 29 (so often urged and used): that no free man of England 'shall be passed upon, tried, or condemned, but by the lawful judgement of his equals, or by the law of the land', which, as says Sir Edward Coke in his exposition of Magna Carta, p. 28, last line, is '*per pares*, by his peers, that is, by his equals'. And page 46, branches 1, 2 and 5, in these words:[5]

> 1. That no man be taken or imprisoned, but *per legem terrae*, that is by the common law, statute law, or custom of England. For these words, *per legem terrae* being towards the end of this chapter, do refer to *all* the pretended matters in this chapter; and this has the first place, because the liberty of a man's person is more precious to him than all the rest that follow; and therefore it is great reason that he should by law be relieved therein, if he be wronged, as hereafter shall be showed.
> 2. No man shall be disseised, that is, put out of seisin, or dispossessed of his freehold (that is, lands or livelihood) or of his liberties or free customs (that is, of such franchises and freedoms, and free customs, as belong to him by his free birthright) unless it be by the lawful judgement, that is verdict of his equals (that is of men of his own condition) or by the law of the land (that is, to speak it once for all) by the due course and processes of law.
> 3. No man shall be in any sort destroyed unless it be by the verdict of his equals or according to the law of the land.

And, chapter 29 of Magna Carta, it is said, '*secundum legem et consuetudinem Angliae*' (after the law and custom of England) '*non regis Angliae*' (not of the *king* of England) – 'lest it might be thought to bind the king only, *nec populi Angliae*, not the people of England; 'but that the law might tend to all, it is said, *per legem terra*, by the law of the land'.[6]

'Against this ancient and fundamental law, and in the very face thereof', says Sir Edward Coke, he found an act of the parliament made in the 11 Hen. VII cap. 3:

> that as well Justices of the Peace, without any finding or presentment by the verdict of twelve men, upon the bare information for the king before them – should have full power and authority by their discretions to hear and determine all offences and contempts committed or done by any person or persons against the form, ordinance, and effect of any statute made and not repealed. By

---

[5] Coke, *The second part of the institutes of the lawes of England* (1642).
[6] Coke actually says this differently and better: 'And it is not said, *legem & Consuetudinem Regis Angliae, &c*, [the laws and customs of the king of England] lest it might be thought to bind the king only, nor *populi Angliae*, [of the people of England] lest it might be thought to bind them only, but that the law might extend to all, it is said *per legem terrae . . .*'.

colour of which act, shaking this fundamental law, it is not credible (says he) what horrible oppressions and exactions – to the undoing of infinite numbers of people – were committed by Sir Richard Empson, Knight, and Edmund Dudley, being Justices of the Peace through England; and upon this unjust and injurious act (as commonly in the like cases it falls out) a new office was erected, and they made Masters of the King's Forfeitures.

But at the parliament held in 1 Hen. VIII (cap. 6), this Act of Henry VII is recited, made void and repealed; and the reason thereof is yielded: for that by force of the said act it was manifestly known that many sinister, crafty, and forged informations had been pursued against divers of the king's subjects, to their great damage and unspeakable vexation – a thing most frequent and usual at this day and in these times – the ill success whereof, together with the most fearful end of these great oppressors, should deter others from committing the like and should admonish parliaments in the future, that instead of this ordinary and precious trial *per legem terra* they bring not in an absolute and partial trial by discretion.[7]

And to this end the judgement upon Simon de Beresford, a commoner, in the fourth year of Edward III's reign, is an excellent precedent for these times (as is to be seen upon record in the Tower in the second roll of parliament held the same year of the said king and delivered into the Chancery by Henry de Edenston, Clerk of the Parliament) – for that the said Simon de Beresford having counselled, aided and assisted Roger de Mortimer to the murder of the father of the said king, the king commanded the earls and barons in the said parliament assembled to give right and lawful judgement unto the said Simon de Beresford. But the earls, barons and peers came before the lord the king in the same parliament and said with one voice that the aforesaid Simon was not their peer or equal, wherefore they were not bound to judge him as a peer of the land. Yet notwithstanding all this, the earls, barons and peers (being over-swayed by the king) *did* award and adjudge (as judges of parliament, by the assent of the king in the said parliament) that the said Simon as a traitor and enemy of the realm should be hanged and drawn; and execution accordingly was done. But as by the said roll appears, it was by full parliament condemned and adjudged as illegal, and as a precedent not to be drawn into example. The words of the said roll are these, viz.

---

[7] Coke, *Institutes*, p. 51.

59

And it is assented and agreed by our lord the king and all the grandees in full parliament: that albeit the said peers as judges in full parliament took upon them in presence of our lord the king to make and give the said judgement by the assent of the king upon some of them that were not their peers (to wit commoners) by reason of the power of the liege lord, and destruction of him which was so near of the blood royal and the king's father; that therefore the said peers which now are, or the peers which shall be for the time to come, be not bound or charged to give judgement upon others than upon their peers, nor shall do it; but of that for ever be discharged and acquitted; and that the aforesaid judgement now given be not drawn into example or consequent for the time to come, by which the said peers may be charged hereafter to judge others than their peers, being against the law of the land, if any such case happen, which God defend.

Agrees with the Record.
William Collet.[8]

But notwithstanding all this our lords in parliament take upon them as judges in parliament to pass judgement and sentence (even of themselves) upon the commoners which are not their peers – and that to fining, imprisonment, etc. And *this* doth not only content them, but they even send forth their armed men, and beset, invade, assault their houses and persons in a warlike manner and take what plunder they please, before so much as any of their pretended, illegal warrants be showed – as was lately upon 11 August 1646 perpetrated against me and mine, which was more than the king himself by his legal prerogative ever could do. For neither by verbal commands or commissions under the Great Seal of England could he ever give any lawful authority to any general, captain or person whatsoever, without legal trial and conviction, forcibly to assault, rob, spoil or imprison any of the free commoners of England. And in case any free commoner by such his illegal commissions, orders or warrants, before they be lawfully convicted, should be assaulted, spoiled, plundered, imprisoned, etc., in such cases his agents and ministers ought to be proceeded against, resisted, apprehended, indicted and condemned (notwithstanding such commissions) as trespassers, thieves, burglars, felons, murderers, both

---

[8] Lilburne later said that he obtained a copy of this record from the Keeper of the Tower, and gave it to Marten. Probably he either gave a copy to Overton or wrote some or all of this section on the Lords himself.

by statute and common law, as is enacted and resolved by Magna Carta, cap. 29; 15 Eliz. 3 stat. 1. caps. 1, 2, 3; 42 Eliz. 5 cap. 1, 13; 28 Eliz. 1 *Artic. sup. chartas*, cap. 2; 4 Eliz. 3 cap. 4; 5 Eliz. 3 cap. 2; 24 Eliz. 3 cap. 1; 2 Rich II cap. 7; 5 Rich. II cap. 5; 1 Hen V cap. 6; 11 Hen II caps. 1–6; 24 Hen. VIII cap. 5; 21 Jacob. cap. 3.

And if the king himself have not this arbitrary power, much less may his peers or companions, the lords, over the free commons of England. And therefore notwithstanding such illegal censures and warrants either of king or of Lords (no legal conviction being made) the persons invaded and assaulted by such open force of arms may lawfully arm themselves, fortify their houses (which are their castles in the judgement of the law) against them; yea, disarm, beat, wound, repress and kill them in their just necessary defence of their own persons, houses, goods, wives and families, and not be guilty of the least offence – as is expressly resolved by the Statute of 21 Edw. *de malefactoribus in parcis*; by 24 Hen. VIII cap. 5; 11 Hen. VI cap. 16; 14 Hen. VI cap. 24; 35 Hen. VI cap. 12; Edward IV cap. 6.

And therefore (sir) as even by nature and by the law of the land I was bound, I denied subjection to these lords and their arbitrary creatures thus by open force invading and assaulting my house, person, etc. – no legal conviction preceding, or warrant then shown. But and if they had brought and shown a thousand such warrants, they had all been illegal, antimagisterial and void in this case; for they have no legal power in that kind, no more than the king, but such their actions are utterly condemned and expressly forbidden by the law. Why therefore should you of the representative body sit still and suffer these lords thus to devour both us and our laws?

Be awakened, arise and consider their oppressions and encroachments and stop their lordships in their ambitious career. For they do not cease only here, but they soar higher and higher and now they are become arrogators to themselves of the natural sovereignty the represented have conveyed and issued to their *proper* representers. They even challenge to themselves the title of the supremest court of judicature in the land – as was claimed by the Lord Hunsden when I was before them, which you may see more at large in a printed letter published under my name, entitled *A defiance against all arbitrary usurpations*[9] – which challenge of his (I think I may be bold to assert) was a

---

[9] Written in August 1646; published in September. Overton names it '*A defiance &c.*' in the text.

most illegal, anti-parliamentary, audacious presumption, and might better be pleaded and challenged by the king singly than by all those lords in a distinction from the Commons. But it is more than may be granted to the king himself; for the parliament, and the whole kingdom whom it represents, is truly and properly the highest supreme power of all others – yea above the king himself.

And therefore much more above the Lords. For they can question, cancel, disannul and utterly revoke the king's own royal charters, writs, commissions, patents, etc., though ratified with the Great Seal – even against his personal will, as is evident by their late abrogation of sundry patents, commissions, writs, charters, loan, ship-money etc. Yea the body representative have power to enlarge or retract the very preroga-tive of the king, as the Statute *de prerog. Reg.*[10] and the parliament roll of I Hen. IV, num.[11]18. doth evidence; and therefore their power is larger and higher than the king's; and if above the king's, much more above the Lords', who are subordinate to the king. And if the king's writs, charters, etc. which entrench upon the weal of the people may be abrogated, nulled and made void by the parliament – the representa-tive body of the land – and his very prerogatives bounded, restrained and limited by them, much more may the orders, warrants, commit-ments etc. of the Lords, with their usurped prerogatives over the Com-mons and people of England be restrained, nulled and made void by them. And therefore these lords must needs be inferior to them.

Further, the legislative power is not in the king himself but only in the kingdom and body representative, who has power to make or to abrogate laws, statutes etc. even without the king's consent. For by law he has not a negative voice either in making or reversing, but by his own coronation oath he is sworn to 'grant, fulfil, and defend all rightful laws, which the commons of the realm shall choose, and to strengthen and maintain them after his power';[12] by which clause of the oath is evident that the Commons (not the king or Lords) have power to choose what laws themselves shall judge meetest,[13] and thereto of

---

[10] The apocryphal statute, *Praerogativa Regis.*

[11] num. not cap. because not printed in the Statutes.

[12] This is a tendentious translation of '*leges . . . quas vulgus elegerit corroborandas*', which in fact rather implies that laws cannot be made without the confirmation of the king. Parliament had used Overton's anti-monarchical translation in a declaration of May 1642.

[13] meetest = most appropriate.

necessity the king must assent. And this is evident by most of our former kings and parliaments, and especially by the reigns of the Edwards I to IV, Richard II and the Henrys IV to VI. So that it cannot be denied but that the king is subordinate and inferior to the whole kingdom and body representative. Therefore if the king, much more must the lords veil their bonnets to the Commons and may not be esteemed the Upper House, or supreme court of judicature of the land.[14]

So that seeing the sovereign power is not originally in the king, or personally terminated in him, then the king at most can be but chief officer or supreme executioner of the laws, under whom all other legal executioners, their several executions, functions and offices are subordinate; for indeed the representers (in whom that power is inherent and from whence it takes its original) can only make conveyance thereof to their representers, vicegerents or deputies, and cannot possibly further extend it. For so they should go beyond themselves, which is impossible, for *ultra posse non est esse*: there is no being beyond the power of being. That which goes beyond the substance and shadow of a thing cannot possibly be the thing itself either substantially or virtually; for that which is beyond the representers is not representative, and so not the kingdom's or people's, either so much as in shadow or substance.

Therefore the sovereign power, extending no further than from the represented to the representers[15] – all this kind of sovereignty challenged by any (whether of king, Lords or others) is usurpation, illegitimate and illegal, and none of the kingdom's or people's. Neither are the people thereto obliged. Thus (sir) seeing the sovereign or legislative power is only from the represented to the representers, and cannot possibly legally further extend, the power of the king cannot be legislative but only executive, and he can communicate no more than he has himself. And the sovereign power not being inherent in him, it cannot be conveyed by or derived from him to any; for could he, he would have carried it away with him when he left the parliament. So that his mere prerogative creatures cannot have that which their lord

---

[14] veil = to doff or take off. The claim seems to be that the king did something of the kind with his hat when in the presence of the Commons, as a sign of respect to them. I can find no evidence of this. The Commons did however, stand bareheaded before the Lords.

[15] Here, as sometimes in this text and others, spelled 'representors'.

and creator never had, has, or can have: namely, the legislative power. For it is a standing rule in nature, *omne simile generas simile*: every like begets its like.

And indeed they are as like him as if they were spit out of his mouth. For their proper station will not content them, but they must make incursions and inroads upon the people's rights and freedoms and extend their prerogative patent beyond their master's compass. Indeed all other courts might as well challenge that prerogative of sovereignty, yea better, than this court of lords. But and if any court or courts in this kingdom should arrogate to themselves that dignity to be the supreme court of judicatory of the land, it would be judged no less than high treason, to wit, for an inferior subordinate power to advance and exalt itself above the power of the parliament.

And (sir) the oppressions, usurpations, and miseries from this prerogative head are not the sole cause of our grievance and complaint, but in especial, the most unnatural, tyrannical, blood-thirsty desires and continual endeavours of the clergy against the contrary-minded in matters of conscience – which have been so veiled, gilded and covered over with such various, fair and specious pretences that by the common discernings such wolfish, cannibal, inhuman intents against their neighbours, kindred, friends and countrymen, as is now clearly discovered was little suspected (and less deserved) at their hands. But now I suppose they will scarce hereafter be so hard of belief. For now in plain terms and with open face, the clergy here discover themselves in their kind, and show plainly that inwardly they are no other but ravening wolves, even as roaring lions wanting their prey, going up and down, seeking whom they may devour.[16]

For (sir) it seems these cruel minded men to their brethren, have, by the powerful agitation of Mr Tate and Mr Bacon[17] (two members of the House) procured a most Romish inquisition ordinance[18] to obtain an admission into the House, there to be twice read, and to be referred

---

[16] Matthew 7: 15: 'Beware of false prophets, which come to you in sheep's clothing, but inwardly are ravening wolves.'

[17] Zouch Tate and Francis Bacon, two Presbyterians.

[18] This ordinance, ordered on 27 May to be prepared by a committee, introduced into the Commons on 2 September, was finally to emerge on 2 May 1648 as the Blasphemy Ordinance. It prescribed death to felonious heretics (defined on arcane theological grounds, and the evidence of two witnesses being good as to the facts) by hanging, drawing and quartering. Other heretics – those who professed almost anything except strict Presbyterian orthodoxy – were to be imprisoned.

to a committee, which is of such a nature, if it should be but confirmed, enacted and established, as would draw all the innocent blood of the saints from righteous Abel unto this present upon this nation and fill the land with more martyrdoms, tyrannies, cruelties and oppressions than ever was in the bloody days of Queen Mary, yea or ever before, or since. For I may boldly say that the people of this nation never heard of such a diabolical, murdering, devouring ordinance, order, edict or law in their land as is that.

So that it may be truly said unto England: 'Woe to the inhabitants thereof, for the devil is come down unto you (in the shape of the letter B.) having great wrath, because he knows he has but a short time.'[19] For never before was the like heard of in England. The cruel, villainous, barbarous martyrdoms, murders and butcheries of God's people under the papal and episcopal clergy were not perpetrated or acted by any law so devilish, cruel and inhumane as this. Therefore what may the free people of England expect at the hands of their Presbyterian clergy, who thus discover themselves more fierce and cruel than their fellows? Nothing but hanging, burning, branding, imprisoning, etc. is like to be the reward of the most faithful friends to the kingdom and parliament if the clergy may be the disposers – notwithstanding their constant magnanimity, fidelity and good service both in the field and at home, for them and the state.

But sure this ordinance was never intended to pay the soldiers their arrears. *If* it be, the Independents are like to have the best share, let them take *that* for their comfort.[20] But I believe there was more tithe-providence than state-thrift in the matter;[21] for if the Independents, Anabaptists, and Brownists were but sincerely addicted to the due payment of tithes, it would be better to them in this case than two-subsidy-men to acquit them of felony.[22]

---

[19] Revelation 12: 12. According to the Blasphemy ordinance, blasphemy was to be punished by branding a letter B – for Beelzebub, prince of the devils – on the left cheek of the blasphemer.

[20] Arrears of pay was a continual problem. Overton seems to be claiming that Independents made up the largest proportion of the members of the New Model, and would therefore benefit most from people's being forced by the ordinance back into their parish churches to resume paying tithes – assuming that the money so collected went to the soldiers.

[21] I.e. Parliament was more interested in preserving tithes to their owners than with the financial problems of the state.

[22] The subsidy was the traditional parliamentary form of tax. When 'a subsidy' (or 'a subsidy and 1/15ths') was voted by parliament, land and real estate was rated at one-

For were it not for the loss of their trade and spoiling their custom, an Anabaptist, Brownist, Independent and presbyter were all one to them; then might they without doubt have the mercy of the clergy; then would they not have been entered into their Spanish Inquisition Calendar for absolute felons, or need they have feared the popish soul-murdering, antiChristian Oath of Abjuration,[23] or branding in the left cheek with the letter B – the new Presbyterian mark of the beast: for you see the devil is now again entered amongst us in a new shape, not like an angel of light (as both he and his servants can transform themselves when they please)[24] but even in the shape of the letter B. From the power of which Presbyterian Beelzebub, good Lord deliver us all and let all the people say Amen. Then needed they not to have feared their prisons, their fire and faggot, their gallows and halters, etc. (the strongest texts in all the Presbyterian new model of clergy divinity for the maintenance and reverence of their cloth, and confutation of errors). For he that doth but so much as question that priest-fattening ordinance for tithes, oblations,[25] obventions,[26] etc. doth flatly deny the fundamentals of presbyters, for it was the first stone they laid in their building;[27] and the second stone was the prohibition of all to teach God's word but themselves[28] – and so are *ipso facto* all felons etc.

By this (sir) you may see what bloody-minded men those of the black presbytery be: what little love, patience, meekness, longsuffering and forbearance they have to their brethren. Neither do they as they would be done to or do to others as is done to them. For they would not be so served themselves of the Independents, neither have the Independents ever sought or desired any such things upon them, but would bear with them in all brotherly love if they would be but contented to live peaceably and neighbourly by them, and not thus to brand, hang,

---

tenth of annual rental value (on prices as under Henry VIII), income at one-fifteenth. I suppose a 'two-subsidy-man' was one who paid both one-tenths and one-fifteenths.

[23] Those to be tried by the proposed ordinance might abjure their beliefs or actions when tried and thus escape death or branding.

[24] 2 Corinthians 11: 14–15.

[25] oblations = offerings.

[26] obventions = fees.

[27] In the face of great resistance to paying tithes, enforced on 8 November 1644 by *An ordinance for the true payment of tithes and other such duties.*

[28] An ordinance of 26 April 1645 forbade any to preach 'who is not ordained as a minister either in this or in some other reformed church, except such (as intending the ministry) shall be allowed trial of their gifts thereunto by both Houses of parliament'. It was a dead letter.

judge and condemn all for felons that are not like themselves. Sure (sir) you cannot take this murdering, bloody, disposition of theirs for the spirit of Christianity; for Christian charity 'suffers long, is kind, envieth not, exalteth not itself, seeketh not its own, is not easily provoked, thinketh no evil; beareth all things, believeth all things, hopeth all things, endureth all things'.[29] But these their desires and endeavours are directly contrary.

Therefore (sir) if you should suffer this bloody inroad of martyrdom, cruelties and tyrannies upon the free commoners of England with whose weal you are betrusted; if you should be so inhumane, undutiful, yea and unnatural unto us, our innocent blood will be upon you, and all the blood of the righteous that shall be shed by this ordinance, and you will be branded to future generations for England's Bloody Parliament.

If you will not think upon us, think upon your posterities. For I cannot suppose that any one of you would have your children hanged in case they should prove Independents, Anabaptists, Brownists – I cannot judge you so unnatural and inhumane to your own children. Therefore (sir) if for our own sakes we shall not be protected, save us for your children's sakes (though you think yourselves secure). For ye may be assured their and our interest is interwoven in one; if we perish, they must not think to escape. And (sir) consider that the cruelties, tyrannies and martyrdoms of the papal and episcopal clergy was one of the greatest instigations to this most unnatural war; and think you, if you settle a worse foundation of cruelty, that future generations will not taste of the dregs of that bitter cup?

Therefore *now* step in or never, and discharge your duties to God and to us and tell us no longer that 'such motions are not yet seasonable' and we must still wait; for have we not waited on your pleasures many fair seasons and precious occasions and opportunities these six years, even till the halters are ready to be tied to the gallows, and now must we hold our peace and wait till we be all imprisoned, hanged, burnt and confounded?

Blame us not (sir) if we complain against you – speak, write and plead thus – with might and main for our lives, laws and liberties; for they are our earthly *summum bonum*,[30] wherewith you are chiefly betrusted, and whereof we desire a faithful discharge at your hands in

---

[29] 1 Corinthians 13.
[30] *summum bonum* = highest good.

especial. Therefore be not you the men that shall betray the blood of us and our posterities into the hands of those bloody black executioners. For God is just and will avenge our blood at your hands. And let heaven and earth bear witness against you, that for this end, that we might be preserved and restored, we have discharged our duties to you – both of love, fidelity and assistance and in what else ye could demand or devise in all your several needs, necessities and extremities – not thinking our lives, estates, nor anything too precious to sacrifice for you and the kingdom's safety. And shall we now be thus unfaithfully, undutifully and ungratefully rewarded? For shame. Let never such things be spoken, far less recorded, to future generations.

Thus sir, I have so far emboldened myself with you, hoping you will let grievances be uttered (that if God see it good they may be redressed), and give losers leave to speak[31] without offence as I am forced to at this time, not only in the discharge of my duty to myself in particular but to yourselves and to our whole country in general for the present and for our several posterities for the future. And the Lord give you grace to take this timely advice from so mean and unworthy an instrument.

One thing more (sir) I shall be bold to crave at your hands: that you would be pleased to present my appeal, here enclosed, to your honourable House. Perchance the manner of it may beget a disaffection in you or at least a suspicion of disfavour from the House. But howsoever I beseech you that you would make presentation thereof, and if any hazard and danger ensue let it fall upon me; for I have cast up mine accounts. I know the most that it can cost me is but the dissolution of this fading mortality, which once must be dissolved; but after – blessed be God – comes righteous judgement.

Thus (sir) hoping my earnest and fervent desires after the universal freedoms and properties of this nation in general, and especially of the most godly and faithful in their consciences, persons and estates, will be a sufficient excuse with you for this my tedious presumption upon your patience, I shall commit the premises to your deliberate thoughts – and the issue thereof unto God, expecting and praying for His blessing upon all your faithful and honest endeavours in the prosecution thereof. And rest,

---

[31] This odd expression ('loosers' in the original) prefigures *The young men's and apprentices' outcry*, 'give losers leave to complain' (text 13) and in *The Moderate*, no. 36 (13–20 March 1649), front page: 'Give loosers leave to speak.'

From the most contemptuous gaol of Newgate (the Lords' benediction)
25 September 1646

In bonds for the just rights and freedoms of the commons of England, theirs and your faithful friend and servant, Richard Overton

To the high and mighty states, the knights, citizens and burgesses in parliament assembled (England's legal sovereign power). The humble appeal and supplication of Richard Overton, prisoner in the most contemptible gaol of Newgate.

Humbly shows,

That whereas your petitioner, under the pretence of a criminal fact being in a warlike manner brought before the House of Lords to be tried, and by them put to answer to interrogatories concerning himself – both which your petitioner humbly conceives to be illegal, and contrary to the natural rights, freedoms and properties of the free commoners of England (confirmed to them by Magna Carta, the Petition of Right and the Act for the abolishment of the Star Chamber) – he therefore was emboldened to refuse subjection to the said House both in the one and the other, expressing his resolution before them that he would not infringe the private rights and properties of himself or of any one commoner in particular, or the common rights and properties of this nation in general. For which your petitioner was by them adjudged contemptuous, and by an order from the said House was therefore committed to the gaol of Newgate, where, from the 11 of August 1646 to this present he has lain, and there commanded to be kept till their pleasures shall be further signified (as a copy of the said order hereunto annexed doth declare) which may be perpetual if they please, and may have their wills. For your petitioner humbly conceives as hereby he is made a prisoner to their wills, not to the law – except their wills may be a law.

Wherefore your liege petitioner doth make his humble appeal unto this most sovereign House (as to the highest court of judicatory in the land, wherein all the appeals thereof are to centre and beyond which none can legally be made) humbly craving (both in testimony of his acknowledgement of its legal regality and of his due submission thereunto) that your honours therein assembled would take his cause (and in his, the cause of all the free commoners of England, whom you represent and for whom you sit) into your serious consideration and legal determination, that he may *either* by the mercy of the law be repossessed of his just liberty and freedoms – and thereby the whole commons of England of theirs, thus unjustly (as he humbly conceives) usurped and invaded by the House of Lords – with due reparations of all such damages to sustained, *or else* that he may undergo what penalty shall in equity by the impartial severity of the law be adjudged against him by this honourable House in case by them he shall be legally found a transgressor herein.

And your petitioner (as in duty bound) shall ever pray, etc.

Die martis 11 Augusti, 1646[32]

It is this day ordered by the Lords in parliament assembled, that Overton, brought before a committee of this House for printing scandalous things against this House,[33] is hereby committed to the prison of Newgate for his high contempt offered to this House and to the said committee by his contemptuous words and gesture, and refusing to answer unto the Speaker. And that the said Overton shall be kept in safe custody by the Keeper of Newgate or his deputy until the pleasure of the House be further signified.

To the Gentleman Usher attending this House, or his deputy, to be delivered to the Keeper of Newgate or his deputy	John Brown Cleric. Parl. Examinat. per Ra. Brisco Clericu. de Newgate

---

Postscript

Sir,

Your unseasonable absence from the House, chiefly while Mistress Lilburne's petition[34] should have been read (you having a report to

---

[32] Tuesday 11 August.

[33] Notably his *An alarum to the House of Lords* (31 July 1646) in which he had come to Lilburne's defence.

[34] John's wife Elizabeth (née Dewell), as usual active in his defence. Her petition of 23 September, *To the chosen and betrusted knights, citizens, and burgesses*, reads as if it were written by John.

make in her husband's behalf) whereby the hearing thereof was deferred and retarded did possess my mind with strong jealousies and fears of you that you either preferred your own pleasure or private interest before the execution of justice and judgement, or else withdrew yourself on set purpose (through the strong instigation of the Lords) to evade the discharge of your trust to God and to your country. But at your return, understanding that you honestly and faithfully did redeem your absent time, I was dispossessed of those fears and jealousies. So that for my over-hasty censorious esteem of you I humbly crave your excuse, hoping you will rather impute it to the fervency of my faithful zeal to the common good than to any malignant disposition or disaffection in me towards you. Yet (sir) in this my suspicion I was not single, for it was even become a general surmise.

Wherefore (sir) for the awarding[35] your innocency for the future from the tincture of such unjust and calumnious suspicions, be you diligent and faithful, instant in season and out of season;[36] omit no opportunity (though with never so much hazard to your person, estate or family) to discharge the great trust in you reposed, with the rest of your fellow members, for the redemption of your native country from the arbitrary domination and usurpations, either of the House of Lords or any other.

And since by the divine providence of God it has pleased that honourable assembly whereof you are a member to select and sever you out from amongst themselves to be of that committee which they have ordained to receive the commoners' complaints against the House of Lords granted upon the foresaid most honourable petition, be you therefore impartial and just, active and resolute, care neither for favours nor smiles, and be no respecter of persons.[37] Let not the greatest peers in the land be more respected with you than so many old bellows-menders, broom-men, cobblers, tinkers, or chimney-sweepers, who are all equally freeborn with the hugest men and loftiest Anakims in the land.[38] Do nothing for favour of the one or fear of the other. And have a care of the temporary sagacity of the new sect of opportunity politicians, whereof we have got at least two or three too many. For delays

---

[35] awarding = protecting.
[36] 2 Timothy 4: 2: 'Preach the word; be instant in season, out of season.'
[37] Acts 10: 34. 'Then Peter opened his mouth, and said, Of a truth I perceive that God is no respecter of persons.'
[38] Lilburne's sentence from *Just mans justification* (1646), p. 10.

and demurrers of justice are of more deceitful and dangerous consequence than the flat and open denial of its execution; for the one keeps
in suspense, makes negligent and remiss, the other provokes to speedy
defence, makes active and resolute. Therefore be wise, quick, stout and
impartial: neither spare, favour, or connive at friend or foe, high or
low, rich or poor, lord or commoner.

And let even the saying of the Lord, with which I will close this
present discourse, close with your heart and be with you to the death.
Leviticus 19:15. 'Ye shall do no unrighteousness in judgement: thou
shall not respect the person of the poor, nor honour the person of the
mighty, but in righteousness shalt thou judge thy neighbour.'

12 October 1646

FINIS

6

Gold tried in the fire, or the burnt petitions revived

A Preface

Courteous Reader,

I shall give thee a short narrative of some passages upon the following petitions.[1] First concerning the *Large Petition*, divers printed copies thereof were sent abroad to gain subscriptions, one whereof was intercepted by an informer[2] and so brought to the hands of Mr Glynn,[3] Recorder of London and a member of the Commons' House, who was pleased to call it a scandalous and seditious paper. Whereupon it was referred[4] to Colonel Leigh's committee (it being that committee appointed to receive informations against those men who preached without licence from the ordainers)[5] to find out the authors of the said petition. Upon this a *Certificate* was drawn up and intended by the petitioners to have been delivered to the said committee for vindication of the said petition – as will appear by the certificate herewith printed – and notice being taken of one of the petitioners named Nicholas Tew,[6] who read the said certificate in the Court of Requests[7] for the concurrence of friends who had not formerly seen nor subscribed the certificate; and for his so doing he was sent for presently before the said committee; and for refusing to answer to interrogatories, was presently by them committed[8] and still remains in prison, it being at the least three months since his first commitment.

---

[1] What is printed as a single pamphlet here was divided into three in the course of publication.

[2] The petition was detected by an informer when it was read out to the General Baptist congregation of Thomas Lambe (see pp. 205–6) at their regular Sunday meeting on 14 March 1647.

[3] John Glynn. As Recorder of London as well as an MP, he was at this time a highly influential supporter of a presbyterian church settlement.

[4] On 15 March 1647.

[5] Colonel Sir Edward Leigh's Committee of Examinations had since January 1647 been harassing Particular Baptists for their publications and activities.

[6] Or Tue (see p. 211).

[7] The old Court of Requests – a court of equity had been abolished in 1641 – but its chamber, the White Hall, adjoining the Common's House, continued in use.

[8] 18 March.

Likewise Major Tulidah,[9] was, upon complaint of that committee, the next day committed by the House – but since discharged upon bail – without any just cause shown for either of their commitments. And others of the petitioners were abused and vilified by that committee, some of them offering to draw their swords upon the petitioners. All which, with more, was ready to be proved to the whole House, but could by no means be obtained, though earnestly desired by a *Petition presently delivered*[10] into the House humbly desiring the examination of these miscarriages; but – after eight weeks' attendance with much importunity, after many promises and days appointed to take their petition into consideration – they obtained a very slight answer which was that they 'could not like of their petition', occasion being taken suddenly after to commit one of the petitioners named Mr Brown[11] to the prison of Newgate, for his importunity in desiring an answer to that petition.

After many promises and delays, shortly after the slight answer obtained to the said petition, the petitioners thought good to deliver a *Second petition* to the House to see if it were possible to obtain a better answer to their just desires, hoping that they would better consider of things.[12] But after attendance and importunity, they obtained an answer in these words. That the parliament had voted it a breach of privilege, 'scandalous, and seditious'; and that petition (and the Large Petition) to be burned by the hand of the hangman; which was accordingly done by order of the house, in these words.

Die Jovis[13] 20 May, 1647

Resolved etc. That the sheriffs of London and Middlesex be required to take care that the petition and paper be burnt: which accordingly was done before the Exchange two days after the said vote and order of the House.[14]

And shortly after this the petitioners prepared a *third petition*, which is the last petition herewith printed. And after much importunity with

---

[9] Major Alexander Tulidah (see p. 211–12).

[10] 20 March.

[11] 30 April. 'Mr Brown' was possibly David Brown, a friend of Lilburne's and a member of John Duppa's Separatist church.

[12] 20 May.

[13] Thursday.

[14] In 1649 Walwyn was to complain that 'most of the upper-most Independents stood aloof and look't on' while the Levellers tried to promote their *Large Petition*, probably because of its demand that tithes should be abolished without compensation.

the members of the House after almost two days' attendance obtained
so much favour from one of the members as to present that petition to
the House; and after all this could obtain no other answer to that petition, but the House after long dispute thereupon passed this vote upon
the 2nd of June 1647: 'that no answer shall be given to the petition at
the present'.

And two days after, the petitioners attended the House for a further
answer, delivering copies of their petition to the several members of
the House, but could obtain no further answer thereunto but received
many vilifying and disgraceful speeches from several members of the
House. And so after a whole day's attendance, departed without any
hope to receive any answer to their just desires in the said petition.

And thus I have faithfully and truly (though briefly) given ye an
account of the proceedings upon the ensuing petitions.

Now let the judicious and considerate reader judge whether the petitioners have received equal and even dealing herein from this present
parliament – the petitioners being such who have laid out themselves,
both in their persons and purses, far above their abilities; who have not
valued their lives, their children's lives, nor their servants' lives, nor
estates too dear for the service of the parliament and commonwealth.
And is this the reward they shall receive after they have thus laid out
themselves? Nay, they have just cause to fear that they and their friends
are men appointed to utter ruin and destruction. Otherwise what means
all the railing, reviling, and reproachful speeches of their ministers and
agents out of the pulpit and press to stir up the rude multitude to fall
upon them and destroy them? Is not this ingratitude in the highest
degree? Shall not the very heathen rise up in judgement against such a
generation of degenerate men as these, who could say, *Si ingratum
dixeris, omnia dixeris?*[15]

You cannot choose but take notice of several remonstrances and petitions presented to the House from these men who call themselves Lord
Mayor, Aldermen and Commons of the city of London in Common
Council assembled – what high affronts *they* have offered to the parliament.[16] Yet they have in some measure by steps and degrees answered

[15] *Si ingratum dixeris, omnia dixeris* = who speaks of the ungrateful speaks of all of them.
[16] From September 1645, encouraged by conservative citizen sentiment, the Common
Council had begun a series of petitions to parliament. These featured pleas for the
creation of a full-blooded Presbyterian church settlement, the suppression of lay preaching and the end to toleration of sects. In the famous 'City Remonstrance' (*A humble*

the remonstrances and granted their petitions; and you may observe what answer they have given to their last petition for raising of horse, etc. (the tendency whereof may be of very dangerous consequence if well weighed). Which is thus: 'Mr Speaker by command of the House, expressed unto them the true sense the House has of their constant good affections to this parliament; and that no alterations whatsoever can work any change in their duty and love; for which he is to give them the heartiest thanks of this house.'[17]

I could enlarge myself but I affect brevity, and the judicious and considerate reader may enlarge himself in his own thoughts, well weighing the matter in the said remonstrances and petitions; and upon due consideration may judge whether their petitions, or the petitions burnt, vilified, and disgraced, deserve most thanks or tend most to the safety of the parliament and commonwealth – and will henceforth conclude that, as there is little good to be hoped for from such parliaments as need to be petitioned, so there is none at all to be expected from those that burn such petitions as these.

If the endeavours of good commonwealthsmen in the House could have prevailed, these petitions had not been burnt nor the petitioners abused. But the sons of Zeruiah[18] were too strong for them – that is to say, the malignants, and delinquents, the lawyers (some few excepted), the monopolising merchants, the sons and servants of the Lords. All these joining together over-voted them about sixteen voices. But God in time, will, we trust, deliver the people of this nation from their deceit and malice; and therefore let us not sorrow as men without hope, nor be discouraged, but go on and persist for the just liberties of England. A word to the wise is sufficient. Farewell.

---

remonstrance and petition) of 26 May 1646 they further asked that the king's powers be preserved, that the City be given back control of its own militia – in the hands of Independents since 1643 – and that no-one disaffected with Presbyterianism should be employed by the government. On 19 December 1646 the Common Council forwarded a further citizens' petition to the Commons accompanying it with a shorter one of its own, which added to all this that they wanted the New Model abolished as a stronghold of sectaries, and reiterated the demand for control of the London militia. Its tone angered many parliamentarians, but no action was taken against the petitioners.

[17] During the winter and spring of 1646–7 parliament had moved in a Presbyterian direction. On 17 January 1647 the City was empowered, following the petition of December 1646, to raise a troop of horse; in April and May control of the London militia was given to the City and the City's purge of Independent members of the militia committee was confirmed by parliament.

[18] The warrior sons of a warrior father, see 2 Samuel especially.

By a well-wisher to truth and peace

Printed in the year 1647

To the right honourable and supreme authority of this nation, the commons in parliament assembled. The humble petition of many thousands, earnestly desiring the glory of God, the freedom of the commonwealth, and the peace of all men[19]

Shows,

That as no government is more just in the constitution than that of parliaments – having its foundation in the free choice of the people – and as the end of all government is the safety and freedom of the governed, even so the people of this nation in all times have manifested most hearty affection unto parliaments as the most proper remedy of their grievances. Yet such have been the wicked policies of those who from time to time have endeavoured to bring this nation into bondage that they have in all times, either by the disuse or abuse of parliaments, deprived the people of their hopes. For testimony whereof the late times foregoing this parliament will sadly witness: when it was not only made a crime to mention a parliament, but either the pretended negative voice[20] (the most destructive to freedom) or a speedy dissolution[21] blasted the fruit and benefit thereof, whilst the whole land was overspread with all kinds of oppression and tyranny extending both to soul and body; and that in so rooted and settled a way that the complaints of the people in general witnessed that they would have given anything in the world for one six months' freedom of parliament. Which has been since evidenced in their instant and constant readiness of assistance to this present parliament, exceeding the records of all former ages, and wherein God has blessed them with their first desires, making this parliament the most absolute and free of any parliament that ever was, and enabling it with power sufficient to deliver the whole nation from all kinds of oppressions and grievances, though of never so long continuance, and to make it the most absolute and free nation in the world.

---

[19] This is the 'Large Petition'.

[20] The power of the king to veto bills proposed to him by the two Houses, and so preventing them becoming statutes.

[21] The king's prerogative included the rights to call, prorogue and dissolve parliaments.

And it is most thankfully acknowledged that ye have in order to the freedom of the people suppressed the High Commission, Star Chamber and Council Table,[22] called home the banished, delivered such as were imprisoned for matters of conscience, and brought some delinquents to deserved punishment;[23] that ye have suppressed the bishops and popish lords,[24] abolished episcopacy and that kind of prelatic persecuting government; that ye have taken away ship-money,[25] and all the new illegal patents. Whereby the hearts of all the well-affected were enlarged and filled with a confident hope that they should have seen long ere this a complete removal of all grievances, and the whole people delivered from all oppressions over soul or body. But such is our misery, that after the expense of so much precious time, of blood, and treasure, and the ruin of so many thousands of honest families in recovering our liberties, we still find this nation oppressed with grievances of the same destructive nature as formerly, though under other notions; and which are so much the more grievous unto us because they are inflicted in the very time of this present parliament – under God, the hope of the oppressed. For, as then all the men and women in England were made liable to the summons, attachments, sentences and imprisonments of the lords of the Council Board, so we find by woeful experience and sufferings of many particular persons that the present Lords do assume and exercise the same power – than which nothing is, or can be, more repugnant and destructive to the commons' just liberties. As the unjust power of Star Chamber was exercised in compelling of men and women to answer to interrogatories tending to accuse themselves and others, so is the same now frequently practised upon divers persons – even your cordial friends, that have been, and still are, punished for refusing to answer to questions against themselves and nearest relations.

[22] All abolished by statutes of July 1641.
[23] At the calling of the Long Parliament in November 1640 many sectarians returned from exile in the Low Countries, and such prisoners as Lilburne, Prynne, John Bastwick and Henry Burton were released from captivity. Proceedings for treason were soon begun against the earl of Strafford, the bishops, and leading royal councillors, many of whom fled into continental exile.
[24] Bishops were removed from the Lords in February 1642, though the order was not abolished until October 1646. Catholic peers effectively lost their votes in November 1641.
[25] August 1641.

As then the great oppression of the High Commission[26] was most evident in molesting of godly peaceable people for non-conformity or different opinion and practice in religion – judging all who were contrary-minded to themselves to be heretics, sectaries, schismatics, seditious, factious, enemies to the state, and the like; and under great penalties forbidding all persons not licensed by them to preach or publish the gospel – even so now at this day, the very same if not greater molestations are set on foot and violently prosecuted by the instigation of a clergy no more infallible than the former: to the extreme discouragement and affliction of many thousands of your faithful adherents, who are not satisfied that controversies in religion can be trusted to the compulsive regulation of any, and after the bishops were suppressed, did hope never to have seen such a power assumed by any in this nation any more.

And although all new illegal patents are by you abolished, yet the oppressive monopoly of Merchant Adventurers and others do still remain to the great abridgement of the liberties of the people and to the extreme prejudice of all such industrious people as depend on clothing or other woollen manufacture (it being the staple commodity of this nation), and to the great discouragement and disadvantage of all sorts of tradesmen, seafaring men, and hindrance of shipping and navigation. Also the old tedious and chargeable way of deciding controversies or suits in law is continued to this day, to the extreme vexation and utter undoing of multitudes of families: a grievance as great and as palpable as any in the world. Likewise that old but most unequal punishment of malefactors is still continued, whereby men's lives and liberties are as liable to the law, and corporal pains as much inflicted for small as for great offences, and that most unjustly upon the testimony of one witness – contrary both to the law of God and common equity: a grievance very great but little regarded. Also tithes and other enforced maintenance are still continued, though there be no ground for either under the gospel and though the same have occasioned multitudes of suits, quarrels, and debates, both in former and later times.[27] In like

---

[26] The supreme court in church matters, deeply implicated in attacks on Puritans, including Lilburne. Like the Star Chamber, its judges questioned the accused directly, and under oath – 'upon interrogatories' as the Levellers called the process. They were thus, they argued, forced to condemn themselves, which God's command to preserve themselves forbade, or to endanger others, which was similarly forbidden.

[27] Opposition to tithes was a staple of Leveller literature. Their basic belief was that ministers should be sustained by the voluntary contributions of their congregations.

manner, multitudes of poor distressed prisoners for debt lie still unregarded in a most miserable and woeful condition throughout the land, to the great reproach of this nation. Likewise prison-keepers or gaolers are as presumptuous as ever they were both in receiving and detaining of prisoners illegally committed; as cruel and inhumane to all, especially to such as are well-affected; as oppressive and extorting in their fees. And they are attended with under-officers of such vile and unChristian demeanour as is most abominable. Also thousands of men and women are still (as formerly) permitted to live in beggary and wickedness all their life long and to breed[28] their children to the same idle and vicious course of life, and no effectual means used to reclaim either or to reduce them to any virtue or industry.

And last, as those who found themselves aggrieved formerly at the burdens and oppressions of those times – that did not conform to the church-government then established, refused to pay ship-money, or yield obedience to unjust patents – were reviled and reproached with nicknames of 'Puritans', 'heretics', 'schismatics', 'sectaries', or were termed 'factious' or 'seditious', 'men of turbulent spirits, despisers of government', and 'disturbers of the public peace'; even so is it at this day in all respects, with those who show any sensibility of the forerecited grievances, or move in any manner or measure for remedy thereof; all the reproaches, evils, and mischiefs that can be devised are thought too few or too little to be laid upon them, as 'roundheads', 'sectaries', 'independents', 'heretics', 'schismatics', 'factious', 'seditious', 'rebellious', 'disturbers of the public peace', 'destroyers of all civil relation, and subordinations'. Yea, and beyond what was formerly, non-conformity is now judged a sufficient cause to disable any person (though of known fidelity) from bearing any office of trust in the commonwealth,[29] whilst neuters, malignants and disaffected are admitted and continued.[30] And though it be not now made a crime to mention a parliament, yet is it little less to mention the supreme power of this honourable House.[31]

---

[28] breed = bring up.

[29] In February and March 1647, following the citizens' and corporations' pleas and with an eye to the demands of the Scots, there were moves in both Houses to remove from civil and military office those who refused to take the Solemn League and Covenant and to conform to Presbyterian church government.

[30] 'Neuters' are those who stand for neither king nor parliament, 'malignants' are royalists, 'disaffected' are proto-royalist Presbyterians eager for a settlement.

[31] That the petition was addressed to 'the supreme authority of this nation, the Commons in parliament assembled' gave great offence to its opponents.

So that in all these respects this nation remains in a very sad and disconsolate condition – and the more, because it is thus with us after so long a session of so powerful and so free a parliament, and which has been so made and maintained by the abundant love and liberal effusion of the blood of the people.

And therefore, knowing no danger nor thralldom like unto our being left in this most sad condition by this parliament, and observing that ye are now drawing the great and weighty affairs of this nation to some kind of conclusion, and fearing that ye may ere long be obstructed by something equally evil to a negative voice, and that ye may be induced to lay by that strength which (under God) has hitherto made you powerful to all good works;[32] whilst we have yet time to hope, and ye power to help, and lest by our silence we might be guilty of that ruin and slavery which without your speedy help is like to fall upon us, yourselves and the whole nation, we have presumed to spread our cause thus plainly and largely before you; and do most earnestly entreat that ye will stir up your affections to a zealous love and tender regard of the people who have chosen and trusted you, and that ye will seriously consider that the end of their trust was freedom and deliverance from all kind of grievances and oppressions.

1. And that therefore in the first place, ye will be exceeding careful to preserve your just authority from all prejudices of a negative voice in any person or persons whomsoever which may disable you from making that happy return unto the people which they justly expect; and that ye will not be induced to lay by your strength until ye have satisfied your understandings in the undoubted security of yourselves and of those who have voluntarily and faithfully adhered unto you in all your extremities and until ye have secured and settled the commonwealth in solid peace and true freedom, which is the end of the primitive institution of all governments.

2. That ye will take off all sentences, fines, and imprisonments imposed on commoners, by any whomsoever, without due course of law or judgement of their equals, and give due reparations to all those who have been so injuriously dealt withal; and for preventing the like for time to come, that ye will enact all such arbitrary proceedings to be capital crimes.

---

[32] I.e. induced to support plans to abolish the New Model, as Denzil Holles, Sir Philip Stapleton and other Presbyterian leaders in parliament were setting out to do, not without the support from those many independents who saw the Army as a threat to parliament's authority.

3. That ye will permit no authority whatsoever to compel any person or persons to answer to questions against themselves or nearest relations, except in cases of private interest between party and party in a legal way; and to release all such as suffer by imprisonment or otherwise for refusing to answer to such interrogatories.

4. That all statutes, oaths, and covenants may be repealed so far as they tend, or may be construed, to the molestation and ensnaring of religious, peaceable, well-affected people for non-conformity or different opinion or practice in religion.[33]

5. That no man, for preaching or publishing his opinion in religion in a peaceable way, may be punished or persecuted as heretical by judges – that are not infallible but may be mistaken as well as other men in their judgements – lest upon pretence of suppressing errors, sects, or schisms, the most necessary truths and sincere professors thereof may be suppressed, as upon the like pretence it has been in all ages.

6. That ye will, for the encouragement of industrious people, dissolve that old oppressive company of Merchant Adventurers and the like, and prevent all such others by great penalties, forever.

7. That ye will settle a just, speedy, plain and unburdensome way for deciding of controversies and suits in law, and reduce all laws to the nearest agreement with Christianity, and publish them in the English tongue; and that all processes and proceedings therein may be true, and also in English, and in the most usual character of writing, without any abbreviations, that each one who can read may the better understand their own affairs; and that the duty of all judges, officers and practisers in the law, and of all magistrates and officers in the commonwealth may be prescribed and their fees limited, under strict penalties, and published in print to the view and knowledge of all men: by which just and equitable means this nation shall be forever freed of an oppression more burdensome and troublesome than all the oppressions hitherto by this parliament removed.

8. That the life of no person may be taken away but under the testimony of two witnesses at least, of honest conversation; and that in an equitable way ye will proportion punishments to offences: that so no man's life may be taken, his body punished, nor his estate forfeited, but upon such weighty and considerable causes as justly deserve such

[33] Parliament's insistence late in 1644 on the taking of the Solemn League and Covenant by military officers had led Lieutenant-Colonel Lilburne to withdraw his military services from their cause.

punishments; and that all prisoners may have a speedy trial, that they be neither starved nor their families ruined by long and lingering imprisonment; and that imprisonment may be used only for safe custody until time of trial, and not as a punishment for offences.

9. That tithes and all other enforced maintenance may be forever abolished and nothing in place thereof imposed, but that all ministers may be paid only by those who voluntarily chose them and contract with them for their labours.

10. That ye will take some speedy and effectual course to relieve all such prisoners for debt as are altogether unable to pay, that they may not perish in prison through the hard-heartedness of their creditors; and that all such as have any estates may be enforced to make payment accordingly and not shelter themselves in prison to defraud their creditors.

11. That none may be prison-keepers but such as are of approved honesty, and that they may be prohibited under great penalties to receive or detain any person or persons without lawful warrant; that their usage of prisoners may be with gentleness and civility, their fees moderate and certain, and that they may give security for the good behaviour of their under-officers.

12. That ye will provide some powerful means to keep men, women, and children from begging and wickedness, that this nation may be no longer a shame to Christianity therein.

13. That ye will restrain and discountenance the malice and impudency of impious persons in their reviling and reproaching the well-affected with the ignominious titles of round-heads, factious, seditious and the like, whereby your real friends have been a long time, and still are, exceedingly wronged, discouraged, and made obnoxious to rude and profane people; and that ye will not exclude any of approved fidelity from bearing office of trust in the commonwealth for non-conformity: rather neuters, and such as manifest disaffection or opposition to common freedom – the admission and continuation of such being the chief cause of all our grievances.

These remedies, or what other shall seem more effectual to your grave wisdoms, we humbly pray may be speedily applied; and in doing thereof ye will be confident of the assistance of your petitioners and of all considerate well-minded people to the uttermost of their best abilities, against all opposition whatsoever, looking upon ourselves as more concerned now at last to make a good end than at the first to have made a good beginning. For what shall it profit us, or what remedy can we expect, if now after so great troubles and miseries this nation should be left by this parliament in so great a thraldom, both of body, mind, and estate?

We beseech you therefore that with all your might whilst ye have time, freedom and power, so effectively to fulfil the true end of parliaments in delivering this nation from these and all other grievances, that none may presume or dare to introduce the like forever.

And we trust that God of your good success will manifest the sincerity of our intentions herein, and that our humble desires are such as tend not only to our own particular but to the general good of the commonwealth, and proper for this honourable House to grant, without which this nation cannot be safe or happy. And that He will bless you with true Christian fortitude, suitable to the trust and greatness of the work ye have undertaken, and make the memory of this parliament blessed to all succeeding generations,

Shall ever be the prayer of your humble petitioners.

To the right honourable, the commons of England assembled in parliament. The humble petition of divers well-affected citizens[34]

Shows,

That as the oppressions of this nation in times fore-going this parliament were so numerous and burdensome as will never be forgotten, so were the hopes of our deliverance by this parliament exceeding great and full of confidence; which, as they were strengthened by many acts of yours in the beginning, especially towards conscientious people without respect unto their judgements or opinions, so did the gratitude of well-minded people exceed all precedent or example, sparing neither estates, limbs, liberties, or lives, to make good the authority of this honourable House as the foundation and root of all just freedom. And although we many times observed to our grief some proceedings holding resemblance rather with our former bondage than with that just freedom we expected, yet did we impute the same to the troublesomeness of the times of war, patiently and silently passing them over, as undoubtedly hoping

[34] This is the *petition presently presented* on 20 March, enclosing the *certificate*.

a perfect remedy so soon as the wars were ended. But perceiving our expectations altogether frustrate, we conceived ourselves bound in conscience and in duty to God to set before you the general grievances of the commonwealth and the earnest desires of ingenious[35] well-minded people; and for that end did engage in promoting the petition in question in the usual and approved way of gathering subscriptions, with full intention to present the same to this honourable House so soon as it should be in readiness. But as it appears, a copy thereof was unduly obtained and tendered to this honourable House under the notion of a dangerous and seditious paper. Whereupon this House was pleased to order the petition to the committee whereof Colonel Leigh is chairman, and Mr Lambe, at whose house it was said to be found, to be there examined concerning the same.

Whereupon your petitioners conceived it their duty to own and avouch the said petition; and for that end in a peaceable manner attended that committee with this humble certificate hereunto annexed to be offered to their wisdoms as opportunity should be ministered. But through some small miscarriage of some few persons (for which your petitioners were much grieved) your committee took so sudden and high displeasure as to command your petitioners to withdraw, threatening to remove them with a guard before they had time to turn themselves.

Whereupon your petitioners caused the certificate to be publicly read in the Court of Requests to take the sense and allowance of many persons who had not before seen the same, with intent still to present it; which though endeavoured to the utmost, was absolutely refused to be received, but to our astonishment, occasion was taken against our friend that read the same, so far as that he stands a prisoner to that committee. And much harsh language, with threatenings and provocations issued from some of the committee towards some other of our friends, purposely (as we verily believe) to get some advantage to present us odious to this honourable House, whose persons and authority has been as dear in our esteem as our very lives. And therefore we have just cause to complain to this honourable House.

1. Of unjust usage from those that endeavoured to interrupt the gathering of hands in a peaceable way or to possess this honourable

[35] He possibly means 'ingenuous', in the sense 'of free and honourable birth'.

House with evil suggestions concerning the intention and purpose of the said petition.

2. Of hard measure from your committee in the particulars forementioned, contrary to what we have deserved – or should have found in former times.

Nevertheless, our liberties to promote petitions to this honourable House are so essential to our freedom (our condition without the same being absolute slavery), and our hope of justice from this honourable House so great in protecting us therein, that we are not discouraged by what has passed, but in confidence thereof do humbly entreat:

First, that ye will be pleased to declare our freedom to promote, and your readiness to receive, the said petition, which we cannot but still look upon as tending the general good of this nation.

Secondly, that our friends may be enlarged, and that ye will discountenance the officiousness of such over-busy informers as have disturbed the just progress of that petition.

We are not ignorant that we have been and are like to be represented unto you as heretics, schismatics, sectaries, seditious persons and enemies to civil-government, and the like; but our said petition is sufficient to stop the mouths of such calumniators and declare us to be not only solicitors for our own particulars but for the general good of the commonwealth, and will minister a just occasion to suspect the designs of those that so frequently asperse us, though their pretences be never so specious. And we trust your wisdoms will timeously[36] discover and prevent any evil intended against us.

And whereas Major Tulidah stands committed by order of this honourable House for some conceived misbehaviour towards some members of your said committee, we humbly entreat that he may be forthwith called to your bar and be permitted to answer for himself, and that witnesses also may be heard on his behalf; that so this honourable House may be rightly and fully informed concerning his cause and the demeanour of those members: the sudden imprisonment of our friends being very grievous unto us.

And your petitions shall pray.

To the honourable committee of parliament sitting in the Queen's Court at Westminster, Colonel Leigh being chairman[37]

---

[36] timeously = in a timely way.
[37] This is the attached *certificate*.

The humble certificate of divers persons interested in and avouching the petition lately referred to this committee by the right honourable House of Commons. Humbly certifying that the petition (entitled *The humble petition of many thousands, earnestly desiring the glory of God, the freedom of the commonwealth, and the peace of all men, and directed to the right honourable, and supreme authority of this nation, the Commons assembled in parliament*) is no scandalous or seditious paper (as has been unjustly suggested) but a real petition, subscribed, and to be subscribed, by none but constant, cordial friends to parliament and commonwealth, and to be presented to that honourable House with all possible speed as an especial means to procure the universal good of this long enthralled and distracted nation; and we trust this honourable committee will in no measure dishearten the people from presenting their humble considerations, reasons, and petitions to those whom they have chosen (there being no other due and legal way wherein those that are aggrieved can find redress) but that rather you will be pleased to give all encouragement therein. In assured hope whereof, we shall pray.

To the right honourable, the commons of England assembled in parliament. The humble petition of divers well-affected people in and about the City of London.[38]

Shows,

That as the authority of this honourable House is entrusted by the people for remedy of their grievances, so has it been their accustomed and undoubted liberty in a peaceable manner to present unto this House whatsoever they deemed to be particular or general grievances. And as ye gave encouragement unto others in the use of this just liberty – reproving such as endeavoured to obstruct the peaceable promoting of petitions – so did we verily hope to have found the like countenance and protection in promoting our Large Petition. But no sooner was the promoting thereof discovered by Mr Glynn, Recorder, as is commonly reported, than he hastily and untimely brought it into this House, exclaiming against it as a most dangerous and seditious paper; and shortly after the Common Council in like manner prejudged it as guilty of danger and sedition, though both without any grounds or reasons affixed that we know of.

---

[38] This is the *second petition* Walwyn speaks of in the preface.

And as the work of Mr Recorder was the occasion (as we conceive) of an inquiry after the promoters, so also of the hard measure we found at Colonel Leigh's Committee, where occasion was suddenly taken to threaten our removal by a guard, to imprison Nicholas Tew, one of the petitioners, the rest being reviled with odious titles of factious and seditious sectaries; and Major Tulidah another of the petitioners, not only reviled and reproached as the rest, but violently hauled, and most boisterously used by Sir Philip Stapleton and Colonel Holles, who made offer as if they would draw their swords upon the petitioners – and Sir Walter Erle,[39] lifting up his cane in a most threatening manner, took another by the shoulder: all which is ready to be certified by sufficient witnesses, and which we do verily believe was done purposely out of their hatred to the matter of the petition, to render us as a turbulent people to this honourable House, to beget a dislike of our petition, and to frustrate our endeavours in promoting thereof.

Unto which their misinformation of this honourable House, as we have cause to suspect, may be imputed the occasion of the sudden imprisonment of Major Tulidah without hearing of him, and our so long and tedious attendance for answer to our last petition and certificate, and the misapprehension of this honourable House of our desires in that petition. For we did not desire (as your answer imports) that this House should declare their liking or disliking of our Large Petition (being not then promoted nor presented by us) but that you would be pleased to vindicate *our liberty to promote* that petition, notwithstanding the hard measure we had found and the aspersions cast upon it; to release the party imprisoned by the committee (meaning Nicholas Tew); to discountenance those that obstructed the gathering of subscriptions; to call Major Tulidah to your bar and to hear witnesses on his behalf, that so ye might also be rightly informed, as of his cause, so of the demeanour of some members of that committee.

Now forasmuch as the more we consider the general grievances of the commonwealth the greater cause we still find of promoting the Large Petition, as not discerning anything of danger therein except to some corruptions yet remaining, nor of sedition except as before this parliament it be in some men's esteems seditious to move – though in the most peaceable manner – for remedy of the most palpable grievances. And forasmuch as we are hopeful this honourable House will in

---

[39] These men (see pp. 203 and 204) were the leading Presbyterian MPs.

due time have good use thereof for discovery of such as are engaged either directly or by relations in those corruptions for removal whereof the petition is intended; and not knowing for what end so great an effusion of the blood of the people has been made except to procure at the least the particulars desired in that petition; and that we might know ourselves so far at least to be free men and not slaves as to be at liberty to promote petitions in a peaceable way, to be judges of the matter thereof and for our time of presenting them to this honourable House, without let or circumvention, we humbly entreat that you will be pleased:

1. To weigh in equal balance the carriage of Mr Recorder and that of the Common Council in this weighty cause of prejudging petitions; and to deal with them as the cause deserves.

2. To consider of how evil consequence it is for your committees to assume a power of imprisoning men's persons without your commission, and that ye will not pass over this in this committee.

3. To receive the testimonies concerning Sir Philip Stapleton, Colonel Holles and Sir Walter Erle, and to deal with them according to the ill consequence of their violent demeanour and misinformation of this honourable House, tending to no less than the obstruction of petitions: the greatest mischief that can befall a people in time of parliament.

4. That Nicholas Tew may be wholly enlarged, and that no man may henceforth be committed by an arbitrary power, as he at the first was, nor without cause showed, though by lawful authority.

5. That ye will as yet suspend your sense of our Large Petition until such time as the petitioners shall judge it fit to present the same as a petition unto your wisdoms.

And as in duty bound, we shall pray etc.

To the right honourable the commons of England assembled in parliament. The humble petition of many thousands of well-affected people[40]

Shows,

That having seriously considered what an uncontrolled liberty has generally been taken publicly to reproach and make odious persons of eminent and constant good affection to parliament and commonwealth,

---

[40] The *third petition*, presented on 2 June.

how prevalent endeavours have been to withhold such from being chosen into places of trust or counsel, how easy to molest or get them into prisons, how exceedingly liable to misconstruction their motions and petitions in behalf of the public have lately been; when we consider what grudgings and repinings have sinistrously[41] been begotten against your most faithful and successful army, what arts and devices to provoke you against them and to make you jealous of them, what hard measure some of them, both officers and soldiers, have found in divers respects in sundry places; when we consider what change of late has importunately (though causelessly) been procured of the committee of militia in the city of London, and how that new committee has already begun to remove from command in the trained bands and auxiliaries persons not to be suspected of disaffection or neutrality but such as have been most zealous in promoting the safety of parliament and city; when we consider how full of armies our neighbour countries are round about us, and what threatenings of foreign forces – when we consider these things[42] we are even astonished with grief, as not able to free ourselves from apprehensions of eminent danger, but are strongly induced to fear some evil intentions of some desperate and wilful persons, yet powerfully working, to blast the just ends of this parliament and re-embroil this late bleeding and much-wasted nation in more violent wars, distempers and miseries.

And as our earnest desires of the quiet and safety of the commonwealth have necessitated these our most sad observations, so are we constrained to believe that so dangerous an alteration could not so generally have appeared but that there is some great alteration befallen both in counsels and authorities throughout the land – which we verily conceive arises from no other cause but from the treacherous policy of enemies and weakness of friends in choosing such thereinto, as having been unfit for those employments: some whereof (as is credibly reported) having served the enemy in arms; some with monies, horse, ammunition, or by intelligence; some in commissions of array; some manifesting constant malignity in their actions, speeches or standing neuters in times of greatest trial; some culpable of notorious crimes; others lying under heavy accusations; some that are under age, or such who are at present engaged in such courses as in the beginning of this parliament were esteemed monopolies.

[41] I.e. in a sinister way.
[42] 'When we consider these things' added.

Now may it please this honourable House, if such as these should remain, or may have privily crept into your counsels or authorities (as by the forecited considerations we humbly conceive cannot but be judged), what can possibly be expected by those who have been most active and faithful in your service, but utter ruin or the worst of bondage?

For prevention whereof, and of those dangers, wars and troubles that are generally feared, we are constrained earnestly to entreat:

1. That you will be pleased instantly to appoint a committee of such worthy members of this honourable House as have manifested most sincere affections to the well-affected, and to authorise them to make speedy and strict inquiry after all such as are possessed of places of counsel, trust, authority or command, who according to law, ordinance, reason, or safety, ought not to be admitted; and that all persons, without exception, may be permitted and encouraged to bring in accusations, witnesses, or testimonies for the more speedy perfecting of the work; and that you will forthwith exclude all such out of all offices of counsel, trust, authority, or command, against whom sufficient cause shall be proved: without which we cannot see how it is possible for the well-affected to live either in peace or safety.

2. That you will countenance, protect, and succour the cordial well-affected in all places according to their several cases and conditions, especially in their addresses with petitions.

3. That you will be pleased to condescend unto all the just and reasonable desires of your commanders, officers and soldiers, by whose courage and faithfulness so great services have been performed, and severely to punish all such as have any way sought to alienate you from them.

4. That the militia of London may be returned to the custody and disposing of those persons of whose faithfulness and wisdom in managing thereof you have had great experience; and that none may be put out of command in the trained bands or auxiliaries who have been and are of known good affection to the commonwealth.

All which we humbly entreat may be speedily and effectually accomplished, according to the great necessity and exigency of these distracted times; and as in duty bound, we shall pray, etc.

FINIS

7
An agreement of the people for a firm and present peace upon grounds of common right and freedom, as it was proposed by the agents of the five regiments of horse, and since by the general approbation of the army offered to the joint concurrence of all the free commons of England

The names of the regiments which have already appeared for the case of the *Case of the army truly stated*, and for this present Agreement,[1] viz.

(Of Horse)

1. The General's Regiment.
2. The Life Guard.
3. The Lieutenant-General's Regiment.
4. The Commissary-General's Regiment.
5. Colonel Whalley's Regiment.
6. Colonel Rich's Regiment.

---

[1] General Fairfax had put the *Case of the army* before the General Council of the Army on 21 October. It had been greeted with hostility by Cromwell and Ireton, who probably suspected the hands of Henry Marten and Thomas Rainborough – dangerous Independent MP radicals – in it, and who were anyway at the time trying to reach an accommodation with the king and could not have approved of its anti-monarchical overtones. It was repudiated by the accredited agitators of the Army, refused a reading, and sent to a committee which was to prepare a vindication of the Army and, presumably, to prepare legal charges against the 'new agents' who had prepared it. But it soon became clear that some regular agents supported the pamphlet; and it also emerged that Charles was dealing with the Scots behind Cromwell's back; so the committee decided to send the regular agitators William Sexby, William Allen and Nicholas Lockyer (see pp. 202 and 211) to present the new agents with an account of the Army's objections to what they had put their hands to, and to invite them 'in a friendly way' to come and discuss them. This *Agreement* is the new agents' answer. Approved by the new agents of five regiments at a meeting attended by John Wildman, a civilian and a lawyer (and the main author of the *Case of the army*) it seems to have been largely written by Walwyn (see p. 212), though Wildman, Lilburne and Overton very likely had hands in it.

7. Colonel Fleetwood's Regiment.
8. Colonel Harrison's Regiment.
9. Colonel Twistleton's Regiment.

(Of Foot)

1. The General's Regiment.
2. Colonel Sir Hardress Waller's Regiment.
3. Colonel Lambert's Regiment.
4. Colonel Rainsborough's Regiment.
5. Colonel Overton's Regiment.
6. Colonel Lilburne's Regiment.
7. Colonel Baxter's Regiment.

Anno Domini 1647

_____ [2]

An Agreement of the people for a firm and present peace upon grounds of common right

Having by our late labours and hazards made it appear to the world at how high a rate we value our just freedom, and God having so far owned our cause as to deliver the enemies thereof into our hands, we do now hold ourselves bound in mutual duty to each other to take the best care we can for the future to avoid both the danger of returning into a slavish condition and the chargeable remedy of another war. For as it cannot be imagined that so many of our countrymen would have opposed us in this quarrel if they had understood their own good, so may we safely promise to ourselves that when our common rights and liberties shall be cleared, their endeavours will be disappointed that seek to make themselves our masters. Since therefore our former oppressions and scarce-yet-ended troubles have been occasioned either by want of frequent national meetings in council or by rendering those meetings ineffectual, we are fully agreed and resolved to provide that hereafter our representatives be neither left to an uncertainty for the time, nor made useless to the ends for which they are intended. In order whereunto we declare:

1. That the people of England being at this day very unequally distributed by counties, cities and boroughs for the election of their deputies in parliament, ought to be more indifferently proportioned according

[2] End of title page.

to the number of the inhabitants: the circumstances whereof, for number, place, and manner, are to be set down before the end of this present parliament.

2. That to prevent the many inconveniences apparently arising from the long continuance of the same persons in authority, this present parliament be dissolved upon the last day of September, which shall be in the year of our Lord, 1648.

3. That the people do of course choose themselves a parliament once in two years, viz. upon the first Thursday in every second March, after the manner as shall be prescribed before the end of this parliament, to begin to sit upon the first Thursday in April following at Westminster or such other place as shall be appointed from time to time by the preceding representatives, and to continue till the last day of September then next ensuing, and no longer.

4. That the power of this and all future representatives of this nation is inferior only to theirs who choose them, and doth extend, without the consent or concurrence of any other person or persons, to the enacting, altering, and repealing of laws; to the erecting and abolishing of offices and courts; to the appointing, removing, and calling to account magistrates and officers of all degrees; to the making war and peace; to the treating with foreign states; and generally, to whatsoever is not expressly or impliedly reserved by the represented to themselves.

Which are as follows:

1. That matters of religion and the ways of God's worship are not at all entrusted by us to any human power, because therein we cannot remit or exceed a tittle of what our consciences dictate to be the mind of God, without wilful sin. Nevertheless the public way of instructing the nation – so it be not compulsive – is referred to their discretion.

2. That the matter of impressing and constraining any of us to serve in the wars is against our freedom; and therefore we do not allow it in our representatives; the rather, because money (the sinews of war) being always at their disposal, they can never want numbers of men apt enough to engage in any just cause.

3. That after the dissolution of this present parliament, no person be at any time questioned for anything said or done in reference to the late public differences, otherwise than in execution of the judgements of the present representatives (or House of Commons).

4. That in all laws made or to be made, every person may be bound alike; and that no tenure, estate, charter, degree, birth, or place do confer any exemption from the ordinary course of legal proceedings whereunto others are subjected.

5. That as the laws ought to be equal, so they must be good and not evidently destructive to the safety and well-being of the people.

These things we declare to be our native rights; and therefore are agreed and resolved to maintain them with our utmost possibilities against all opposition whatsoever: being compelled thereunto, not only by the examples of our ancestors – whose blood was often spent in vain for the recovery of their freedoms, suffering themselves through fraudulent accommodations to be still deluded of the fruit of their victories – but also by our own woeful experience, who having long expected and dearly earned the establishment of these certain rules of government, are yet made to depend for the settlement of our peace and freedom upon him[3] that intended our bondage and brought a cruel war upon us.

For the noble and highly honoured the freeborn people of England, in their respective counties and divisions, these:

Dear countrymen and fellow-commoners,

For your sakes, our friends, estates and lives have not been dear to us. For your safety and freedom we have cheerfully endured hard labours and run most desperate hazards. And in comparison to your peace and freedom we neither do nor ever shall value our dearest blood; and we profess our bowels are and have been troubled and our hearts pained within us in seeing and considering that you have been so long bereaved of these fruits and ends of all our labours and hazards. We cannot but sympathise with you in your miseries and oppressions. It's grief and vexation of heart to us to receive your meat or monies whilst you have no advantage, nor yet the foundations of your peace and freedom surely laid. And therefore, upon most serious considerations that your principal right most essential to your well-being is the clearness, certainty, sufficiency and freedom of your power in your representatives in parliament; and considering that the original of most of your oppressions and

---

[3] him = the king, with whom Cromwell and Ireton were still continuing to treat though with increasingly less optimism.

miseries have been either from the obscurity and doubtfulness of the power you have committed to your representatives in your elections, or from the want of courage in those whom you have betrusted to claim and exercise their power (which might probably proceed from their uncertainty of your assistance and maintenance of their power); and minding that for this right of yours and ours we engaged our lives (for the king raised the war against you and your parliament upon this ground: that he would not suffer your representatives to provide for your peace, safety and freedom that were then in danger, by disposing of the militia and otherwise, according to their trust); and for the maintenance and defence of that power and right of yours, we hazarded all that was dear to us. And God has borne witness to the justice of our cause.

And further minding that the only effectual means to settle a just and lasting peace, to obtain remedy for all your grievances, and to prevent future oppressions is the making clear and secure the power that you betrust to your representatives in parliament – that they may know their trust, in the faithful execution whereof you will assist them.

Upon all these grounds we propound your joining with us in the agreement herewith sent unto you, that by virtue thereof we may have parliaments certainly called and have the time of their sitting and ending certain and their power or trust clear and unquestionable; that hereafter they may remove your burdens and secure your rights without oppositions or obstructions and that the foundations of your peace may be so free from uncertainty that there may be no grounds for future quarrels or contentions to occasion war and bloodshed. And we desire you would consider that as these things wherein we offer to agree with you are the fruits and ends of the victories which God has given us, so the settlement of these are the most absolute means to preserve you and your posterity from slavery, oppression, distraction, and trouble. By this, *those whom yourselves shall choose* shall have power to restore you to, and secure you in, all your rights; and they shall be in a capacity to taste of subjection as well as rule, and so shall be equally concerned with yourselves in all they do. For they must equally suffer with you under any common burdens and partake with you in any freedoms. And by this they shall be disenabled to defraud or wrong you – when the laws shall bind all alike, without privilege or exemption. And by this your consciences shall be free from tyranny and oppression, and those occasions of endless strifes and bloody wars shall be perfectly removed. Without controversy, by your joining with us in this agreement all your particular and common grievances will be redressed forthwith without delay. The parliament must then make your relief and common good their only study.

Now because we are earnestly desirous of the peace and good of all our countrymen – even of those that have opposed us – and would to our utmost possibility provide for perfect peace and freedom and prevent all suits, debates, and contentions that may happen amongst you in relation to the late war, we have therefore inserted it into this agreement that no person shall be questionable for anything done in relation to the late public differences after the dissolution of this present parliament, further than in execution of their[4] judgement: that thereby all may be secure from all sufferings for what they have done, and not liable hereafter to be troubled or punished by the judgement of another parliament – which may be to their ruin unless this agreement be joined in, whereby any acts of indemnity or oblivion shall be made unalterable and you and your posterities be secure.

But if any shall inquire why we should desire to join in an agreement with the people to declare these to be our native rights – and not rather petition to the parliament for them – the reason is evident. No Act of parliament is or can be unalterable, and so cannot be sufficient security to save you or us harmless from what another parliament may determine if it should be corrupted. And besides, parliaments are to receive the extent of their power and trust from those that betrust them; and therefore the people are to declare what their power and trust is – which is the intent of this agreement. And it's to be observed that though there has formerly been many Acts of parliament for the calling of parliaments every year, yet you have been deprived of them and enslaved through want of them. And therefore, both necessity for your security in these freedoms that are essential to your well-being, and woeful experience of the manifold miseries and distractions that have been lengthened out since the war ended through want of such a settlement, require this agreement. And *when* you and we shall be joined together therein we shall readily join with you to petition the parliament – as they are our fellow-commoners equally concerned – to join with us.

And if any shall inquire why we undertake to offer this agreement, we must profess we are sensible that you have been so often deceived with declarations and remonstrances and fed with vain hopes that you

---

[4] I.e. parliament's judgement.

have sufficient reason to abandon all confidence in any persons whatsoever from whom you have no other security of their intending your freedom than bare declaration. And therefore, as our consciences witness that in simplicity and integrity of heart we have proposed lately in the *Case of the army stated* your freedom and deliverance from slavery, oppression and all burdens, so we desire to give you satisfying assurance thereof by this agreement – whereby the foundations of your freedoms provided in the *Case of the army* shall be settled unalterably. And we shall as faithfully proceed to – and all other most vigorous actings for your good that God shall direct and enable us unto. And though the malice of our enemies and such as they delude would blast us by scandals, aspersing us with designs of 'anarchy' and 'community', yet we hope the righteous God will, not only by this our present desire of setting an equal just government but also by directing us unto all righteous undertakings simply for public good, make our uprightness and faithfulness to the interest of all our countrymen shine forth so clearly that malice itself shall be silenced and confounded. We question not but the longing expectation of a firm peace will incite you to the most speedy joining in this agreement – in the prosecution whereof, or of anything that you shall desire for public good, you may be confident you shall never want the assistance of,

Your most faithful fellow-commoners now in arms for your service.
Edmund Bear
Robert Everard (Lieutenant-General's Regiment).
George Garret
Thomas Beverley (Commissary-General's Regiment).
William Pryor
William Bryan (Colonel Fleetwood's Regiment).
Matthew Weale
William Russell (Colonel Whalley's Regiment).
John Dover
William Hudson (Colonel Rich's Regiment).
Agents coming from other regiments unto us have subscribed the agreement to be proposed to their respective regiments and you.

For our much honoured and truly worthy fellow-commoners and soldiers, the officers and soldiers under command of his excellency Sir Thomas Fairfax

Gentlemen and fellow soldiers,

The deep sense of many dangers and mischiefs that may befall you in relation to the late war whensoever this parliament shall end – unless sufficient prevention be now provided – has constrained us to study the most absolute and certain means for your security. And upon most serious considerations we judge that no Act of Indemnity can sufficiently provide for your quiet, ease, and safety, because – as it has formerly been – a corrupt party, chosen into the next parliament by your enemies' means may possibly surprise the House and make any Act of Indemnity null,[5] seeing they cannot fail of the king's assistance and concurrence in any such actings against you that conquered him.

And by the same means, your freedom from impressing also may in a short time be taken from you though for the present it should be granted.[6] We apprehend no other security by which you shall be saved harmless for what you have done in the late war than a mutual agreement between the people and you that no person shall be questioned by any authority whatsoever for anything done in relation to the late public differences after the dissolution of the present House of Commons, further than in execution of their judgement; and that your native freedom from constraint to serve in war, whether domestic or foreign, shall never be subject to the power of parliaments – or any other. And for this end we propound the agreement that we herewith send to you to be forthwith subscribed.

---

[5] In response to and largely acceding to Army demands, parliament had passed an *Ordinance of indemnity* on 21 May 1647. A standing committee of parliament was set up to ensure that soldiers and civilians 'not able to defend a suit at common law' or 'aggrieved' at the results of such a suit (which they often were because of hostility to soldiers in the localities) could have their appeals heard at Westminster. This was a definite improvement from the solders' point of view. But the ordinance declared indemnity for only a narrow range of actions, 'done by the authority of this present parliament or for the benefit thereof'; and though a further ordinance of 7 June substituted (for soldiers) 'all such actions the exigency of war hath necessitated them unto', there was still the journey to Westminster. In December the Army was to begin an unsuccessful campaign to persuade parliament to appoint county committees for indemnity.

[6] Conscription by impressment to the military forces, administered by the London Militia Committee and by deputy lieutenants and committees in the counties, targeted the poor. Exempt were men (and sons of men) rated at £5 in goods or £3 in lands, clergymen, scholars, students at law or at the universities, esquires' sons, MPs and peers and tax officials. Mariners, watermen and fishermen were exempt for reasons of state economy.

And because we are confident that 'in judgement and conscience'[7] ye hazarded your lives for the settlement of such a just and equal government that you and your posterities and all the freeborn people of this nation might enjoy justice and freedom; and that you are really sensible that the distractions, oppressions and miseries of the nation, and your want of your arrears, do proceed from the want of the establishment both of such certain rules of just government and foundations of peace as are the price of blood and the expected fruits of all the people's cost; therefore in this agreement we have inserted the certain rules of equal government under which the nation may enjoy all its rights and freedoms securely. And as we doubt not but your love to the freedom and lasting peace of the yet-distracted country will cause you to join together in this agreement.

So we question not but every true Englishman that loves the peace and freedom of England will concur with us. And then your arrears and constant pay (while you continue in arms) will certainly be brought in, out of the abundant love of the people to you; and then shall the mouths of those be stopped that scandalise you and us as endeavouring anarchy or to rule by the sword; and then will so firm an union be made between the people and you that neither any homebred or foreign enemies will dare to disturb our happy peace.

We shall add no more but this; that the knowledge of your union in laying this foundation of peace, this agreement, is much longed for by,
Yours, and the people's most faithful servants.

Postscript

Gentlemen,
We desire you may understand the reason of our extracting some principles of common freedom out of those many things proposed to you in the *Case of the army truly stated* and drawing them up into the form of an agreement. It's chiefly because for these things we first engaged against the king. He would not permit the people's representatives to provide for the nation's safety – by disposing of the militia, and other ways, according to their trust – but raised a war against them; and we engaged for the defence of that power and right of the people in their representatives. Therefore these things in the agreement, the people

---

[7] An echo of the *Declaration or remonstrance* of 14 June: 'And so we took up arms in judgement and conscience.'

are to claim as their native right and price of their blood, which you are obliged absolutely to procure for them.

And these being the foundations of freedom, it's necessary that they should be settled unalterably, which can be by no means but this agreement with the people.

And we cannot but mind[8] you that the ease of the people in all their grievances depends upon the setting those principles or rules of equal government for a free people; and, were but this agreement established, doubtless all the grievances of the Army and people would be redressed immediately and all things propounded in your *Case of the army* stated to be insisted on, would be forthwith granted.

Then should the House of Commons have power to help the oppressed people, which they are now bereaved of by the chief oppressors; and then they shall be equally concerned with you and all the people in the settlement of the most perfect freedom – for they shall equally suffer with you under any burdens or partake in any freedom.

We shall only add that the sum of all the agreement which we herewith offer to you is but in order to the fulfilling of our Declaration of 14 June wherein we promised to the people that we would with our lives vindicate and clear their right and power in their parliaments.

Edmond Bear
Robert Everard (Lieutenant-General's Regiment).
George Garret
Thomas Beverley (Commissary-General's Regiment).
William Pryor
William Bryan (Colonel Fleetwood's Regiment).
Matthew Wealey
William Russell (Colonel Whalley's Regiment).
John Dober
William Hudson (Colonel Rich's Regiment).
Agents coming from other regiments unto us have subscribed the agreement to be proposed to their respective regiments and you.

---

[8] mind = remind.

8

At the General Council of the Army, Putney, 29 October 1647

(The paper called the *Agreement* read. Afterwards the first article read by itself: 'That the people of England being at this day very unequally distributed by counties, cities and boroughs for the election of their deputies in parliament, ought to be more indifferently proportioned according to the number of inhabitants . . . ')

Commissary-General Henry Ireton: The exception that lies in it is this. It is said they ('the people of England etc.') are to be distributed according to the number of the inhabitants. This does make me think that the meaning is that every man that is an inhabitant is to be equally considered, and to have an equal voice in the election of the representers – those persons that are for the General Representative. And if that be the meaning then I have something to say against it. But if it be only that those people that by the civil constitution of this kingdom, which is original and fundamental, and beyond which I am sure no memory of record does go . . .

Commissary Nicholas Cowling (interrupting): Not before the Conquest.[1]

Ireton: But before the Conquest it was so. If it be intended that those that by that constitution that was before the Conquest that has been beyond memory, such persons that have been before by that constitution the electors should be still the electors, I have no more to say against it . . . *Ireton* then asked whether those men whose hands are to *the Agreement*, or those that brought it, 'do know so much of the matter as to know whether they mean that all that had a former right of election are to be electors, or that those that had *no right before* are to come in?'

Cowling: In the time before the Conquest. Since the Conquest the greatest part of the kingdom was in vassalage.

Maximilian Petty: We judge that all inhabitants that have not lost their birthright should have an equal voice in elections.

---

[1] I.e. the constitution did not exist before the Norman Conquest, and was imposed by the will of the conqueror.

Colonel Thomas Rainborough: I desired that those that had engaged in it might be included. For really I think that the poorest he that is in England has a life to live as the greatest he; and therefore truly, sir, I think it's clear that every man that is to live under a government ought first by his own consent to put himself under that government; and I do think that the poorest man in England is not at all bound in a strict sense to that government that he has not had a voice to put himself under. And I am confident that when I have heard the reasons against it, something will be said to answer those reasons – insomuch that I should doubt whether he was an Englishman or no that should doubt of these things.

Ireton: *That's* the meaning of this 'according to the number of the inhabitants'? Give me leave to tell you that if you make this the rule, I think you must fly for refuge to an absolute natural right and you must deny all civil right; and I am sure it will come to that in the consequence. This, I perceive, is pressed as that which is so essential and due: the right of the people of this kingdom, and as they *are* the people of this kingdom, distinct and divided from other people; and that we must for this right lay aside all other considerations; this is so just, this is so due, this is so right to them. And that those that they do thus choose must have such a power of binding all, and loosing all, according to those limitations. This is pressed as so due and so just as it is argued that it is an engagement paramount to all others, and you must for it lay aside all others. If you have engaged any otherwise you must break it. We must so look upon these as thus held out to us; so it was held out by the gentleman that brought it yesterday.[2]

For my part, I think it is no right at all. I think that no person has a right to an interest or share in the disposing or determining of the affairs of the kingdom, and in choosing those that shall determine what laws we shall be ruled by here – no person has a right to this that has not a permanent fixed interest in this kingdom; and *those* persons

---

[2] Robert Everard (see biographies for him and the other protagonists at Putney) had brought the *Agreement* to headquarters on 27 October. It had been approved by the agents of the five regiments, by other soldiers, by John Wildman and by 'divers country-gentlemen'. Wildman had told the meeting the day before that, 'according to the best knowledge I have of their apprehensions, they do apprehend that whatever obligation is past must afterwards be considered when it is urged whether the *Engagement* be just or no; and if [that obligation] were not just it does not oblige the persons, if it be an oath itself . . . I conceive the first thing is to consider the honesty of what is offered; otherwise it cannot be considered of any obligation that does prepossess'.

together are properly the represented of this kingdom and consequently are also to make up the representers of this kingdom, who, taken together, do comprehend whatsoever is of real or permanent interest in the kingdom. And I am sure otherwise I cannot tell what any man can say why a foreigner coming in amongst us – or as many as will coming in amongst us, or by force or otherwise settling themselves here, or at least by our permission having a being here – why they should not as well lay claim to it as any other. We talk of 'birthright'. Truly by birthright there is *thus* much claim. Men may justly have by birthright (by their very being born in England) that we should not seclude them out of England, that we should not refuse to give them air and place and ground and the freedom of the highways and other things to live amongst us – not to any man that is born here, though by his birth there come nothing at all that is part of the permanent interest of this kingdom to him. *That* I think is due to a man by birth. But that by a man's being born here he shall have a share in that power that shall dispose of the lands here, and of all things here, I do not think it a sufficient ground.

I am sure, if we look upon that which is the utmost within *any* man's view of what was originally the constitution of this kingdom, upon that which is most radical and fundamental, and which if you take away there is no man has any land, any goods, or any civil interest, that is this: that those that choose the representers for the making of laws by which this state and kingdom are to be governed are the persons who, taken together, *do* comprehend the local interest of this kingdom, that is the persons in whom all land lies and those in corporations in whom all trading lies. This is the most fundamental constitution of this kingdom and that which if you do not allow, you allow none at all. This constitution has limited and determined it that only those shall have voices in elections. It is true – as was said by a gentleman near me – the meanest man in England ought to have a voice in the election of the government he lives under. But *only if* he has some local interest. I say this: that those that have the meanest local interest – that man that has but forty shillings a year – he has as great voice in the election of a knight for the shire as he that has ten thousand a year or more, if he had never so much; and therefore there is that regard had to it. But this local interest, still³ the constitution of this government has had an

---

³ still = always.

eye to. And what other government has not an eye to this? It does not relate to the interest of the kingdom if it do not lay the foundation of the power that's given to the representers in those who have a permanent and a local interest in the kingdom, and who taken all together do comprehend the whole interest of the kingdom. There is all the reason and justice that can be in this. If I will come to live in a kingdom being a foreigner to it, or live in a kingdom having no permanent interest in it, and if I will desire as a stranger or claim as one freeborn here, the air, the free passage of highways, the protection of laws, and all such things – if I will either desire them or claim them, then I (if I have no permanent interest in that kingdom) must submit to those laws and those rules which they shall choose, who, taken together, do comprehend the whole interest of the kingdom. And if we shall go to take away this we shall plainly go to take away all property and interest that any man has, either in land by inheritance or in estate by possession, or anything else – I say, if you take away this fundamental part of the civil constitution.

Rainborough: Truly sir, I am of the same opinion I was, and am resolved to keep it till I know reason why I should not. I confess my memory is bad, and therefore I am fain to make use of my pen. I remember that – in a former speech which this gentleman brought before this meeting – he was saying that in some cases he should not value whether there were a king or no king, whether lords or no lords, whether a property or no property.[4] For my part I differ in that. I do very much care whether there be a king or no king, lords or no lords, property or no property; and I think, if we do not all take care, we shall all have none of these very shortly.

But as to this present business. I do hear nothing at all that can convince me why any man that is born in England ought not to have his voice in election of burgesses. It is said that if a man have not a 'permanent interest' he can have no claim; and that we must be no freer than the laws will let us be; and that there is no law in any chronicle will let us be freer than that we now enjoy. Something was said to this yesterday. I do think that the main cause why Almighty God gave men reason, it was that they should make use of that reason, and that they should improve it for that end and purpose that God gave it them. And truly, I think that half a loaf is better than none if a

---

[4] Earlier in the afternoon's debate, before the *Agreement* was read.

man be an-hungry. This gift of reason without other property may seem a small thing, yet I think there is nothing that God has given a man that anyone else can take from him. And therefore I say that either it must be the Law of God or the law of man that must prohibit the meanest man in the kingdom to have this benefit as well as the greatest. I do not find anything in the Law of God that a lord shall choose twenty burgesses, and a gentleman but two,[5] or a poor man shall choose none. I find no such thing in the law of nature, nor in the law of nations. But I *do* find that all Englishmen must be subject to English laws; and I do verily believe that there is no man but will say that the foundation of all law lies in the people; and if it lie in the people, I am to seek for this exemption.

And truly I have thought something else: in what a miserable distressed condition would many a man that has fought for the parliament in this quarrel be! I will be bound to say that many a man whose zeal and affection to God and this kingdom has carried him forth in this cause, has so spent his estate that, in the way the state and the Army are going, he shall not hold up his head, if, when his estate is lost and not worth forty shillings a year, a man shall not have any 'interest'. And there are many other ways by which the estates men have – if that be the rule which God in his providence does use – do fall to decay. A man, when he has an estate, has an interest in making laws; but when he has none, he has no power in it; so that a man cannot lose that which he has for the maintenance of his family but he must also lose that which God and nature has given him! And therefore I do think, and am still of the same opinion, that every man born in England cannot, ought not, neither by the Law of God nor the law of nature, to be exempted from the choice of those who are to make laws for him to live under – and for him, for aught I know, to lose his life under. And therefore I think there can be no great stick in this.

Truly I think that there is not this day reigning in England a greater fruit or effect of tyranny than this very thing would produce. Truly I know nothing free but only the knight of the shire; nor do I know anything in a parliamentary way that is clear from the height and fullness of tyranny, but only that. As for this of corporations which you also mentioned, it is as contrary to freedom as may be. For, sir, what is it? The king he grants a patent under the Broad Seal of England to

---

[5] The number of MPs for each county.

such a corporation to send burgesses. He grants to such a city to send burgesses. When a poor base corporation from the king's grant shall send two burgesses; when five hundred men of estate shall not send one; when those that are to make their laws are called by the king, or cannot act but by such a call: truly I think that the people of England have little freedom.

Ireton: I think there was nothing that I said to give you occasion to think that I did contend for this: that such a corporation as that should have the electing of a man to the parliament. I think I agreed to this matter, that all should be equally distributed.[6] But the question is whether it should be distributed to *all persons*, or whether the *same* persons that are the electors now should be the electors still, and it be equally distributed amongst *them*. I do not see anybody else that makes this objection; and if nobody else be sensible of it I shall soon have done. Only I shall a little crave your leave to represent the consequences of it, and clear myself from one thing that was misrepresented by the gentleman that sat next me. I think if the gentleman remember himself, he cannot but remember that what I said was to this effect: that if I saw the hand of God leading so far as to destroy king, and destroy lords, and destroy property, and leave no such thing at all amongst us, I should acquiesce in it; and so I did not care if no king, no lords, or no property should be, in comparison of the tender care that I have of the honour of God and of the people of God, whose good name is so much concerned in this army. This I did deliver *so* and not absolutely.

All the main thing that I speak for is because I would have an eye to property. I hope we do not come to contend for victory; but let every man consider with himself that he do not go that way to take away all property. For here is the case of the most fundamental part of the constitution of the kingdom, which if you take away, you take away all

---

[6] As he indeed had. Ireton was one of the leading authors of the *Heads of the proposals* (see n. 20 below). There it was proposed that parliaments should be called biennially and that 'the elections of the Commons for succeeding parliaments may be distributed to all counties or other parts or divisions of the kingdom according to some rule of equality or proportion, so as all counties may have a number of parliament members allowed to their choice proportionable to the respective rates they bear in the common charges and burdens of the kingdom, [or] according to some other rule of equality or proportion, to render the House of Commons (as near as may be) an equal representative of the whole; and in order thereunto, that a present consideration be had to take off the election of burgesses for poor decayed or inconsiderable towns, and to give some present addition to the number of parliament members for the great counties that have now less than their due proportion'.

by that. Here men of this and this quality are determined to be the electors of men to the parliament, and they are all those who have any permanent interest in the kingdom, and who, taken together, do comprehend the whole permanent, local interest of the kingdom.

I mean by 'permanent' and 'local', that it is not able to be removed anywhere else, as for instance he that has a freehold and that freehold cannot be removed out of the kingdom; and also there's a freeman of a corporation, – a place which has the privilege of a market and trading – which if you should allow to all places equally, I do not see how you could preserve any peace in the kingdom: and that is the reason why in the constitution we have but some few market towns. Now those people that have freeholds and those that are the freemen of corporations, were looked upon by the former constitution to comprehend the permanent interest of the kingdom. For firstly, he that has his livelihood by his trade and by his freedom of trading in such a corporation – which he cannot exercise in another – he is tied to that place, for his livelihood depends upon it. And secondly, that man has an interest – has a *permanent* interest there, upon which he may live, and live a freeman without dependence. These things the constitution of this kingdom has looked at.

Now I wish we may all consider of what right you will challenge that all the people should have right to elections. Is it by the right of nature? If you will hold forth that as your ground, then I think you must deny all property too, and this is my reason. For thus: by that same right of nature (whatever it be) that you pretend, by which you can say that one man has an equal right with another to the choosing of him that shall govern him – by the same right of nature he has the same equal right in any goods he sees: meat, drink, clothes, to take and use them for his sustenance. He has a freedom to the land, to take the ground, to exercise it, till it; he has the same freedom to anything that anyone does account himself to have any propriety in. Why now I say then, if you, against the most fundamental part of the civil constitution (which I have now declared), will plead the law of nature that a man should (paramount to this, and contrary to this[7]) have a power of choosing those men that shall determine what shall be law in this state, though he himself have no permanent interest in the state but whatever interest he hath he may carry about with him – if this be allowed (because by

---

[7] I.e. overriding the civil constitution, and contradictory to it.

the right of nature we are free; we are equal; one man must have as much voice as another), then show me what step or difference there is why I may not by the same right take your property, though not of necessity to sustain nature. It is for my better being, and the better settlement of the kingdom? Possibly not for it,[8] neither. Possibly I may not have so real a regard to the peace of the kingdom as that man who hath a permanent interest in it. He that is here today and gone tomorrow, I do not see that he hath such a permanent interest. Since you cannot plead to it by anything but the law of nature, or for anything but for the end of better being, and since that better being is not certain, and what is more, destructive to another: upon these grounds, if you do, paramount to all constitutions, hold up this law of nature, I would fain have any man show me their bounds, where you will end, and why you should not take away all property.

Rainborough: I shall now be a little more free and open with you than I was before. I wish we were all true-hearted, and that we did all carry ourselves with integrity. If I did mistrust you I would not use such asseveration. I think it does go on mistrust, and things are thought too readily matters of reflection that were never intended. For my part, as I think, *you* forgot something that was in *my* speech; and you do not only yourselves believe that we are inclining to anarchy, but you would make all men believe that. And, sir, to say because a man pleads that every man has a voice by right of nature, that therefore it destroys by the same argument all property, this is to forget the Law of God. That there's a property, the Law of God says it – else why has God made that law 'Thou shalt not steal'?[9]

I am a poor man, therefore I must be *oppressed*? If I have no interest in the kingdom, I must suffer by all their laws – be they right or wrong? Nay thus: a gentleman lives in a country and has three or four lordships – as some men have (God knows how they got them) – and when a parliament is called he must be a parliament-man. And it may be he sees some poor men – they live near this man. He can crush them; I have known an invasion to make sure he has turned the poor men out of doors; and I would fain know whether the potency of rich men do not this, and so keep them under the greatest tyranny that was ever thought of in the world. And therefore I think that to that it is

---

[8] I.e. possibly not for the better settlement of the kingdom.
[9] The eighth of the Ten Commandments, Exodus 20.

fully answered: God has set down that thing as to propriety with this law of his: 'Thou shalt not steal.' For my part I am against any such thought; and, as for yourselves, I wish you would not make the world believe that we are for anarchy.

Lieutenant-General Oliver Cromwell: I know nothing but this, that they that are the most yielding have the greatest wisdom; but really, sir, this is not right as it should be. No man says that you have a mind to anarchy, but that the *consequence* of this rule tends to anarchy, must *end* in anarchy. For where is there any bound or limit set if you take away this limit: that men that have no interest but the interest of breathing shall have no voice in elections? Therefore I am confident on't, we should not be so hot one with another.

Rainborough: I know that some particular men we debate with believe we are for anarchy.

Ireton: I profess I must clear myself as to that point. I would not desire – I cannot allow myself – to lay the least scandal upon anybody. And truly, for that gentleman that did take so much offence, I do not know why he should take it so. We speak to the paper and to the matter of the paper – not to persons. And I hope that no man is so much engaged to the matter of the paper – I hope that our persons and our hearts and judgements are not so pinned to papers but that we are ready to hear what good or ill consequence will flow from it.

I have, with as much plainness and clearness of reason as I could, showed you how I did conceive the doing of this that the paper advocates: takes away that which is the most original, the most fundamental civil constitution of this kingdom, and which is, above all, that constitution by which I have any property. If you will take away that, and set up as a thing paramount whatever a man may claim by the law of nature – though it be not a thing of necessity to him for the sustenance of nature[10] – if you do make this your rule, I desire clearly to understand where then remains property.

Now then – I would misrepresent nothing – the answer which had anything of matter in it (the great and main answer upon which that

---

[10] The normal natural law argument, as in Aquinas (and later in Locke), was that there was a natural duty of charity, according to which, in Locke's words: 'twould always be a sin in any man of estate to let his brother perish for want of affording him relief out of his plenty', gave the poor a claim where the necessity of preservation demanded it. Ireton is not disagreeing with *that* argument, rather he is claiming that there is no necesssity operating here.

which hath been said against this objection rests) seemed to be that it will not make a breach of property, for this reason: that there is a Law, 'Thou shalt not steal.' But the same law says, 'Honour thy father and thy mother',[11] and that law does likewise hold out that it does extend to all that (in that place where we are in) are our governors: so that by that there is a forbidding of breaking a civil law when we may live quietly under it – and that by a divine law.

Again it is said – indeed was said before – that there is no law, no divine law, that tells us that such a corporation must have the election of burgesses, such a shire of knights, or the like.

Divine law extends not to particular things. And so, on the other side, if a man were to demonstrate his right to property by divine law, it would be very remote. Our right to property descends from other things, as well as[12] our right of sending burgesses. That divine law does not determine particulars but generals in relation to man and man and to property and all things else; and we should be as far to seek if we should go to prove a property in a thing[13] by divine law as to prove that I have an interest in choosing burgesses of the parliament by divine law. And truly, under favour, I refer it to all whether there be anything of solution to that objection that I made, if it be understood. I submit it to any man's judgement.

Rainborough: To the thing itself – property in the franchise. I would fain know how it comes to be the property of some men and not of others. As for estates and those kind of things – and other things that belong to men – it will be granted that they are property. But I deny that *that* is a property – to a lord, to a gentleman, to any man more than another in the kingdom of England. *If* it be a property, it is a property by a law; neither do I think[14] that there is very little property in this thing by the law of the land, because I think that the law of the land in that thing is the most tyrannical law under heaven. And I would fain know what we have fought for – for a law which denies the people the franchise? And *this* is the old law of England, and that which enslaves the people of England: that they should be bound by laws in which they have no voice at all!

---

[11] The fifth of the Ten Commandments (on honouring parents) was routinely glossed as a command to obey all superiors, including governors.

[12] I.e. as also does.

[13] I.e. the ownership by a *particular* person of a *particular* thing.

[14] neither do I think = and I think.

With respect to the divine law which says 'Honour thy father and thy mother', the great dispute is who is a right father and a right mother? I am bound to know *who* is my father and mother; and – I take it in the same sense you do – I would have a distinction, a character, whereby God commands me to honour them. And for my part I look upon the people of England so, that wherein they have not voices in the choosing of their governors – their civil fathers and mothers – they are not bound to that commandment.

Petty: I desire to add one word concerning the word 'property'. It is for *something* that anarchy is so much talked of. For my own part I cannot believe in the least that it can be clearly derived from that paper. 'Tis true that somewhat may be derived in the paper against the king – the power of the king – and somewhat against the power of the Lords. And the truth is, when I shall see God going about to throw down king and Lords and property, then I shall be contented. But I hope that they may live to see the power of the king and the Lords thrown down that yet may live to see property preserved. And for this of changing the Representative of the nation, of changing those that choose the Representative – making of them more full, taking more into the number than formerly – I had verily thought we had all agreed in it that more should have chosen, that all had desired a more equal representation than we now have. For now those only choose who have forty shillings freehold. A man may have a lease for one hundred pounds a year, a man may have a lease for three lives, but he has no voice. But as for this argument that it destroys all right to property that every Englishman that is an inhabitant of England should choose and have a voice in the representatives, *I* suppose it is, on the contrary, the only means to preserve all property. For I judge every man is naturally free; and I judge the reason why men chose representatives when they were in so great numbers that every man could not give his voice directly was that they who were chosen might preserve property for all; and therefore men agreed to come into some form of government that they might preserve property. And I would fain know, if we were to begin a government, whether you would say: 'You have not forty shillings a year, therefore you shall not have a voice.' Whereas *before* there was a government, every man *had* such a voice, and afterwards – and for this very cause – they did choose representatives and put themselves into forms of government that they may preserve property; and therefore it is not to destroy it, to give every man a voice.

Ireton: I think we shall not be so apt to come to a right understanding in this business, if one man, and another man, and another man do speak their several thoughts and conceptions to the same purpose, as if we do consider where the *objection* lies, and what the answer is which is made to it; and therefore I desire we may do so.

To that which this gentleman spoke last. The main thing that he seemed to answer was this: that he would make it appear that the going about to establish this government – or such a government – is not a destruction of property, nor does not tend to the destruction of property, because the people's falling into a government is for the *preservation* of property. What weight there is in it lies in this: since there is a falling into a government, and government is to preserve property, therefore this cannot be against property. But my objection does not lie in that – the making of the representation more equal – but in the introducing of men into an equality of interest in this government who have no property in this kingdom, or who have no local permanent interest in it. For if I had said that I would not wish at all that we should have any enlargement of the bounds of those that are to be the electors, then you might have excepted against it. But what I said was that I would not go to enlarge it *beyond all bounds*, so that upon the same ground you may admit of so many men from foreign states as would outvote you. The objection lies *still* in this. I do not mean that I would have it restrained to that proportion that now obtains, but to restrain it still to men who have a local, a permanent interest in the kingdom, who have such an interest that they may live upon it as freemen, and who have such an interest as is fixed upon a place, and is not the same everywhere equally. If a man be an inhabitant upon a rack rent for a year, for two years, or twenty years, you cannot think that man has any fixed or permanent interest. That man, if he pay the rent that his land is worth, and has no advantage but what he has by his land, is as good a man – may have as much interest – in another kingdom as here. I do not speak of not enlarging this representation at all, but of keeping this to the most fundamental constitution in this kingdom, that is, that no person that has not a local and permanent interest in the kingdom should have an equal dependence in election with those that have. But if you go beyond this law – if you admit any man that has a breath and being – I did show you how this will destroy property. It may come to destroy property thus. You may have such men chosen, or at least the major part of them, as have no local and permanent interest. Why may not those men vote against all property? Again you may admit strangers by this rule (if you admit them once to inhabit), and those that have interest in the land may be voted out of their land. It may destroy property that way. But here is the rule that you go by. You infer this to be the right of the people, of every inhabitant, because man has such a right in nature, though it be not of necessity for the preserving of his being; and therefore you are to overthrow the most fundamental constitution for this. By the same rule, show me why you will not by the same right of nature make use of anything that any man has, though it be not for the necessary sustenance of men? Show me what you will stop at, wherein you will fence any man in a property by this rule.

Rainborough: I desire to know how this comes to be a property in some men and not in others.

Colonel Nathaniel Rich: I confess there is weight in that objection that the Commissary-General last insisted upon; for you have five to one in this kingdom that have no permanent interest. Some men have ten, some twenty servants – some more, some less. If the master and servant shall be equal electors, then clearly those that have no interest in the kingdom will make it their interest to choose those that have no interest. It may happen that the majority may, by law – not in a confusion – destroy property; there may be a law enacted that there shall be an equality of goods and estate. I think that either of the extremes may be urged to inconveniency: that is, that men that have no interest as to estate should have no interest as to election and that they should have an *equal* interest. But there may be a more equitable division and distribution than that he that has nothing should have an equal voice; and certainly there may be some other way thought of that there may be a representative of the poor as well as the rich, and not to exclude all. I remember there were many workings and revolutions, as we have heard, in the Roman Senate; and there was never a confusion that did appear – and that indeed *was* come to – till the state came to know this kind of distribution of election. That is how the people's voices were bought and sold, and that by the poor; and thence it came that he that was the richest man, and a man of some considerable power among the soldiers, and one they resolved on, made himself a perpetual dictator. And if we strain too far to avoid monarchy in kings let us take heed that we do not call for emperors to deliver us from more than one tyrant.

Rainborough: I should not have spoken again. I think it is a fine gilded pill. But there is much danger and it may seem to some that there is some kind of remedy possible. I think that we are better as we are if it can be really proved that the poor shall choose many and still the people be in the same case, be over-voted still. But of this, and much else, I am unsatisfied; and therefore truly, sir, I should desire to go close to the business; and the first thing that I am unsatisfied in is how it comes about that there is such a propriety in some freeborn Englishmen, and not in others.

Cowling demanded whether the younger son have not as much right to the inheritance as the eldest.

Ireton: Will you decide it by the light of nature?

Cowling: Why election was given only to those with freeholds of forty shillings a year (which was then worth more than forty pounds a year now), the reason was that the commons of England were overpowered by the lords who had abundance of vassals; but that still they might make their laws good against encroaching prerogatives by this means, therefore they did exclude all slaves. Now the case is not so. All slaves have bought their freedoms, and they are more free that in the commonwealth are more beneficial. Yet there are men of substance in the country with no voice in elections. There is a tanner in Staines worth three thousand pounds, and another in Reading worth three horseskins. The second has a voice; the first, none.

Ireton: In the beginning of your speech you seem to acknowledge that by law, by civil constitution, the propriety of having voices in election was fixed in certain persons. So then your exception of your argument does not prove that by civil constitution they have *no* such propriety, but your argument does acknowledge that by civil constitution they *have* such propriety. You argue against this law only that this law is not good.

John Wildman: Unless I be very much mistaken, we are very much deviated from the first question. Instead of following the first proposition to inquire what is just, I conceive we look to prophecies, and look to what may be the event, and judge of the justness of a thing by the consequence. I desire we may recall ourselves to the question whether it be right or no. I conceive all that has been said against it will be reduced to this question of consequences. And to another reason: that it is against a fundamental law that every person choosing ought to have a permanent interest, because it is not fit that those should choose parliaments that have no lands to be disposed of by parliament.

Ireton: If you will take it by the way, it is not fit that the representees should choose as the representers – the persons who shall make the law in the kingdom – those who have not a permanent fixed interest in the kingdom. The reason is the same in the two cases.

Wildman: Sir, I do so take it; and I conceive that that is brought in for the same reason: that foreigners might otherwise not only come to have a voice in our elections as well as the native inhabitants, but to be elected.

Ireton: That is upon supposition that these foreigners should be all inhabitants.

Wildman: I shall begin with the last first. The case is different with the native inhabitant and the foreigner. If a foreigner shall be admitted to be an inhabitant in the nation (so he will submit to that form of government as the natives do) he has the same right as the natives but in this particular. *Our* case is to be considered thus: that we have been under slavery; that's acknowledged by all; our very laws were made by our conquerors. And whereas it's spoken much of chronicles, I conceive there is no credit to be given to any of them: and the reason is because those that were our lords and made us their vassals would suffer nothing else to be chronicled.

We are now engaged for our freedom. That's the end of parliaments: not to constitute what is already established but to act according to the just rules of government. Every person in England has as clear a right to elect his representative as the greatest person in England. I conceive that's the undeniable maxim of government: that all government is in the free consent of the people. If so, then upon that account there is no person that is under a just government – or has justly his own – unless he by his own free consent be put under that government. This he cannot be unless he be consenting to it; and therefore, according to this maxim, there is never a person in England but ought to have a voice in elections. If such as that gentleman says be true, there are no laws that in this strictness and rigour of justice any man is bound to that are not made by those whom he does consent to. And therefore I should humbly move that if the question be stated in a way which would soonest bring things to an issue, it might rather be thus: whether any person can justly be bound by law, who does not give his consent that such persons shall make laws for him?

Ireton: Let the question be so, whether a man can be bound to any law that he does not consent to, and I shall tell you that he may and ought to be bound to a law that he does not give a consent to, nor does not choose any to consent to; and I will make it clear. If a foreigner come within this kingdom, if that stranger will have liberty to dwell here who has no local interest here, he, as a man, it's true, has air, the passage of highways, the protection of laws, and all that by nature. We must not expel him our coasts, give him no being amongst us, nor kill him because he comes upon our land, comes up our stream, arrives at our shore. It is a piece of hospitality, of humanity, to receive that man amongst us. But if that man be received to a being amongst us, I think that man may very well be content to submit himself to the law of the land – that is, the law that is made by those people that have a property, a fixed property, in the land. I think, if any man will receive protection from this people – though neither he nor his ancestors, not any betwixt him and Adam, did ever give concurrence to this constitution – I think this man ought to be subject to those laws, and to be bound by those laws, so long as he continues amongst them. That is my opinion. A man ought to be subject to a law that did not give his consent. But with this reservation: that if this man do think himself unsatisfied to be subject to this law he may go into another kingdom. And so the same reason does extend, in my understanding, to that man that has no permanent interest in the kingdom. If he has money, his money is as good in another place as here; he has nothing that does locally fix him to this kingdom. If that man will live in this kingdom, or trade amongst us, that man ought to subject himself to the law made by the people who have the interest of this kingdom in them. And yet I do acknowledge that which you take to be so general a maxim, that in every kingdom, within every land, the original of power of making laws, of determining what shall be law in the land, *does* lie in the people – but by 'the people' is meant those that are possessed of the permanent interest in the land. But whoever is extraneous to this, that is, as good a man in another land, that man ought to give such a respect to the property of men that live in the land. *They* do not determine that I shall live in this land. Why should I have any interest in determining what shall be the law of this land?

Major William Rainborough: I think if it can be made to appear that it is a just and reasonable thing, and that it is for the preservation of all the native freeborn men that they should have an equal voice in election – I think it ought to be made good unto them. And the reason is that the chief end of this government is to preserve *persons* as well as estates, and if any law shall take hold of my person it is more dear than my estate.

Colonel Thomas Rainborough: I do very well remember that the gentleman in the window – Colonel Rich – said that if it were so, there were no propriety to be had, because five parts of the nation – the poor people – are now excluded and would then come in. So one on the other side said that if it were otherwise, then rich men only shall be chosen. *Then*, I say, the one part shall make hewers of wood and drawers of water[15] of the other five, and so the greatest part of the nation be enslaved. Truly I think we are still where we were; and I do not hear any argument given but only that it is the present law of the kingdom. I say still: what shall become of those many men that have laid out themselves for the parliament of England in this present war, that have ruined themselves by fighting, by hazarding all they had? They are Englishmen. They have now nothing to say for themselves.

Rich: I should be very sorry to speak anything here that should give offence – or that may occasion personal reflections that we spoke against just now. I did not urge anything so *far* as was represented; and I did not *at all* urge that there should be a consideration had of rich men only, and that a man that is poor shall be without consideration, or that he deserves to be made poorer and not to live in independence at all. All that I urged was this: that I think it worthy consideration, whether they should have an *equality* in their interest. However, I think we have been a great while upon this point; and if we be as long upon all the rest it were well if there were no greater difference than this.

Mr Hugh Peter: I think that this matter of the franchise may be easily agreed on – that is, there may be a way thought of. I think you would do well to sit up all night if thereby you could effect it, but I think that three or four might be thought of in this company to form a committee. You will be forced only to put characters upon electors or elected; therefore I do suppose that if there be any here that can make up a Representative to your mind, the thing is gained. But I would fain know whether that will answer the work of your meeting. The question is whether you can state any *one* question for removing the present

---

[15] Joshua 10: 21, 23, 27. They are 'bondsmen . . . hewers of wood and drawers of water for the congregation'.

danger of the kingdom – whether any one question or no will dispatch the work.

Sir, I desire, if it be possible, that some question may be stated to finish the present work, to cement us in the points wherein lies the distance; and if the thoughts be of the commonwealth and the people's freedom, I think that's soon cured. I desire that all manner of plainness may be used, that we may not go on with the lapwing and carry one another off the nest. There is something else that must cement us where the awkwardness of our spirits lies.

Col. Rainborough: For my part, I think we cannot engage one way or other in the Army if we do not think of the people's liberties. If we can agree where the liberty and freedom of the people lies, that will do all.

Ireton: I cannot consent so far. As I said before: when I see the hand of God destroying king, and Lords – and Commons too, or any foundation of human constitution – when I see God has done it, I shall, I hope, comfortably acquiesce in it. But first, I cannot give my consent to it, because it is not good. And secondly, as I desire that this army should have regard to engagements wherever they are lawful, so I would have them have regard to this as well: that they should not bring that scandal upon the name of God and the saints, that those that call themselves by that name – those whom God has owned and appeared with – that we should represent ourselves to the world as men so far from being of that peaceable spirit which is suitable to the gospel, as we should have bought peace of the world upon such terms as we would not have peace in the world but upon such terms as should destroy all property. If the principle upon which you move this alteration, or the ground upon which you press that we should make this alteration, do destroy all kind of property or whatsoever a man has by human constitution, I cannot consent to it. The Law of God does not give me property, nor the law of nature, but property is of human constitution. I have a property and this I shall enjoy. Constitution founds property. If either the thing itself that you press or the consequence of that you press do destroy property, though I shall acquiesce in having no property, yet I cannot give my heart or hand to it because it is a thing evil in itself and scandalous to the world, and I desire this army may be free from both.

Captain Edward Sexby: I see that though liberty were our end, there is a degeneration from it. We have engaged in this kingdom and ventured our lives, and it was all for this: to recover our birthrights and privileges as Englishmen; and by the arguments urged there *are* none. There are many thousands of us soldiers that have ventured our lives. We have had little propriety in the kingdom as to our estates, yet we have had a birthright. But it seems now, except a man has a fixed estate in this kingdom, he has no right in this kingdom. I wonder we were so much deceived. If we had not a right to the kingdom we were mere mercenary soldiers. There are many in my condition that have as good a condition as I have. It may be little estate they have at present, and yet they have as much a birthright as those, too, who are their lawgivers – as any in this place. I shall tell you in a word my resolution. I am resolved to give my birthright to none. Whatsoever may come in the way, and whatsoever may be thought, I will give it to none. If this thing be denied the poor that with so much pressing after they have sought, it will be the greatest scandal.

There was one thing spoken to this effect: that if the poor and those in low condition were given their birthright it would be the destruction of this kingdom. I think this was but a distrust of providence. I do think the poor and meaner of this kingdom – I speak as in relation to the condition of soldiers, in which we are – have been the means of the *preservation* of this kingdom. I say, in their stations, and really I think to their utmost possibility; and their lives have not been held dear for purchasing the good of the kingdom. And now they demand the birthright for which they fought. Those that act to this end are as free from anarchy or confusion as those that oppose it, and they have the Law of God and the law of their conscience with them. But truly I shall only sum up in this. I desire that we may not spend so much time upon these things. We must be plain. When men come to understand these things, they will not lose that which they have contended for. That which I shall beseech you is to come to a determination of this question.

Ireton: I am very sorry we are come to this point, that from reasoning one to another we should come to express our resolutions. I profess for my part, what I see is good for the kingdom and becoming a Christian to contend for, I hope through God I shall have strength and resolution to do my part towards it. And yet I will profess direct contrary in some kind to what that gentleman said. For my part, rather than I will make a disturbance to a good constitution of a kingdom wherein I may live in godliness and honesty and peace and quietness, I will part with a great deal of my birthright. I will part with my own property rather than I will be the man that shall make a disturbance in the kingdom for my property. And therefore if all the people in this kingdom, or the representatives of them all together, should meet and should give away my property, I would submit to it; I would give it away. But that gentleman – and I think every Christian – ought to bear that spirit, to carry that in him, that he will not make a public disturbance upon a private prejudice.

Now let us consider where our difference lies. We all agree that you should have a Representative to govern, and this Representative to be as equal as you can make it. But the question is, whether this distribution can be made to all persons equally, or whether equally amongst those that have the interest of England in them – that which I have declared is my opinion still. I think we ought to keep to that constitution which we have now, both because it is a civil constitution – it is the most fundamental constitution that we have – and because there is so much justice and reason and prudence in it as I dare confidently undertake to demonstrate that there are many more evils that will follow in case you do alter it than there can be in the standing of it.

But I say but this in the general: that I do wish that they that talk of birthrights – we *any* of us when we talk of birthrights – would consider what really our birthright is. If a man mean by birthright whatsoever he can challenge by the law of nature (supposing there were no constitution at all, supposing no civil law and no civil constitution) and that I am to contend for against constitution, then you leave no property, nor no foundation for any man to enjoy anything. But if you call that your birthright which is the most fundamental part of your constitution, then let him perish that goes about to hinder you or any man of the least part of your birthright or will desire to do it. But if you will lay aside the most fundamental constitution, which is as good for aught you can discern as anything you can propose – at least it is a constitution, and I will give you consequence for consequence of good upon that constitution as you can give upon your birthright without it. And if you, merely upon pretence of a birthright, of the right of nature – which is only true as for your being, and not for your better being – if you will upon that ground pretend that this constitution, the most fundamental constitution, the thing that has reason and equity in it, shall not stand in your way, it is the same principle to me, say I, as if but for your better satisfaction you shall take hold of anything that another man calls his own.

Col. Rainborough: Sir, I see that it is impossible to have liberty but all property must be taken away. If it be laid down for a rule, and if you will say it, it must be so. But I would fain know what the soldier has fought for all this while? He has fought to *enslave* himself, to give power to men of riches, men of estates, to make him a perpetual slave? We do find in all presses that go forth none must be pressed[16] that are freehold men. When these gentlemen fall out among themselves they shall press the poor scrubs[17] to come and kill one another for them.

Ireton: I confess I see so much right in the business that I am not easily satisfied with flourishes. If you will not lay the stress of the business upon the consideration of reason, or right relating to anything of human constitution, or anything of that nature, but will put it upon consequences, I will show you greater ill consequences. I see enough to say that, to my apprehensions, I can show you greater ill consequences to follow upon that alteration which you would have, by extending voices to all that have a being in this kingdom, than any that can come by this present constitution – a great deal. That that you urge of the present constitution is a *particular* ill consequence. This that I object against your proposal is a *general* ill consequence, and this is as great as that or any ill consequence else whatsoever, though I think you will see that the validity of that argument must be that for one ill that lies upon that which now is, I can show you a thousand upon this that you propose.

Give me leave to say but this one word. I will tell you what the soldier of the kingdom has fought for. First, the danger that we stood in was that one man's will must be a law. The people of the kingdom must have this right at least, that they should not be concluded but by the representative of those that had the interest of the kingdom. Some men fought in this because they were immediately concerned and engaged in it. Other men who had no other interest in the kingdom but this, that they should have the benefit of those laws made by the representative, yet fought that they should have the benefit of this Representative. They thought it was better to be concluded by the common consent of those that were fixed men, and settled men that had the interest of this kingdom in them. 'And from that way', said they, 'I shall know a law and have a certainty.' Every man that was born in the

---

[16] I.e. impressed into military service. See *Agreement* above, n. 6 on p. 99.
[17] scrubs = insignificant people.

country, that is a denizen in it, that has a freedom, he was capable of trading to get money, to get estates by; and therefore this man, I think, had a great deal of reason to build up such a foundation of interest to himself: that is, that the will of one man should not be a law, but that the law of this kingdom should be by a choice of persons to represent, and that choice to be made by the generality of the kingdom. *Here* was a right that induced men to fight; and those men that had this interest, though this be not the utmost interest that other men have, yet they had some interest. Now tell me why we should go to plead whatsoever we can challenge by the right of nature against whatsoever any man can challenge by constitution. I do not see where that man will stop, as to point of property, so that he shall not use against other property that right he has claimed by the law of nature against that constitution. I desire any man to show me where there is a difference.

I have been answered: 'now we see liberty cannot stand without destroying property'. Liberty *may* be had and property not be destroyed. First, the liberty of all those that have the permanent interest in the kingdom, that is provided for by the constitution. And secondly, by an appeal to the law of nature, liberty cannot be provided for in a general sense, if property be preserved. For if property be preserved by acknowledging a natural right in the possessor – so that I am not to meddle with such a man's estate, his meat, his drink, his apparel, or other goods – then the right of nature destroys liberty. By the right of nature I am to have sustenance rather than perish; yet property destroys it for a man to have this by the right of nature, even suppose there be *no* human constitution.

Peter: I do say still, under favour, there is a way to cure all this debate. I will mind you of one thing: that upon the will of one man abusing us, we reached agreement; and if the safety of the Army be in danger so we may again. I hope it is not denied by any man that any wise, discreet man that has preserved England is worthy of a voice in the government of it. So that I profess to you for my part I am clear the point of election should be amended in that sense. I think they will desire no more liberty. If there were time to dispute it, I think they would be satisfied, and all will be satisfied.

Cromwell: I confess I was most dissatisfied with that I heard Mr Sexby speak, of any man here, because it did savour so much of *will*. But I desire that all of us may decline that; and if we meet here really to agree to that which is for the safety of the kingdom, let us not spend so much time in such debates as these are, but let us apply ourselves to such things as are conclusive: and that shall be this. Everybody here would be willing that the representative might be mended, that is, that it might be made better than it is. Perhaps it may be offered in that other paper[18] too lamely. If the thing there insisted upon be too limited, why perhaps there are a very considerable part of copyholders by inheritance that ought to have a voice; and there may be somewhat in that paper too that reflects upon the generality of the people in denying them a voice. I know our debates are endless if we think to bring it to an issue this way. If we may but resolve upon a committee, things may be done. If I cannot be satisfied to go so far as these gentlemen that bring this paper, I say it again and I profess it, I shall freely and willingly withdraw myself; and I hope to do it in such a manner that the Army shall see that I shall, by my withdrawing, satisfy the interest of the Army, the public interest of the kingdom, and those ends these men aim at. And I think if you do bring this to a result it were well.

Col Rainborough: If these men must be advanced, and other men set under foot, I am not satisfied. If *their* rules must be observed, and other men that are not in authority be silenced, I do not know how this can stand together with the idea of a free debate. I wonder how that should be thought wilfulness in one man that is reason in another; for I confess I have not heard anything that does satisfy me; and though I have not so much wisdom, or so many notions in my head, I have so many apprehensions that I could tell an hundred such of the ruin of the people. I am not at all against a committee's meeting; and as you say – and I think every Christian ought to do the same – for my part I shall be ready, if I see the way that I am going, and the thing that I would insist on will destroy the kingdom, I shall withdraw from it as soon as any. And therefore, till I see that, I shall use all the means I can, and I think it is no fault in any man to refuse to sell that which is his birthright.

Sexby: I desire to speak a few words. I am sorry that my zeal to what I apprehend is good should be so ill-resented. I am not sorry to see that which I apprehend is truth disputed; but I am sorry the Lord has darkened some so much as not to see it, and that is in short this. Do you not think it were a sad and miserable condition, that we have fought all this time for nothing? All here – both great and small – do

---

[18] In *The heads of the proposals* (see nn. 6 and 20 on pp. 107 and 126).

think that we fought for something. I confess, many of us fought for those ends which, we since saw, were not those which caused us to go through difficulties and straits and to venture all in the ship with you. It had been good in you to have advertised us of it, and I believe you would have had fewer under your command to have commanded. But if this be the business, that an estate does make men capable – it is no matter which way they get it, they are capable – to choose those that shall represent them, I think there are many that have not estates that in honesty have as much right in the freedom of their choice as any that have great estates. Truly, sir, as for your putting off this question and coming to some other, I dare say, and I dare appeal to all of them, that they cannot settle upon any other until this be done. It was the ground that we took up arms on, and it is the ground which we shall maintain.

Concerning my making rents and divisions in this way. As a particular,[19] if I were but so, I could lie down and be trodden there; but truly I am sent by a regiment, and if I should not speak, guilt shall lie upon me, and I should think I were a covenant-breaker. I do not know how we have been answered in our arguments; and as for our engagements, I conceive we shall not accomplish them to the kingdom when we deny them to ourselves. I shall be loath to make a rent and division, but for my own part, unless I see this put to a question, I despair of an issue.

[text omitted]

Ireton: I should not speak again, but reflections do necessitate it, do call upon us to vindicate ourselves. As if we, who have led men into engagements and services, had divided from them because we did not concur with them! I will ask that gentleman that spoke (whom I love in my heart): whether when they drew out to serve the parliament in the beginning, whether when they engaged with the Army at Newmarket, whether then they thought of any more interest or right in the kingdom than this; whether they did think that they should have as great interest in parliament-men as freeholders had, or whether from the beginning we did not engage for the liberty of parliaments, and that we should be concluded by the laws that such did make. Unless somebody did make you believe before now that you should have an equal interest in the kingdom – unless somebody did make that to be believed – there is no reason to blame men for leading you so far as

---

[19] I.e. as an individual not as a representative.

they have done; and if any man was far enough from such an apprehension, that man has not been deceived.

And truly, I shall say but this word more for *myself* in this business – because the whole objection seems to be pressed to me, and maintained against me. I will not arrogate that I was the first man that put the Army upon the thought either of successive parliaments or more equal parliaments; yet there are some here that know who they were that put us upon that foundation of liberty of putting a period to this parliament, in order that we might have successive parliaments, and that there might be a more equal distribution of elections.[20] There are many here that know who were the first movers of that business in the Army. I shall not arrogate that to myself; but I can argue this with a clear conscience: that no man has prosecuted that with more earnestness, and will stand to that interest more than I do, of having parliaments successive and not perpetual, and the distribution of elections more equal.

But notwithstanding, my opinion stands good that it ought to be a distribution amongst the fixed and settled people of this nation. It's more prudent and safe, and more upon this ground of right for it to be so. Now it is the fundamental constitution of this kingdom; and that which if you take away, you take away for matter of wilfulness.

Notwithstanding, as for this universal conclusion that all inhabitants shall have voices as it stands in the Agreement, I must declare that though I cannot yet be satisfied, yet for my part I shall acquiesce. I will not make a distraction in this army. Though I have a property in being one of those that should be an elector, though I have an interest in the birthright, yet I will rather lose that birthright and that interest than I will make it my business to oppose them, if I see but the generality of those whom I have reason to think honest men and conscientious men and godly men to carry themselves another way. I will not oppose, though I be not satisfied to join with them. And I desire to say this. I am agreed with you if you insist upon a more equal distribution of elections; I will agree with you, not only to dispute for it, but to fight for it and contend for it. Thus far I shall agree with you. On the other

---

[20] *The heads of proposals* were first mooted about 7 July, when parliamentary commissioners to the Army asked the Army to present their desires for a settlement in a consolidated form. Ireton, with Colonel John Lambert as his assistant, did so, in close co-operation with Lords Wharton and Saye and Sele, and perhaps with Sir Henry Vane the Younger – leaders of the parliamentary Independents.

hand, to those who differ in their terms and say 'I will not agree with you except you go farther', I make answer, 'thus far I can go with you; I will go with you as far as I can'. If you will appoint a committee of some few to consider of that – so as you preserve the equitable part of that constitution that now is, securing a voice to those who are like to be free men, men not given up to the wills of others, and thereby keeping to the latitude which is the equity of constitutions – I will go with you as far as I can. And where I cannot I will sit down. I will not make any disturbance among you.

Col. Rainborough: If I do speak my soul and conscience I do think that there is not an objection made but that it has been answered; but the speeches are so long. I am sorry for some passion and some reflections, and I could wish where it is most taken amiss that cause had not been given. It is a fundamental of the constitution of the kingdom that there be parliamentary boroughs; I would fain know whether the choice of burgesses in corporations should not be altered. But the end wherefore I speak is only this. You think we shall be worse than we are if we come to a conclusion by a sudden vote. If it be put to the question we shall at least all know one another's mind. If it be determined, and the common resolutions known, we shall take such a course as to put it in execution. This gentleman says, if he cannot go he will sit still. He thinks he has a full liberty to do so; we think we have not. There is a great deal of difference between us two. If a man has all he does desire, he may *wish* to sit still; but if I think I have nothing at all of what I fought for, I do not think the argument holds that I must desist as well as he.

Petty: The rich would very unwillingly be concluded by the poor. And there is as much reason that the rich should conclude the poor as the poor the rich – and indeed that is no reason at all. There should be an equal share in both. I understood your engagement was that you would use all your endeavours for the liberties of the people, that they should be secured. If there is such a constitution that the people are not free, that constitution should be annulled. That constitution which is now set up is a constitution of forty shillings a year; but this constitution does not make the people free.

Cromwell: Here's the mistake: you make the whole question to be whether that's the better constitution in that paper, or that which now is. But if you will go upon such a ground as that, although a better constitution was *really* offered for the removing of the worse, yet some gentlemen are resolved to stick to the worse and there might be a great deal of prejudice upon such an apprehension. I think you are by this time satisfied that it is a clear mistake; for it is a *dispute* whether or no this proposed constitution be better – nay, whether it be not destructive to the kingdom.

[Text omitted]

Lieutenant Edmund Chillenden: In the beginning of this discourse there were overtures made of imminent danger. This way we have taken this afternoon is not the way to prevent it. I would humbly move that we should put a speedy end to this business, and that not only to this main question of the paper, but also according to the Lieutenant-General's motion that a committee may be chosen seriously to consider the things in that paper and compare them with divers things in our declarations and engagements, that so we may show ourselves ready, as we have all professed, to lay down ourselves before God. If we take this course of debating upon one question a whole afternoon, and if the danger be so near as it is supposed, it were the ready way to bring us into it. I desire that things may be put into a speedy dispatch.

Captain John Clarke: I presume that the great stick here is this: that if everyone shall have his natural propriety of election it does bereave the kingdom of its principal fundamental constitution that it now has. I presume that all people and all nations whatsoever have a liberty and power to alter and change their constitutions if they find them to be weak and infirm. Now if the people of England shall find this weakness in their constitution, they may change it if they please. Another thing is this: it is feared that if the light of nature be only followed in this, it may destroy the propriety which every man can call his own. But it will not. And the reason is this: because this principle and light of nature does give all men their own – as, for example, the clothes upon my back because they are not another man's. Finally, if every man has this propriety of election to choose those who shall make the laws, you fear it may beget inconveniences. I do not conceive that anything may be so nicely and precisely done but that it may admit of inconveniency. If it be that there is inconveniency in that form of the constitution wherein it is now, there may some of those inconveniences rise from the changes that are apprehended from them. For my part I know nothing of fatal consequence in the relation of men but the want of love in it; and then, if difference arises, the sword must decide it. I too shall desire that before the question be stated it may be moderated as for foreigners.

[Text omitted]

Ireton: I have declared that you will alter that constitution from a better to a worse, from a just to a thing that is less just, in my apprehension; and I will not repeat the reasons of that, but refer to what I have declared before. To me, if there were nothing but this, that there is a constitution, and that constitution which is the very last constitution, which if you take away you leave nothing of constitution, and consequently nothing of right or property, it would be enough. I would not go to alter this, though a man could propound that which in some respects might be better, unless it could be demonstrated to me that this were unlawful or that this were destructive. Truly, therefore, I say for my part, to go on a sudden to make such a limitation as that to inhabitants in general is to make no limitation at all. If you do extend the latitude of the constitution so far that any man shall have a voice in election who has not that interest in this kingdom that is permanent and fixed, who has not that interest upon which he may have his freedom in this kingdom without dependence, you will put it into the hands of men to choose, not of men desirous to preserve their liberty, but of men who will give it away.

I am confident, our discontent and dissatisfaction if ever they do well, they do in this. If there be anything at all that is a foundation of liberty it is this, that those who shall choose the law-makers shall be men freed from dependence upon others. I have a thing put into my heart which I cannot but speak. I profess I am afraid that if we – from such apprehensions as these are of an imaginable right of nature opposite to constitution – if we will contend and hazard the breaking of peace upon this business of that enlargement, I think if we, from imaginations and conceits, will go about to hazard the peace of the kingdom to alter the constitution in such a point, I am afraid we shall find the hand of God will follow it and we shall see that that liberty which we so much talk of and have so much contended for, shall be nothing at all by this our contending for it, by our putting it into the hands of those men that will give it away when they have it.

Cromwell: If we should go about to alter these things, I do not think that we are bound to fight for every particular proposition. Servants, while servants, are not included. Then you agree that he that receives alms[21] is to be excluded?

---

[21] I.e. he who depends on the charity of the parish for maintenance.

Lieutenant-Colonel Thomas Reade[22]: I suppose it's concluded by all that the choosing of representatives is a privilege. Now I see no reason why any man that is a native ought to be excluded that privilege, unless from voluntary servitude.

Petty: I conceive the reason why we would exclude apprentices, or servants, or those that take alms, is because they depend upon the will of other men and should be afraid to displease them. For servants and apprentices, they are included in their masters, and so for those that receive alms from door to door; but if there be any general way taken for those that are not so bound to the will of other men, it would be well.

---

[22] Of Cromwell's regiment. Not an agitator but often a member of the Council of War 1647–8.

9

To the right honourable, the Commons of England in parliament assembled. The humble petition of divers well-affected persons inhabiting the City of London, Westminster, the Borough of Southwark, Hamlets and places adjacent

With the Parliament's Answer thereunto[1]

Shows,

That although we are as earnestly desirous of a safe and well-grounded peace and that a final end were put to all the troubles and miseries of the commonwealth as any sort of men whatsoever, yet, considering upon what grounds we engaged on your part in the late and present wars and how far by our so doing we apprehend ourselves concerned, give us leave before you conclude (as by the treaty in hand)[2] to acquaint you: first with the ground and reason which induced us to aid you against the king and his adherents; secondly what our apprehensions are of this treaty; thirdly, what we expected from you and still do most earnestly desire.

Be pleased therefore to understand that we had not engaged on your part but that we judged this honourable House to be the supreme authority of England, as chosen by and representing the people and entrusted with absolute power for redress of grievances and provision for safety, and that the king was but at the most the chief public officer of this kingdom and accountable to this House, the representative of the people, from whom all just authority is or ought to be derived for the discharge of his office. And if we had not been confident hereof,

---

[1] The petition was presented to the Commons on 11 September 1648, and was referred to a committee, never to re-emerge. It was probably mostly written by Lilburne and Walwyn and is said to have obtained 40,000 signatures.

[2] The Treaty of Newport was soon to be entered into by parliamentary commissioners with the king at the Isle of Wight on 18 September. This had been made possible on 24 August by the repeal of the vote that parliament should make no further addresses to the king – the 'Vote of No Addresses'.

we had been desperately mad to have taken up arms or to have been aiding assisting in maintaining a war against him – the laws of the land making it expressly a crime no less than treason for any to raise war against the king.

But when we considered the manifold oppressions brought upon the nation by the king, his Lords and bishops, and that this honourable House declared their deep sense thereof, and that – for the continuance of that power which had so oppressed us – it was evident the king intended to raise forces and make war, and that if he did set up his standard it tended to the dissolution of the government: upon this, knowing the safety of the people to be above law and that to adjudge thereof appertained to the supreme authority and not to the supreme magistrate, and being satisfied in our consciences that the public safety and freedom was in imminent danger, we concluded we had not only a just cause to maintain, but the supreme authority of the nation to justify, defend and indemnify us in time to come in what we should perform by direction thereof – though against the known law of the land, or any inferior authority, though the highest.

And as this our understanding was begotten in us by principles of right reason, so were we confirmed therein by your own proceedings: as by your condemning those judges who in the case of ship-money had declared the king to be judge of safety;[3] and by your denying him to have a negative voice in the making of law, where you wholly exclude the king from having any share in the supreme authority;[4] then by your casting the bishops out of the House of Lords, who by tradition also had been accounted an essential part of the supreme authority;[5] and by your declaring to the Lords that if they would not join with you in

---

[3] On 7 August 1641, Parliament passed an Act declaring the illegality of ship-money, a prerogative tax, as 'contrary to and against the laws and statutes of this realm, the right of property, the liberty of the subjects, former resolutions in parliament, and the Petition of Right made in the third year of the reign of his Majesty that now is'.

[4] The two Houses made their first ordinance on 20 August 1641 in the (brief) absence of the king; but it was in the March and April of 1642 that the Houses put into deadly effect (with the passage and execution of Militia Ordinance without the king's consent) the claim of parliament's more enthusiastic supporters: that the two Houses could legislate without the king.

[5] The bishops or 'spiritual Lords' were accounted either one of the three 'estates' of parliament (the others being Commons and lay Lords, with the king as 'head' of the estates), or alternatively, they were thought to be an essential part of the Lords when that House was conceived as one of the three 'estates' together with king and Commons. They were excluded from the House of Lords by statute in February 1642.

settling the militia (which they long refused) you would settle it without them – which you could not justly have done and they had[6] any real share in the supreme authority.

These things we took for real demonstrations that you undoubtedly knew yourselves to be the supreme authority – ever weighing down in us all other your indulgent expressions concerning the king or Lords – it being indeed impossible for us to believe that it can consist either with the safety or the freedom of the nation to be governed either by three, or two, supremes, especially where experience has proved them so apt to differ in their judgements concerning freedom or safety that the one has been known to punish what the other has judged worthy of reward, when not only the freedom of the people is directly opposite to the prerogatives of king and Lords, but the open enemies of the one have been declared friends by the other (as the Scots were by the House of Lords).[7]

And whenas most of the oppressions of the commonwealth have in all times been brought upon the people by the king and Lords, who nevertheless would be so equal in the supreme authority as that there should be no redress of grievances, no provision of safety, but at their pleasure: for our parts, we profess ourselves so far from judging this to be consistent with freedom and safety, that we know no great cause wherefor we assisted you in the late wars but in hope to be delivered by you from so intolerable, so destructive a bondage, so soon as you should through God's blessing upon the armies raised by you be enabled. But to our exceeding grief we have observed that no sooner God vouchsafed you victory and blessed you with success, and thereby enabled you to put us and the whole nation into an absolute condition of freedom and safety, but, according as ye have been accustomed – passing by the ruin of the nation and all that blood that has been spilt by the king and his party – ye betake yourselves to a treaty with him, thereby putting him that is but one single person and a public officer of the commonwealth in competition with the whole body of the people whom ye represent, not considering that it is impossible for you to

---

[6] 'and they had any share' = 'if they had had any share'. John Pym, the Commons' leader, was reported as telling the Lords, when they balked at agreeing to the Militia Ordinance on 25 January 1642, that the Commons would be glad of their help 'in saving the kingdom, but if they fail of it, it should not discourage them in doing their duty'.

[7] On 22 July 1648 the Commons alone published a declaration to the effect that the Scots (who were in England and were being approached by Cromwell's Army) were enemies. The Lords had refused to agree with them in their intention of doing this.

erect any authority equal to yourselves, and declared to all the world that you will not alter the ancient government from that of king, Lords and Commons – not once mentioning (in case of difference) which of them is supreme, but leaving that point (which was the chiefest cause of all our public differences, disturbances, wars and miseries) as uncertain as ever.

Insomuch as we who upon these grounds have laid out ourselves every way to the uttermost of our abilities – and all others throughout the land, soldiers and others who have done the like in defence of our supreme authority and in opposition to the king – cannot but deem ourselves in the most dangerous condition of all others: left without all plea of indemnity for what we have done, as already many have found by the loss of their lives and liberties either for things done or said against the king, the law of the land frequently taking place and precedency against and before your authority, which we esteemed supreme, and against which no law ought to be pleaded. Nor can we possibly conceive how any that in any ways assisted you can be exempt from the guilt of murders and robbers by the present laws in force if you persist to disclaim the supreme authority, though their own consciences do acquit them as having opposed none but manifest tyrants, oppressors and their adherents.

And whereas a personal treaty, or any treaty with the king has been long time held forth as the only means of a safe and well-grounded peace, it is well known to have been cried up principally by such as have been disaffected unto you. And though you have contradicted it, yet it is believed that you much fear the issue – as you have cause sufficient except you see greater alteration in the king and his party than is generally observed, there having never yet been any treaty with him but was accompanied with some underhand dealing, and whilst the present force upon him (though seeming liberty)[8] will in time to come be certainly pleaded against all that shall or can be agreed upon. Nay, what can you confide in[9] if you consider how he has been provoked, and what former kings have done – after oaths, laws, charters,

---

[8] The king had been liberated on parole from his confinement in Carisbrooke Castle and was allowed to occupy a house in Newport. (The treating was to take place in the Town Hall.) The petitioners were correct in thinking that he (and his son) would plead that any agreement he made was made under duress and was therefore not binding on him. He was soon (about 8 October) to plan an escape with the aid of his host, William Hopkins.

[9] confide in = have confidence in.

bonds, excommunications and all ties of reconciliations – to the destruction of all those that had provoked and opposed them; yea when yourselves so soon as he had signed those bills in the beginning of this parliament saw cause to tell him 'That even about the time of passing those bills, some design or other was one fact which if it had taken effect would not only have rendered those bills fruitless but have reduced you to a worse condition of confusion than that wherein the parliament found you.'[10]

And if you consider what news wars, risings, revolting invasions and plottings have been since this last cry for a personal treaty, you will not blame us if we wonder at your hasty proceedings thereunto, especially considering the wonderful victories which God has blessed the Army withal. We profess we cannot choose but stand amazed to consider the inevitable danger we shall be in, though all things in the propositions were agreed unto: the resolutions of the king and his party have been perpetually, violently and implacably prosecuted and manifested against us, and that with such scorn and indignation that it must be more than ordinary bonds that must hold them. And it is no less a wonder to us that you can place your own security therein or that you can ever imagine to see a free parliament any more in England.

The truth is – and we see we must now speak it or for ever be silent – we have long expected things of another nature from you, and such as we are confident would have given satisfaction to all serious people of all parties.

1. That you would have made good the supremacy[11] of the people in this honourable House from all pretences of negative voices either in king or Lords.

2. That you would have made laws for election of Representatives yearly and of course without writ or summons.

3. That you would have set express times for their meeting, continuance and dissolution – as not to exceed 40 or 50 days at the most, and to have a fixed, expressed, time for the ending of this present parliament.

4. That you would have exempted matters of religion and God's worship from the compulsive or restrictive power of any authority upon earth, and reserved to the supreme authority an uncompulsive power

---

[10] *To the king's most excellent majesty, the humble petition of the Lords and Commons* (March 1642), in *Exact collection*, p. 124.

[11] 'supreme of the people' in the original.

only of appointing a way for the public – whereby abundance of misery, prosecution and heart-burning would for ever be avoided.

5. That you would have disclaimed in yourselves and all future Representatives a power of pressing and forcing any sort of men to serve in wars, there being nothing more opposite to freedom, nor more unreasonable in an authority empowered for raising monies in all occasions, for which (and a just cause) assistants need not be doubted – the other way serving rather to maintain injustice and corrupt parties.

6. That you would have made both kings, queens, princes, dukes, earls, lords and all persons alike liable to every law of the land, made or to be made; that so all persons, even the highest, might fear and stand in awe, and neither violate the public peace nor private right of person and estate – as has been frequent – without being liable to account as other men.

7. That you would have freed all commoners from the jurisdiction of the Lords in all cases; and have taken care that all trials should be only of twelve sworn men, and no conviction but upon two or more sufficient, known, witnesses.

8. That you would have freed all men from being examined against themselves, and from being questioned or punished for doing of that against which no law has been provided.

9. That you would have abbreviated the proceedings in law, mitigated and made certain the charge of all particulars.

10. That you would have freed all trade and merchandising from all monopolising and engrossing by Companies or otherwise.

11. That you would have abolished excise and all kinds of taxes except subsidies, the old and only just way of England.

12. That you would have laid open all late enclosures of fens and other commons, or have enclosed them only or chiefly for the benefit of the poor.[12]

13. That you would have considered the many thousands that are ruined by perpetual imprisonment for debt, and provided to their enlargement.

14. That you would have ordered some effectual course to keep people from begging and beggary in so fruitful a nation as through God's blessing this is.

---

[12] Not a common Leveller demand – they were in general not much interested in rural problems. But the issue of enclosure was a live one.

15. That you would have proportioned punishments more equal to offences that so men's lives and estates might not be forfeited upon trivial and slight occasions.

16. That you would have removed the tedious burden of tithes, satisfying all impropriators and providing a more equal way of maintenance for the public ministers.[13]

17. That you would have raised a stock of money out of those many confiscated estates you have had for payment of those who contributed voluntarily above their abilities before you provided for those that disbursed out of their superfluities.

18. That you would have bound yourselves and all future parliaments from abolishing propriety, levelling men's estates or making all things common.[14]

19. That you would have declared what the duty or business of the kingly office is, and what not, and ascertained the revenue past increase or diminution, that so there might never be more quarrels about the same.

20. That you would have rectified the election of public officers for the City of London[15] and of every particular Company therein, restoring the commonalty their just rights most unjustly withheld from them, to the producing and maintaining of corrupt interest opposite to common freedom and exceedingly prejudicial to the trade and manufactures of this nation.

21. That you would have made full and ample reparations to all persons that had been oppressed by sentences in High Commission, Star Chamber and Council Board, or by any kind of monopolisers or projectors – and that out of the estates of those that were authors, actors or

---

[13] In a petition of January 1648, the typical Leveller demand for the abolition of tithes without compensation to those who had a right to them was absent. As Wildman said, this was so as 'not to disengage any considerable party' – he meant the independent congregations, some of which relied on tithes for their sustenance. Here a middle position is taken, one still reconcilable with the Independents' interests. Impropriators were lay owners of rights to tithes.

[14] These are things that parliament would never have contemplated. The prohibition on Levelling appears here for the first time in a Leveller policy statement, obviously designed as a piece of defensive propaganda.

[15] London was governed by a Mayor, a Court of Aldermen and a Common Council – a combination Lilburne compared with king, Lords and Commons in *Londons liberty in chains discovered* (1646). He argued (much as he would soon on the national level) for a diminution of aldermanic power (derived from their control of the guilds and power to elect the mayor); and he argued for the supreme power of a Common Council elected on a franchise extended to all the freemen of London.

promoters of so intolerable mischiefs (and that without much attendance).[16]

22. That you would have abolished all committees and have conveyed all business into the true method of the usual trials of the commonwealth.

23. That you would not have followed the example of former tyrannous and superstitious parliaments in making orders, ordinances or laws, or in appointing punishments concerning opinions or things supernatural, styling some 'blasphemies', others 'heresies', whenas you know yourselves easily mistaken and that divine truths need no human helps to support them – such proceedings having been generally invented to divide the people amongst themselves and to affright men from that liberty of discourse by which corruption and tyranny would soon be discovered.

24. That you would have declared what the business of the Lords is, and ascertain their condition, not derogating[17] them the liberties of other men, that so there might be an end of striving about the same.

25. That you would have done justice upon the capital authors and promoters of the former or late wars, many of them being under your power, considering that mercy to the wicked is cruelty to the innocent and that all your lenity doth but make them all the more insolent and presumptuous.

26. That you would have provided constant pay for the Army now under the command of the Lord General Fairfax, and given rules to all judges and all other public officers throughout the land for their indemnity and for saving harmless all that have any ways assisted you, or that have said or done anything against the king, queen, or any of his party since the beginning of this parliament – without which, any of his party are in a better condition than those who have served you, nothing being more frequent with them than their reviling of you and your friends.

The things and worthy acts which have been done and achieved by this army and their adherents – however ungratefully suffered to be scandalised as sectaries and men of corrupt judgements – in defence of the just authority of this honourable House and of the common liberties of the nation and in opposition to all kind of tyranny and oppression, being so far from meriting an odious Act of Oblivion[18] that they rather

---

[16] I.e. not much attendance at law courts to see the cases through.
[17] derogating = taking away from.
[18] A reference perhaps to the 7 June indemnity ordinance. *Agreement*, n. 5 on p. 99.

deserve a most honourable Act of Perpetual Remembrance to be a pattern of public virtue, fidelity and resolution to all posterity.

27. That you would have laid to heart all the abundance of innocent blood that has been spilt and the infinite spoil and havoc that has been made of peaceable, harmless people by the express commissions of the king, and seriously to have considered whether the justice of God be likely to be satisfied or his yet-continuing wrath appeased by an Act of Oblivion.

These and the like we have a long time hoped you would have minded, and have made such an establishment for the general peace and contentful satisfaction of all sorts of people as should have been the happiness of all future generations, and which we most earnestly desire you would set yourselves speedily to effect, whereby the almost dying honour of this most honourable House would be again revived and the hearts of your petitioners and all other well-affected people be afresh renewed unto you. The freedom of this nation (now in perpetual hazard) would be firmly established, for which you would once more be so strengthened with the love of the people that you should not need to cast your eyes any other ways (under God) for your security. But if all this avails nothing, God be our guide – for men show us not a way for our preservation.

The House received this petition, and returned answer thereunto which was to this effect, viz. that the House gave them thanks for their great pains and care to the public good of the kingdom, and would speedily take their humble desires into their serious consideration.[19]

---

[19] This does not seem to represent the House's actual feelings about the petition. On 13 September, officers and citizens had to bring a new petition to the House, riotously demanding the immediate consideration of the petition of the 11th.

10

England's new chains discovered: or the serious apprehensions of a part of the people in behalf of the commonwealth; (being presenters, promoters and approvers of the Large Petition of 11 September 1648)

Presented to the supreme authority of England, the representers of the people in parliament assembled, by Lieutenant-Colonel John Lilburne and divers other citizens of London and borough of Southwark, 26 February 1649[1] Whereunto his speech delivered at the bar is annexed

---

Since you have done the nation so much right and yourselves so much honour as to declare that 'the people (under God) are the original of all just powers',[2] and given us thereby fair grounds to hope that you really intend their freedom and prosperity; yet the way thereunto being frequently mistaken, and through haste or error of judgement, those who mean the best are many times misled so far to the prejudice of those that trust them as to leave them in a condition nearest to bondage when they have thought they had brought them into a way of freedom. And since woeful experience has manifested this to be a truth, there seems no small reason that you should seriously lay to heart what at present we have to offer for discovery and prevention of so great a danger. And because we have been the first movers in and concerning an Agreement of the People as the most proper and just means for the setting the long and tedious distractions of this nation occasioned by nothing more than the uncertainty of our government, and since there has been an Agreement prepared and presented by some officers of the

---

[1] 1648 (Old Style) in original.
[2] A resolution of the Commons, 4 January 1649: 'The Commons of England in parliament assembled do declare that the people are, under God, the original of all just power; and also declare that the Commons of England in parliament assembled, being chosen by and representing the people, have the supreme power in the nation; and also declare that whatsoever is enacted or declared for law by the Commons of England in parliament assembled hath the force of law, and the people of England are concluded thereby although the consent and concurrence of the king or House of Peers be not had thereto.'

Army to this honourable House,[3] as what they thought requisite to be agreed unto by the people (you approving thereof) we shall in the first place deliver our apprehensions thereupon.

That an agreement between those that trust and those who are trusted has appeared a thing acceptable to this honourable House, his excellency, and the officers of the Army, is much to our rejoicing, as we conceive it just in itself and profitable for the commonwealth, and cannot doubt but that you will protect those of the people who have no ways forfeited their birth-right in their proper liberty of taking this or any other agreement as God and their own considerations shall direct them.

Which we the rather mention, for that many particulars in the Agreement before you, are upon serious examination thereof dissatisfactory to most of those who are very earnestly desirous of an agreement; and many very material things seem to be wanting therein, which may be supplied in another. As:

1. They are now much troubled there should be any intervals between the ending of this Representative and the beginning of the next, as being desirous that this present parliament – that has lately done so great things in so short a time tending to their liberties – should sit until with certainty and safety they can see them delivered into the

---

[3] Lilburne refers to *A petition from his excellency Thomas Lord Fairfax and the General Council of the officers of the Army, to the honourable the Commons of England . . . concerning the draught of an Agreement of the People*, presented to the Commons on 20 January 1649. He called the Agreement annexed to the petition the 'officers' agreement', because, although representatives of the Levellers, of the Independent churches in London, of radical MPs and of the Army officers had agreed in early November that an Agreement of the People would form a basis for settlement, Lilburne thought that they had also agreed that the four groups would decide on the detail of the Agreement, and then submit it to the people. But the Army marched on London and Purged Parliament before the Agreement was completed, and after it was (the groups meeting again from about 7–14 December) it was submitted it to the Council of the Army as it turned out for further discussion – not for simple acceptance. Lilburne withdrew from the negotiations, objecting both to the purge and to the Council's further discussing what he thought had been decided. On 15 December he published the groups' version, as *Foundations of freedom*: 'I only amended a clause in the first reserve about religion to the sense of us all but Ireton.' The officers continued discussions in a series of General Council meetings at Whitehall from 15 December to 13 January (agitators had ceased to appear there since November 1647, but Wildman and Walwyn were included in them). The officers' agreement, whatever Lilburne's complaints, was in the result of careful consideration of the Levellers' views and adopts many of their proposals. In the event the Army petitioned the Commons and presented their agreement on the day Charles's public trial began. It was received but never discussed, and the officers showed no concern at this.

hands of another Representative, rather than to leave them (though never so small a time) under the dominion of a Council of State:[4] a constitution of a new and inexperienced nature, and which they fear as the case now stands may design to perpetuate their power and to keep off parliaments for ever.

2. They now conceive no less danger in that it is provided that parliaments for the future are to continue but six months, and a Council of State, eighteen. In which time, if they should prove corrupt, having command of all forces by sea and land, they will have great opportunities to make themselves absolute and unaccountable. And because this is a danger than which there cannot well be a greater, they generally incline to annual parliaments, bounded and limited as reason shall devise; not dissolvable, but to be continued or adjourned as shall seem good in their discretion during that year, but no longer, and then to dissolve of course and give way to those who shall be chosen immediately to succeed them; and in the intervals of their adjournments, to entrust an ordinary committee of their own members, as in other cases limited and bounded with express instructions and accountable to the next session: which will avoid all those dangers feared from a Council of State as at present this is constituted.

3. They are not satisfied with the clause wherein it is said that the power of the representatives shall extend to the erecting and abolishing of courts of justice, since the alteration of the usual way of trials by twelve sworn men of the neighbourhood may be included therein – a constitution so equal and just in itself as that they conceive it ought to remain unalterable. Neither is it clear what is meant by these words,

---

[4] The officers' Agreement asked that the Rump be dissolved by the 28 April 1649 and that an election for a new Representative be held on the first Thursday in May, for a first meeting in June. Thereafter there were to be biennial elections every second May, and the Representative so elected would meet in the June following that May, finally to dissolve in the following December, but in the meantime capable of adjourning or dissolving itself. The Representative would, within twenty days of its meeting, appoint a Council of State to last ten days into the time of the next Representative (unless the next Representative 'put an end to that trust sooner'). The Council was 'for the managing of public affairs . . . according to such instructions as the Representative shall give'. It had the power during adjournments to recall the Representative, and in the intervals between Representatives to call a short-term emergency Representative. The Councillors of State (like salaried officers of the army and of garrisons, together with treasurers and receivers of public monies and lawyers who currently practised) were not eligible to be elected members of the Representative by the people, though members of the Representative (once elected by the people to the Representative) could be elected to the Council by the Representative.

viz. 'that the representatives have the highest final judgement', they conceiving that their authority in these cases is only to make laws, rules, and directions for other courts and persons assigned by law for the execution thereof; unto which every member of the commonwealth – as well those of the Representative as others – should be alike subject; it being likewise unreasonable in itself, and an occasion of much partiality, injustice and vexation to the people that the law-makers should be law-executors.[5]

4. Although it doth provide 'that in the laws *hereafter* to be made, no person by virtue of any tenure, grant, charter, patent, degree, or birth, shall be privileged from subjection thereunto, or from being bound thereby, as well as others', yet doth it not null and make void those *present* protections by law, or otherwise; nor leave all persons – as well lords as others – alike liable in person and estate, as in reason and conscience they ought to be.

5. They are very much unsatisfied with what is expressed as a reserve from the Representative in matters of religion, as being very obscure and full of perplexity, that ought to be most plain and clear – there having occurred no greater trouble to the nation about any thing than by the intermeddling of parliaments in matters of religion.[6]

6. They seem to conceive it absolutely necessary that there be in their Agreement a reserve from ever having any kingly government, and a bar against restoring the House of Lords, both which are wanting in the agreement which is before you.

---

[5] The officers' Agreement proposed: 'That the Representatives have, and shall be understood to have, the supreme trust in order to the preservation and government of the whole, and that their power extend without the consent or concurrence of any other person or persons to the erecting and abolishing of courts of justice and public offices, and to the enacting, altering, repealing and declaring of laws and the highest and final judgement concerning all natural or civil things, but not concerning things spiritual or ecclesiastical.' It then listed six areas where, nevertheless, this supremacy was limited, and powers reserved to the people.

[6] The officers' Agreement, having denied the Representative supremacy over things 'spiritual and evangelical', nevertheless desired a reformed Christian religion ('not popery or prelacy') to be the 'public profession of this nation', and allowed the Representatives to provide for the 'instructing of the people whereunto in a public way (so it be not compulsive)' out of the public treasury – 'and we desire not by tithes'. None should be 'compelled by penalties or otherwise' to that public profession, so that, except for papists and prelatists, 'those such as profess faith in God by Jesus Christ . . . shall be protected in the profession of their faith and exercise of religion according to their consciences . . . so as they abuse not this liberty to the civil injury of others or to the actual disturbance of the public peace on their parts'. This formulation had followed

7. They seem to be resolved to take away all known and burdensome grievances, as tithes[7] (that great oppression of the country's industry and hindrance of tillage), excise and customs (those secret thieves and robbers, drainers of the poor and middle sort of people, and the greatest obstructers of trade, surmounting all the prejudices of ship-money, patents and projects before this parliament); also to take away all monopolising companies of merchants (the hinderers and decayers of clothing and cloth-working, dyeing, and the like useful professions) by which thousands of poor people might be set at work that are now ready to starve, were merchandising restored to its due and proper freedom. They conceive likewise that the three grievances before mentioned, viz. monopolising companies, excise and customs, do exceedingly prejudice shipping and navigation and consequently discourage sea-men and mariners, and which have had no small influence upon the late unhappy revolts[8] which have so much endangered the nation and so much advantaged your enemies. They also incline to direct a more equal and less burdensome way for levying monies for the future – those other forementioned being so chargeable in the receipt as that the very stipends and allowance to the officers attending thereupon would defray a very great part of the charge of the Army, whereas now they engender and support a corrupt interest. They also have in mind to take away all imprisonment of disabled men for debt and to provide some effectual course to enforce all that are able to a speedy payment, and not suffer them to be sheltered in prisons where they live in plenty whilst their creditors are undone. They have also in mind to provide work and comfortable maintenance for all sorts of poor, aged and impotent people, and to establish some more speedy, less troublesome and chargeable way for deciding of controversies in law (whole families having been ruined by seeking right in the ways yet in being): all which, though of greatest and most immediate concernment to the people, are yet omitted in their agreement before you.

These and the like are their intentions in what they purpose for an Agreement of the People, as being resolved (so far as they are able) to

long debates among the Council of Officers and those they had consulted (including Wildman, Walwyn and leading Independent clergy) at Whitehall.
[7] Actually (see previous note) tithes were objected to by the officers, but none of the other reforms were mentioned.
[8] 'The late unhappy revolts' means the second civil war, prominent features of which were the counter-revolutionary activity of Thames watermen, together with the mutiny

lay an impossibility upon all whom they shall hereafter trust of ever wronging the commonwealth in any considerable measure without certainty of ruining themselves, and as conceiving it to be an improper, tedious, and unprofitable thing for the people to be ever running after their representatives with petitions for redress of such grievances as may at once be removed by themselves, or to depend for these things so essential to their happiness and freedom upon the uncertain judgements of several[9] Representatives, the one being apt to renew what the other has taken away.

And as to the use of their rights and liberties herein – as becomes and is due to the people from whom all just powers are derived – they hoped for and expect what protection is in you and the Army to afford. And we likewise in their and our own behalves do earnestly desire that you will publicly declare your resolution to protect those who have not forfeited their liberties[10] in the use thereof – lest they should conceive that the Agreement before you, being published abroad and the commissioners therein nominated being at work in pursuance thereof,[11] is intended to be *imposed* upon them: which, as it is absolutely contrary to the nature of a free agreement, so we are persuaded it cannot enter into your thoughts to use any impulsion therein.

But although we have presented our apprehensions and desires concerning this great work of an agreement and are apt to persuade ourselves that nothing shall be able to frustrate our hopes which we have built thereupon, yet have we seen and heard many things of late which occasion not only apprehensions of other matters intended to be brought upon us of danger to such an agreement but of bondage and ruin to all such as shall pursue it.

Insomuch that we are even aghast and astonished to see that notwithstanding the productions of the highest notions of freedom that ever this nation – or any people in the world – have brought to light, notwithstanding the vast expense of blood and treasure that has been made

of six ships of the fleet on 27 May 1648, which blockaded Dover and gave the royalists control of the Castles of Deal, Sandown and Walmer.

[9] several = different.

[10] I.e. royalists and counter-revolutionaries of 1648.

[11] The officers' Agreement did not actually envisage that the Commons would impose it 'as a law upon the kingdom (for so it would lose the nature of an Agreement of the People)' but that, so far as it agreed with their judgement, it should 'receive your seal of approbation only'. Instead it set up its own system for the taking of subscriptions to the Agreement, and for organising the first election under it.

to purchase those freedoms, notwithstanding the many eminent and even miraculous victories God has been pleased to honour our just cause withal, notwithstanding the extraordinary gripes and pangs this House has suffered more than once at the hands of your own servants, and that at least seemingly for the obtaining these our native liberties.

When we consider what rackings and tortures the people in general have suffered through decay of trade and dearness of food, and very many families in particular (through free-quarter, violence, and other miseries incident to war) having nothing to support them therein but hopes of freedom and a well-settled commonwealth in the end: that yet after all these things have been done and suffered, and whilst the way of an agreement of the people is owned and approved – even by yourselves – and that all men are in expectation of being put into possession of so dear a purchase, behold, in the close of all, we hear and see what gives us fresh and pregnant cause to believe that the contrary is really intended and that all those specious pretences and high notions of liberty, with those extraordinary courses that have of late been taken (as if of necessity for liberty, and which indeed can never be justified but deserve the greatest punishments unless they end in just liberty and an equal government) appear to us to have been done and directed by some secret, powerful influences, the more securely and unsuspectedly to attain an absolute domination over the commonwealth – it being impossible for them, but by assuming our generally approved principles and hiding under the fair show thereof their other designs, to have drawn in so many good and godly men (really aiming at what the other had but in show and pretence) and making them unwittingly instrumental to their own and their country's bondage.

For where is that good, or where is that liberty so much pretended, so dearly purchased, if we look upon what this House has done since it has voted itself the supreme authority and disburdened themselves of the power of the Lords?[12]

First, we find a High Court of Justice erected for trial of criminal causes, whereby that great stronghold of our preservation – the way of trial by twelve sworn men of the neighbourhood – is infringed. All liberty of exception against the triers is over-ruled by a court consisting

---

[12] On 19 March 1649, the Commons passed a resolution that: 'finding by too long experience that the House of Lords is useless and dangerous to the people of England to be continued . . . enact . . . that from henceforth the House of Lords in parliament shall be and is hereby wholly abolished and taken away'.

of persons picked and chosen in an unusual way: the practice whereof we cannot allow of, though against open and notorious enemies,[13] as well because we know it to be an usual policy to introduce by such means all usurpations, first against adversaries, in hope of easier admission; as also, for that the same being so admitted, may at pleasure be exercised against any person or persons whatsoever. This is the first part of our new liberty.

The next is the censuring of a member of this House for declaring his judgement in a point of religion,[14] which is directly opposite to the reserve in the *Agreement* concerning religion. Besides the Act for pressing of seamen,[15] directly contrary to the *Agreement* of the officers. Then the stopping of our mouths from printing is carefully provided for, and the most severe and unreasonable ordinances of parliament that were made in the time of Holles and Stapleton's reign to gag us from speaking truth and discovering the tyrannies of bad men are referred to the care of the General, and by him to his Marshal, to be put in execution in searching, fining, imprisoning, and other ways corporally punishing all that any ways be guilty of unlicensed printing:[16] as they dealing with us as the bishops of old did with the honest Puritan, who were exact in getting laws made against the papist, but really intended them against the Puritan – and made them feel the smart of them – which also has been, and is daily exercised most violently, whereby our liberties have been more deeply wounded than since the beginning of this parliament – and that to the dislike of the soldiery, as by their late petition in that behalf plainly appears.[17] Then whereas

---

[13] Two High Courts of Justice were erected by parliament to try, in January 1649, the king (Lilburne was invited, but refused, to be a member), and in February Arthur, Lord Capel (with whom Lilburne was in supportive correspondence), the earl of Hamilton, the earl of Holland, George Lord Goring and Sir John Owen.

[14] John Frye, for holding doubts about the Trinity. He was readmitted to parliament 3 February 1649, on repudiating his opinions.

[15] *An act for the encouragement of officers and mariners, and impresting seamen* (22 February 1649).

[16] On 5 January 1649 the Commons voted that Fairfax should require the Marshal of the Army to put into execution the ordinance of 30 September 1647 (passed when Presbyterians controlled the House) against unlicensed pamphleteering. On 18 January the Levellers presented a broadsheet petition to the Commons against this, which they then published on the 19th. On 3 February another ordinance was ordered prepared against public preaching and printing of anything against the House or the Council of State.

[17] A soldiers' petition to the Commons, printed in the Levellers' newspaper *The Moderate* (20–27 February) demanded that martial law be mitigated 'for an army of freeborn Englishmen' and the Army not be used for policing the ordinance against unlicensed printers.

it was expected that the Chancery, and courts of justice in Westminster, and the judges and officers thereof, should have been surveyed, and for the present regulated till a better and more equal way of deciding controversies could have been constituted, that the trouble and charge of the people in their suits should have been abated: instead hereof, the old and advanced fees are continued, and new thousand pounds' annual stipends allotted (when in the corruptest times the ordinary fees were thought a great and a sore burden). In the meantime, and in lieu thereof, there is not one perplexity or absurdity in proceedings taken away.

Those petitioners that have moved in behalf of the people, how have they been entertained? Sometimes with the compliment of empty thanks – their desires in the meantime not at all considered. At other times meeting with reproaches and threats for their constancy and public affections, and with violent motions that their petitions be burnt by the common hangman, whilst others are not taken in at all: to so small an account are the people brought, even while they are flattered with notions of being the 'original of all just power'.

And lastly, for completing this new kind of liberty, a Council of State is hastily erected for guardians thereof, who to that end are possessed with power to order and dispose all the forces appertaining to England by sea or land, to dispose of the public treasure, to command any person whatsoever before them, to give oath for the discovering of truth, to imprison any that shall disobey their commands, and such as they shall judge contumacious.[18] What now is become of that liberty 'that no man's person shall be attached or imprisoned, or otherwise disseised of his freehold, or free customs, but by lawful judgement of his equals'?

We entreat you give us leave to lay these things open to your view and judge impartially of our present condition – and of your own also, that by strong and powerful influences of some persons, are put upon these and the like proceedings, which both you and we ere long (if we look not to it) shall be enforced to subject ourselves unto.

Then we have further cause to complain when we consider the persons.[19]

---

[18] An act appointing a Council of State, 13 February 1649. Contumacious = disobedient or insubordinate.

[19] I.e. The persons who had been invited to be members of the Council of State. On 14 February 1649, a committee of the Commons which was set up to nominate the Council

As first: the chief of the Army – directly contrary to what themselves thought meet in their *Agreement for the people*.[20] Secondly, judges of the law and treasurers for monies.[21] Then five that were members of the Lords' House – and most of them such as have refused to approve of your votes and proceedings, concerning the king and lords[22] – two of them judges in the Star Chamber, and approvers of the bloody and tyrannical sentences issuing from thence.[23] Some of your own House, forward men in the treaty, and decliners of your last proceedings.[24] All which do clearly manifest to our understandings that the secret contrivers of those things do think themselves now so surely guarded by the strength of an army, in their daily acts and stratagems to their ends inclined, and the captivation of this House, that they may now take off the veil and cloak of their designs as dreadless of whatever can be done against them.

By this Council of State, all power is got into their own hands – a project which has been long and industriously laboured for, and which being once firmly and to their liking established, their next motions may be (upon pretence of ease to the people) for the dissolution of this parliament, half of whose time is already swallowed up by the said Council now – because no obstacle lies in their way to the full establishment of these their ends but the uncorrupted part of the soldiery that have their eyes fixed upon their engagements and promises of good to the people and resolve by no threats or allurements to decline the same, together with that part of the people in the city and countries[25] that remain constant in their motions for common good and still persist to run their utmost hazards for procurement of the same – by whom all evil men's designs both have, and are still likely to, find a check and discovery.

presented 41 names. But from then until 23 February it was hard to recruit the members because of an Engagement required from the members which would register their approval of the High Court of Justice which tried the king, the king's execution, and the abolition of monarchy and the House of Lords.

[20] Fairfax was indeed elected, as were six other army officers.

[21] The Keepers of the Great Seal, Chief Justices, and Chief Baron of the Exchequer were elected; and office-holding was held no impediment to serving.

[22] The earls of Denbigh, Pembroke and Salisbury refused the Engagement but sat on the Council; the earl of Mulgrave and Lord Grey of Wark refused to serve.

[23] Pembroke and Salisbury.

[24] About 26 of the 41 nominees had opposed Pride's Purge and the trial and execution of the king.

[25] countries = counties.

Hereupon the grand contrivers forementioned (whom we can particular by name) do begin to raise their spleen and manifest a more violent enmity against soldiers and people, disposed as aforesaid, than ever heretofore – as appears by what lately passed at a meeting of officers on 22 February last at Whitehall, where, after expressions of much bitterness against the most conscientious part of the soldiery and others, it was insisted upon (as we are from very credible hands certainly informed) that a motion should be made to this House for the procurement of a law enabling them to put to death all such as they should judge by petitions or otherwise to disturb the present proceedings. And upon urging that the civil magistrate should do it, it was answered, that 'they could hang twenty ere the magistrate one'. It was likewise urged that orders might be given to seize upon the petitioners, soldiers, or others at their meetings – with much exclamation against some of greatest integrity to your just authority, whereof they have given continual and undeniable assurances. A proclamation was likewise appointed, forbidding the soldiers to petition you, or any but their officers, and prohibiting their correspondences; and private orders to be given out for seizing upon citizens and soldiers at their meetings.[26]

And thus after these fair blossoms of hopeful liberty breaks forth this bitter fruit of the vilest and basest bondage that ever Englishmen

[26] Lilburne had heard that at a meeting of the Council of Officers on 22 February 1649 the officers had decided that the Levellers were behind the unrest in the army which had emerged that month, and in particular behind a petition which was circulating among several regiments and addressed to parliament, which, in addition to asking for pay and arrears, also objected to tithes and excise, to the activities of committee-men and excise men, to encroachment on freedom of religion, and asked that 'speedy provision' might be made for 'the continual supply of the necessities of the poor of this nation'. The officers then ordered that soldiers' petitions should be contained within their own regiments. Only the General would decide if any petition should go to parliament. They also wanted to get their hands on the civilians they thought responsible. Colonel Hewson had said: 'We have had trial enough of the civil courts. We can hang twenty before they will hang one.' So the Council had asked Cromwell and Ireton to approach parliament 'for some expedient in this case, and that some severe punishment . . . may be inflicted upon any that shall dare to endeavour to breed any discontent in the army, and (if it be approved) that they may be subject and liable to such punishment as a soldier of the army should be in like case'. Lilburne, who had retired from politics in disgust at the officers' taking over the composition and presentation of the Agreement in December 1648 (and who had been voted a stipend of £300 by parliament to be recovered from the sale of royalist lands in Durham, his native county, whence he had departed) said that hearing all this led him to return to political activity and to reactivate the Leveller party. But in fact he had already returned from Durham in early February, and already on the 8th there were reports that troopers were posting up his pamphlets and petitions in Hitchin, a few miles north of London.

groaned under, whereby this, notwithstanding, is gained viz. an evident and (we hope) a timely discovery of the instruments from whence all the evils, contrivances, and designs (which for above these eighteen months have been strongly suspected) took their rise and original – even ever since the first breach of their promises and engagements made at Newmarket and Triploe Heath with the agitators and people. It being for these ends that they have so violently opposed all such as manifested any zeal for common right or any regard to the faith of the Army: sentencing some to death, others to reproachful punishments,[27] placing and displacing officers according as they showed themselves serviceable or opposite to their designs, enlisting as many as they thought good – even of such as have served in arms against you. And then again, upon pretence of easing the charge of the people, disbanding supernumeraries, by advantage thereof picking out such as were most cordial and active for common good, thereby moulding the Army as far as they could to their own bent and ends premised; exercising martial law with much cruelty, thereby to debase their spirits and make them subservient to their wills and pleasures; extending likewise their power (in many cases) over persons not members of the Army.

And when, in case of opposition and difficult services, they have by their creatures desired a reconciliation with such as at other times they reproached, vilified, and otherwise abased, and through fair promises of good (and dissembled repentance) gained their association and assistance to the great advantage of their proceedings, yet – their necessities being over and the common enemy subdued – they have slighted their former promises and renewed their hate and bitterness against such their assistances, reproaching them with such appellations as they knew did most distaste the people, such as 'Levellers', 'Jesuits', 'anarchists', 'royalists' – names both contradictory in themselves and altogether groundless in relation to the men so reputed; merely relying for belief[28] thereof upon the easiness and credulity of the people. And though – the better to insinuate themselves and get repute with the people, as also to conquer their necessities – they have been fain to make use of those very principles and productions the men they have so much traduced have brought to light, yet the producers themselves they have and do still more eagerly malign than ever, as such whom they know

---

[27] See *Young men's and apprentices' outcry* below for a history of the soldiers' punishments.
[28] 'releese' in original.

to be acquainted to their deceits and deviations and best able to discover the same.

So that now at length, guessing all to be sure and their own – the king being removed, the House of Lords nulled, their long-plotted Council of State erected and this House awed to their ends – the edge of their malice is turning against such as have yet so much courage left them as to appear for the well establishment of England's liberties. And because God has preserved a great part of the Army untainted with the guilt of the designs aforementioned, who cannot without much danger to the designers themselves be suppressed, they have resolved to put this House upon raising more new forces (notwithstanding the present necessities of the people in maintaining those that are already); in doing whereof, though the *pretence* be danger and opposition, yet the *concealed end* is like to be the over-balancing those in the Army who are resolved to stand for true freedom as the end of all their labours, the which (if they should be permitted to do) they would not then doubt of making themselves absolute seizures,[29] lords and masters, both of parliament and people; which, when they have done, we expect the utmost of misery. Nor shall it grieve us to expire with the liberties of our native country. For what good man can with any comfort to himself survive then?

But God has hitherto preserved us; and the justice of our desires, as integrity of our intentions, are daily more and more manifest to the impartial and unprejudiced part of men; insomuch that it is no small comfort to us that – notwithstanding we are upon all these disadvantages that may be, having neither power nor pre-eminence (the common idols of the world) – our cause and principles do through their own natural truth and lustre get ground in men's understandings; so that where there was one, twelve months since, that owned our principles, we believe there are now hundreds: so that though *we* fail, our truths prosper.

And posterity we doubt not shall reap the benefit of our endeavours whatever shall become of us. However, though we have neither strength nor safety before us, we have discharged our consciences and emptied our breasts unto you, knowing well that if you will make use of your power and take unto you that courage which becomes men of your trust and condition, you may yet through the goodness of God prevent

---

[29] seizures = those who have forcibly seized possession.

the danger and mischief intended and be instrumental in restoring this long-enthralled and betrayed nation into a good and happy condition. For which end we most earnestly desire and propose, as the main prop and support of the work:

1. That you will not dissolve this House nor suffer yourselves to be dissolved until as aforesaid you see a new Representative the next day ready to take your room; which you may confidently and safely insist upon, there being no considerable number in the Army or elsewhere that will be so unworthy as to dare to disturb you therein.

2. That you will put in practice the Self-denying Ordinance – the most just and useful that ever was made, and continually cried out for by the people – whereby a great infamy that lies upon your cause will be removed, and men of powerful influences and dangerous designs, deprived of those means and opportunities which now they have to prejudice the public.[30]

3. That you will consider how dangerous it is for one and the same persons to be continued long in the highest commands of a military power, especially acting so long distinct and of themselves as those now in being have done, and in such extraordinary ways whereunto they have accustomed themselves – which was the original of most regalities and tyrannies in the world.

4. That you appoint a committee of such of your own members as have been longest established upon those rules of freedom upon which you now proceed to hear, examine, and conclude all controversies between officers and officers, and between officers and soldiers, to consider and mitigate the law-martial, and to provide that it be not exercised at all upon persons not of the Army; also to release and repair such as have thereby unduly suffered, as they shall see cause; to consider the condition of the private soldiers, both horse and foot, in these dear times, and to allow them such increase of pay as wherewithal they may live comfortably, and honestly discharge their quarters.[31]

That all disbanding be referred to the said committee, and that such of the Army as have served the king may be first disbanded.

5. That you will open the press, whereby all treacherous and tyrannical designs may be the easier discovered and so prevented, which is a

---

[30] The basic idea of the *Self-denying ordinance* (3 April 1645) was to prohibit members of either House from holding military or civil office, thus denying them any personal profit from their service to their country.

[31] discharge their quarters = i.e. pay those civilians who had given them food and lodgings.

liberty of greatest concernment to the commonwealth, and which such only as intend a tyranny are engaged to prohibit: the mouths of adversaries being best stopped by the sensible good which the people receive from the actions of such as are in authority.

6. That you will (whilst you have opportunity) abate the charge of the law, and reduce the stipends of judges and all other magistrates and officers in the commonwealth to a less, but competent, allowance, converting the over-plus to the public treasury, whereby the taxes of the people may be much eased.

7. But above all that you will dissolve this present Council of State, which upon the grounds fore-mentioned so much threatens tyranny, and manage your affairs by committees of short continuance and such as may be frequently and exactly accountable for the discharge of their trusts.

8. That you will publish a strict prohibition and severe penalty against all such – whether committees, magistrates, or officers of what kind soever – as shall exceed the limits of their commission, rules, or directions; and encourage all men in their informations and complaints against them.

9. That you will speedily satisfy the expectations of the soldiers in point of arrears, and of the people in point of accounts, in such a manner as that it may not (as formerly) prove a snare to such as have been most faithful, and a protection to the most corrupt in the discharge of their trust and duties.

10. That the so-many-times complained of Ordinance for Tithes upon treble damages[32] may be forthwith taken away.

All which, together with due regard showed to petitioners – without respect to their number and strength – would so fasten you in the affections of the people and of the honest officers and soldiers, as that you should not need to fear any opposite power whatsoever, and for

---

[32] On 9 August 1647 parliament passed *An ordinance for the true payment of tithes and other duties*. In November 1644 a previous ordinance had lamented the non-payment of tithes due to the 'present distractions' and the absence of ecclesiastical courts to enforce them. It had empowered JPs to hear disputes and to enforce collection, with appeals to the Court of Chancery, which could award 'reasonable damages' to the owner, proprietor or impropriator of the tithes if he was damaged by the delay caused by an appeal, or by non-payment. The 1647 ordinance complained of the many vexatious appeals to Chancery and laid down that there would be no appeal except if the assessed amount were produced at chancery as security and rendered the appellant liable to 'double costs and damages' to the party injured by the appeal.

the time to come of yourselves enjoy the exercise of your supreme authority whereof you have yet but the name only, and be enabled to vindicate your just undertakings: wherein we should not only rejoice to have occasion to manifest how ready we should be to hazard our lives in your behalf, but should also bend all our studies and endeavours to render you honourable to all future generations.

26 February 1649[33]

Being ushered in by the Sergeant-at-Arms, and called to the bar, with all due respects given unto the House, Lieutenant-Colonel John Lilburne, with divers others coming to the bar next the Mace, with the address in his hand, spoke these words – or to this effect – as follows: Mr Speaker,

I am very glad that without any inconvenience unto myself and those that are with me, I may freely and cheerfully address myself to this honourable House as the supreme authority of England. Time was when I could not. And it much refreshes my spirit to live to see this day that you have made such a step to the people's liberties as to own and declare yourselves to be (as indeed you are) the supreme authority of this nation.

Mr Speaker, I am desired by a company of honest men living in and about London, who in truth do rightly appropriate to themselves the title of the contrivers, promoters, presenters, and approvers of the late Large London Petition of 11 September last – which was the first petition I know of in England that was presented to this honourable House against the late destructive personal treaty with the late king – to present you with their serious apprehensions. And give me leave (I beseech you) for myself and them to say thus much: that for the most part of us, we are those that in the worst of times durst own our liberties and freedoms in the face of the greatest of our adversaries, and from the beginning of these wars never shrunk from the owning of our freedoms in the most tempestuous times, nor changed our principles. Nay sir, let me with truth tell you that to the most of us, our wives, our children, our estates, our relations, nay our lives, and all that upon earth we can call ours, have not been so highly valued by us as our liberties and freedoms; which our constant actions (to the apparent

---

[33] 1648 in original.

hazard of our blood and lives) have been a clear and full demonstration of for these many years together.

And Mr Speaker, give me leave to tell you that I am confident our liberties and freedoms (the true and just end of all the late wars) are so dear and precious to us that we had rather our lives should breath out with them than to live one moment after the expiration of them.

Mr Speaker, I must confess I am to present you with a paper, something of a new kind. For we have had no longer time to consider of it than from Thursday last; and warrants (as we are informed) issuing out against us to take us – from those that have no power over us – we durst not well go our ordinary way to work to get subscriptions to it, lest we should be surprised before we could present it to this honourable House, and so be frustrated in that benefit or relief that we justly expect from you; and to present it with a few hands, we judged inconsiderable in your estimation, and therefore choose in the third place (being in so much haste as we were to prevent our eminent and too apparent ruin) in person to bring it to your bar, and avowedly to present it here. And therefore without any further question, give me leave to tell you I own it, and I know so doth all the rest of my friends present; and if any hazard should ensue thereby, give me leave resolvedly to tell you I am sorry I have but one life to lose in maintaining the truth, justice, and righteousness of so gallant a piece.

Mr Speaker, we own this honourable House as of right, the true, guardian of our liberties and freedoms; and we wish and most heartily desire you would rouse up your spirits (like men of gallantry) and now at last take unto yourselves a magnanimous resolution to acquit yourselves without fear or dread like the chosen and betrusted trustees of the people, from whom (as yourselves acknowledge and declare) all just power is derived, to free us from all bondage and slavery and really and truly invest us into the price of all our blood, hazards, and toils: our liberties and freedoms, the true difference and distinction of men from beasts.

Mr Speaker, though my spirit is full in the sad apprehension of the dying condition of our liberties and freedoms, yet at present I shall say no more, but in the behalf of myself and my friends I shall earnestly entreat you to read these our serious apprehensions seriously and debate them deliberately.

Friends,

This we have adventured to publish for the timely information and benefit of all that adhere unto the common interest of the people, hoping that with such, upon due consideration, it will find as large an acceptance as our late petition of 11 September 1648. And we thought good (in regard we were not called in to receive an answer to the same) to acquaint you that we intend to second it with a petition sufficiently subscribed – we doubt not with many thousands – earnestly to solicit for an effectual answer.

FINIS

A manifestation from Lieutenant-Colonel John Lilburne, Mr William Walwyn, Mr Thomas Prince, and Mr Richard Overton (now prisoners in the Tower of London), and others, commonly (though unjustly) styled Levellers

Intended for their full vindication from the many aspersions cast upon them to render them odious to the world and unserviceable to the commonwealth. And to satisfy and ascertain all men whereunto all their motions and endeavours tend, and what is the ultimate scope of their engagement in the public affairs

They also that render evil for good, are our adversaries: because we follow the thing that good is.[1]
Printed in the year of our Lord, 1649

_____ [2]

A manifestation from Lieutenant-Colonel John Lilburne, Mr William Walwyn, Mr Thomas Prince, and Mr Richard Overton (now prisoners in the Tower of London), and others, commonly (though unjustly) styled Levellers
Since no man is born for himself only, but obliged by the laws of nature (which reaches all), of Christianity (which engages us as Christians), and of public society and government, to employ our endeavours for the advancement of a communitive[3] happiness of equal concernment to others as ourselves, here have we (according to that measure of understanding God has dispensed unto us) laboured, with much weakness indeed but with integrity of heart, to produce out of the common calamities such a proportion of freedom and good to the nation as might somewhat compensate its many grievances and lasting sufferings. And although in doing thereof we have hitherto reaped only reproach and

[1] An imperfect rendition of Psalm 38: 20.
[2] End of title page.
[3] communitive = common among a community.

hatred for our good-will, and been fain to wrestle with the violent passions of powers and principalities, yet since it is nothing so much as our blessed Master and his followers suffered before us and but what at first we reckoned upon, we cannot be thereby any whit dismayed in the performance of our duties, supported inwardly by the innocency and evenness of our consciences.

'Tis a very great unhappiness – we well know – to be always struggling and striving in the world, and does wholly keep us from the enjoyment of those contentments our several conditions reach unto. So that if we should consult only with ourselves and regard only our own ease, we should never interpose as we have done in behalf of the commonwealth. But when so much has been done for recovery of our liberties, and seeing God has so blessed that which has been done as thereby to clear the way and to afford an opportunity which these six hundred years[4] has been desired but could never be attained – of making this a truly happy and wholly free nation – we think ourselves bound by the greatest obligations that may be to prevent the neglect of this opportunity and to hinder as much as lies in us that the blood which has been shed be not spilt like water upon the ground, nor that after the abundant calamities which have overspread all quarters of the land, the change be only notional, nominal, circumstantial, whilst the real burdens, grievances, and bondages be continued, even when the monarchy is changed into a republic.

We are no more concerned indeed than other men, and could bear the yoke we believe as easily as others; but since a common duty lies upon every man to be cautious and circumspect in behalf of his country, especially while the government thereof is settling, other men's neglect is so far we think from being a just motive to us of the like sloth and inanimadvertency[5] as that it rather requires of us an *increase* of care and circumspection, which, if it produces not so good a settlement as ought to be, yet certainly it will prevent its being so bad as otherwise it would be if we should all only mind our particular callings and employments. So that although personally we may suffer, yet our solace is that the commonwealth is thereby some gainer, and we doubt not but that God in his due time will so clearly dispel the clouds of ignominy and obloquy which now surround us, by keeping

---

[4] these six hundred years = since the Norman Conquest.
[5] inanimadvertancy = not giving due attention to.

our hearts upright and our spirits sincerely public, that every good man will give us the right hand of fellowship and be even sorry that they have been estranged and so hardly opinionated against us.

We question not but that in time the reason of such misprisions[6] will appear to be in *their* eyes and not in *our* actions – in the false representation of things to them and improper glosses that are put upon everything we do or say. In our own behalves we have as yet said nothing, trusting that either shame and Christian duty would restrain men from making so bold with others' good name and reputation, or that the sincerity of our actions would evince the falsehood of these scandals and prevent the people's belief of them. But we have found that with too much greediness they suck in reports that tend to the discredit of others, and that our silence gives encouragement to bad rumours of us; so that in all places they are spread and industriously propagated, as well amongst them that know us as them that know us not – the first being fed with jealousies that there is more in our designs than appears: that there is something of danger in the bottom of our hearts not yet discovered, that we are driven on by others, that we are even discontented and irresolved, that nobody yet knows what we would have or where our desires will end; whilst they that know us not are made to believe any strange conceit of us: that we would level all men's estates, that we would have no distinction of orders and dignities amongst men, that we are indeed for no government, but a popular confusion; and then again that we have been agents for the king (and now for the queen); that we are atheists, antiscripturists, Jesuits – and indeed anything that is hateful and of evil repute amongst men.

All which we could without observance pass over – remembering what is promised to be the portion of good men – were the damage only personal; but since the ends of such rumours are purposely to make us useless and unserviceable to the commonwealth, we are necessitated to open our breasts and show the world our insides, for removing of those scandals that lie upon us, and likewise for manifesting plainly and particularly what our desires are and in what we will centre and acquiesce: all which we shall present to public view and consideration, not pertinaciously or magisterially as concluding other men's judgements, but manifesting our own for our further vindication

---

[6] misprisions = failures to appreciate value.

and for the procuring of a bond and lasting establishment for the commonwealth.

First then, it will be requisite that we express ourselves concerning levelling – for which we suppose is commonly meant an equality of men's estates, and taking away the proper right and title that every man has to what is his own. This as we have formerly declared against, particularly in our petition of 11 September,[7] so do we again profess that to attempt an inducing the same is most injurious unless there did precede an universal assent thereunto from all and every one of the people. Nor do we, under favour, judge it within the power of a representative itself, because although their power is supreme, yet it is but deputative and of trust, and consequently must be restrained expressly or tacitly to some particular essentials as well to the people's safety and freedom as to the present government.

The community amongst the primitive Christians was voluntary, not coactive.[8] They brought their goods and laid them at the apostles' feet. They were not enjoined to bring them: it was the effect of their charity and heavenly mindedness which the blessed apostles begot in them and not the injunction of any constitution, which, as it was but for a short time done (and in but two or three places) that the scripture makes mention of, so does the very doing of it there and the apostle's answer to him that detained a part, imply that it was not esteemed a duty but reckoned a voluntary act occasioned by the abundant measure of faith that was in those Christians and apostles.[9]

We profess therefore that we never had it in our thoughts to level men's estates, it being the utmost of our aim that the commonwealth be reduced to such a pass that every man may with as much security as may be enjoy his propriety.

We know very well that in all ages those men that engage themselves against tyranny and unjust and arbitrary proceedings in magistrates have suffered under such appellations – the people being purposely frightened from that which is good by insinuations of imaginary evil.

---

[7] 1648. Printed as text above.

[8] not coactive = not forced upon them by others.

[9] Acts 4: 34–6; 5: 1–11. The story *actually* has Peter reprimanding Ananias and his wife Sapphira as lying to God in not giving to the church the full price of the land they had sold and in keeping some aside for themselves. Both died as a consequence of hearing of God's displeasure.

But, be it so, we must notwithstanding discharge our duties, which, being performed, the success is in God's hand to whose good pleasure we must leave the clearing of men's spirits, our only certainty being tranquillity of mind and peace of conscience.

For distinction of orders and dignities: we think them so far needful as they are animosities[10] of virtue or requisite for the maintenance of the magistracy and government. We think they were never intended for the nourishment of ambition or subjugation of the people, but only to preserve the due respect and obedience in the people which is necessary for the better execution of the laws.

That we are for government and against popular confusion we conceive all our actions declare when rightly considered, our aim having been all along to reduce it as near as might be to perfection; and certainly we know very well the pravity[11] and corruption of man's heart is such that there could be no living without it, and that though tyranny is so excessively bad, yet of the two extremes, confusion is the worst. 'Tis somewhat a strange consequence to infer that because we have laboured so earnestly for a *good* government therefore we would have none at all, because we would have the *dead* and *exorbitant branches* pruned and better scions grafted therefore we would pluck the *tree* up by the roots. Yet thus have we been misconceived and misrepresented to the world, under which we must suffer till God sees it fitting in his good time to clear such harsh mistakes, by which many – even good men – keep a distance from us.

For those weak suppositions of some of us being agents for the king or queen, we think it needful to say no more but this: that though we have not been any way violent against the persons of them or their party (as having aimed at the conversion of all, and the destruction of none), yet do we verily believe that those principles and maxims of government which are most fundamentally opposite to the prerogative and the king's interest take their first rise and original from us – many whereof though at first startled at and disowned by those that professed the greatest opposition to him, have yet since been taken up by them and put in practice. And this we think is sufficient, though much more might be said to clear us from any agency for that party.

[10] animosities = things that stir the spirit to virtue.
[11] pravity = perversity.

It is likewise suggested that we are acted by[12] others who have other ends than appear to us. We answer that that cannot be, since everything has its rise amongst ourselves, and since those things we bring to light cannot conduce to the ends of any but the public weal of the nation.

All our desires, petitions and papers are directly opposite to all corrupt interests; none have any credit with us but persons well known, and of certain abodes, and such as have given sound and undeniable testimonies of the truth of their affection to their country. Besides the things we promote are not good only in appearance but *sensibly* so: not moulded, not contrived by the subtle or politic principles of the world, but plainly produced and nakedly sent, without any insinuating arts, relying wholly upon the apparent and universal belief they carry in themselves. And that is it which convinces and engages us in the promotion thereof. So that that suggestion has not indeed any foundation in itself, but is purposely framed, as we conceive, to make us afraid one of another and to disable us in the promotion of those good things that tend to the freedom and happiness of the commonwealth.

For our being Jesuits, either in order or principles[13] (as 'tis severally reported of us): though the easiest negative is hardly proved, yet we can say that those on whom the first is principally fixed are married and were never over sea – and we think marriage is never dispensed withal[14] in that order, and that none can be admitted into the order but such as are personally present. 'Tis hard that we are put to express thus much; and haply we might better pass such reports over in silence, but that we believe the very mentioning of them publicly will be an answer to them and make such as foment them ashamed of such generally condemned ways of discrediting and blasting the reputation of other men. For the principles of Jesuits, we profess we know not what they are. But they are generally said to be full of craft and worldly policy, and therefore exceedingly different from that plainness and simplicity that is apparently visible in all our proceedings.

Whereas it's said we are atheists and antiscripturists, we profess that we believe there is one eternal and omnipotent God, the author and preserver of all things in the world, to whose will and directions,

---

[12] acted by = caused to act by others.
[13] The point of calling them Jesuits was fundamentally to claim that they believed evil governors could be deposed, or assassinated, as well accusing them of the 'craft and worldly policy' mentioned later on.
[14] never dispensed withal = the prohibition against marriage is never waived.

written first in our hearts and afterwards in his blessed word, we ought to square our actions and conversations.[15] And though we are not so strict upon the formal and ceremonial part of His service – the method, manner, and personal injunction being not so clearly made out unto us, nor the necessary requisites which his officers and ministers ought to be furnished withal as yet appearing (to some of us) in any that pretend thereunto[16] – yet for the manifestation of God's love in Christ, it is clearly assented unto by us; and the *practical and most real part of religion* is as readily submitted unto by us as being in our apprehensions the most eminent and the most excellent in the world, and as proceeding from no other but that God who is goodness itself. And we humbly desire His goodness daily more and more to conform our hearts to a willing and sincere obedience thereunto.

For our not being preferred to offices and places of profit and credit – which is urged to be the ground of our dissatisfaction – we say that although we know no reason why we should not be equally capable of them with other men, nor why our public affection should be any bar or hindrance thereunto, yet on the other side we suppose we can truly say of ourselves that we have not been so earnest and solicitous after them as others and that in the catalogue of suitors very few that are reckoned of us are to be found. We are very sorry that so general a change of officers is proposed,[17] which we judge of no small disparagement to our cause; and do think it best that in removals of that kind, the ground should not be difference in opinion either in religious or civil matters, but corruption or breach of trust – considering the misery which befalls whole families upon such changes and that discontents are thereby increased: whereas we hold it necessary that all ways of composure and acquieting those storms which the preceding differences and distractions have begotten be with utmost care and prudence endeavoured.

And whereas 'tis urged that if we were in power we would bear ourselves as tyrannically as others have done: we confess indeed that the experimental[18] defections of so many men as have succeeded in

---

[15] conversations = (not just talking with, but) a way of life among others.

[16] Presbyterians and episcopalians tended to claim divine ordination for their forms of church government, quoting especially from Acts, 1 Timothy and Titus.

[17] It was being proposed that office-holders should be required to take an engagement, which later emerged as one to be 'faithful to the commonwealth as it is now established, without king and Lords'. Refusal would mean loss of office.

[18] experimental = that which has been experienced.

authority, and the exceeding difference we have hitherto found in the same men in a low and in an exalted condition, makes us even mistrust our own hearts and hardly believe our own resolutions of the contrary. And therefore we have proposed such an establishment, as, supposing men to be too flexible and yielding to worldly temptations, they should not yet have a means or opportunity either to injure particulars or prejudice the public without extreme hazard and apparent danger to themselves. Besides, to the objection we have further to say that we aim not at power in ourselves, our principles and desires being in no measure of self-concernment; nor do we rely for obtaining the same upon strength or a forcible obstruction, but solely upon that inbred and persuasive power that is in all good and just things to make their own way in the hearts of men, and so to procure their own establishments.[19]

And that makes us at this time naked and defenceless as we are, and amidst so many discouragements on all hands to persevere in our motions and desires of good to the nation, although disowned therein at such a time when the doing thereof can be interpreted no other but a politic delivering us up to slaughter by such as we took our friends – our brethren of several churches[20] – and for whom with truth of affection we have even in the most difficult times done many services: all which (and whatsoever else can be done against us) we shall reckon but

[19] This may not be true. *Some* Levellers were clearly very interested in seeing 'strength or forcible obstruction' bring their principles into practice. Leveller mutiny was a problem for the New Model in November 1647, and again from March to May 1649. Lilburne and Overton's writings of 1647 and 1649 often sound like a declaration of (real) war against parliament and the Army grandees.

[20] On 25 March 1649, the Leveller leaders had attended particular Baptist congregations to get signatures to *The second part of England's new chains*, an even more aggressive attack on the new regime than *England's new chains*. In doing so they hoped to reactivate an alliance with the congregations which had operated in 1646 and early 1647. But it was not to be. The following Friday or Saturday Samuel Richardson, the Particular Baptist London leader, visited the now-imprisoned authors (plus Walwyn who had had nothing to do with it) and tried to persuade them – perhaps at Cromwell's instigation – to give up their campaign against the government. The Levellers refused, and on Monday 3 April the Particular Baptists, led by William Kiffin, presented a submissive petition of seven churches to the Commons, to be rewarded with the assurance from the Speaker: 'That for yourselves and other christians walking answerable to such professions as in this petition you make, they do assure you of liberty and protection so far as God shall enable them, in all things consistent with Godliness, honesty and civil peace.' After which there was no more alliance between the Levellers and the Independent and Separatist congregations of London. *Walwyn's wiles*, an attack on Walwyn, appeared later in the month under the name not only of John Price, its author, but of seven Congregationalists.

as badges of our sincerity and be no whit discouraged thereby from the discharge of our duties.

For the dissatisfactions that be upon many good men's spirits, for that they are not ascertained whereunto all our motions tend and in what they will centre: though (we conceive) they may have received some general satisfaction from what we have formerly at several times propounded, yet since they were not disposed into such a form and condition as to become practicable, we have with the best care and abilities God has afforded us cast the same into a model and platform which we shall speedily present unto the view and consideration of all as the standard and ultimate scope of our designs, that so (in case of approval) it may be subscribed and returned as agreed upon by the people. And thus far (we conceive) we may without offence or prejudice to authority, proceed; and which we the rather do because we know no better, and indeed no other way or means, but by such an agreement to remove as much as may be all disgusts and heart-burnings and to settle the commonwealth upon the fairest probabilities of a lasting peace and contentful establishment.

The *Agreement of the people* which was presented by his excellency and the officers of the army to the right honourable the commons in parliament, although in many things short (according to our apprehensions) of what is necessary for the good of the commonwealth, and satisfaction of the people – particularly in that it contains no provision for the certain removal of notorious and generally complained of grievances – and although it hath some things of much hazard to the public, yet, had it been put in execution, we should scarcely have interrupted the proceedings thereof, since therein is contained many things of great and important concernment to the commonwealth. But seeing the time proposed therein for reducing the same into practice is now past, and that likewise the generality of the people have not or do not approve of the same – for the reasons (as we suppose) fore-mentioned – we have thought fit to revise it, making only such alterations therein as we conceive really necessary for the welfare, security and safety of the people, together with additional provisions for the taking away of those burdens and grievances which may without real prejudice to the management of public affairs be removed.

And because it is essential to the nature of such an agreement to take its rise from the people, we have therefore purposely declined the presentment thereof to the parliament, and conceive it may speedily proceed to subscription and so to further practice without any interruption to this representative until the season prefixed in the *Agreement* for the assembling another, by whose immediate succession, without any interval, the affairs of the commonwealth may suffer no stop or intermission.

Lastly, we conceive we are much mistaken in being judged impatient and over-violent in our motions for the public good. To which we answer that could we have had any assurance that what is desired should have otherwise, or by any, have been done, and had not had some taste of the relinquishment of many good things that were promised, we should not have been so earnest and urgent for the doing thereof. (Though we know likewise, it has been very customary in such heretofore as never intended any freedom to the nation to except only against the season, and to protract the time so long till they became sufficiently empowered to justify the total denial and refusal thereof.)

However the main reason of our proceeding as we do is because we prefer the way of a settlement by an agreement of the people before any other whatsoever.

And thus the world may clearly see what we are and what we aim at. We are altogether ignorant, and do from our hearts abominate, all designs and contrivances of dangerous consequence which we are said (but God knows, untruly) to be labouring withal. Peace and freedom is our design. By war we were never gainers, nor ever wish to be; and under bondage we have been hitherto sufferers. We desire however, that what is past may be forgotten – provided the commonwealth may have amends made it for the time to come. And this from our soul we desire, having no men's persons in hatred, and judging it needful that all other respects whatsoever are to give way to the good of the commonwealth. And this is the very truth and inside of our hearts.
From the Tower, 14 April 1649
John Lilburne
William Walwyn
Thomas Prince
Richard Overton

An agreement of the free people of England, tendered as a peace-offering to this distressed nation, by Lieutenant-Colonel John Lilburne, Master William Walwyn, Master Thomas Prince and Master Richard Overton, prisoners in the Tower of London, 1 May 1649

Matthew 5:9: 'Blessed are the peacemakers for they shall be called the children of God.'

A preparative to all sorts of people

If afflictions make men wise and wisdom direct to happiness, then certainly this nation is not far from such a degree thereof as may compare, if not far exceed, any part of the world, having for some years by-past drunk deep of the cup of misery and sorrow. We bless God our consciences are clear from adding affliction to affliction, having ever laboured from the beginning of our public distractions to compose and reconcile them, and should esteem it the crown of all our temporal felicity that yet we might be instrumental in procuring the peace and prosperity of this commonwealth, the land of our nativity. And therefore according to our promise in our late *Manifestation*[1] of 14 April 1649, being persuaded of the necessity and justness thereof as a peace-offering to the free people of this nation, we tender this ensuing Agreement, not knowing any more effectual means to put a final period to all our fears and troubles.

It is a way of settlement, though at first much startled at by some in high authority, yet, according to the nature of truth, it hath made its own way into the understanding and taken root in most men's hearts and affections, so that we have real ground to hope – whatever shall become of us – that our earnest desires and endeavours for good to the people will not altogether be null and frustrate. The life of all things is in the right use and application, which is not our work only, but every man's; conscience must look to itself and not dream out more seasons

[1] Text 11 above.

and opportunities. And this we trust will satisfy all ingenuous people that we are not such wild, irrational, dangerous creatures as we have been aspersed to be – this Agreement being the ultimate end and full scope of all our desires and intentions concerning the government of this nation, and wherein we shall absolutely rest satisfied and acquiesce. Nor did we ever give just cause for any to believe worse of us by anything either said or done by us, and which would not in the least be doubted but that men consider not the interest of those that have so unChristian-like made bold with our good names. But we must bear with men of such interests as are opposite to any part of this Agreement, when neither our Saviour nor his apostles' innocency could stop such men's mouths whose interests their doctrines and practices did extirpate. And therefore if friends at least would but consider what interest men relate to whilst they are telling or whispering their aspersions against us, they would find the reason and save us a great deal of labour in clearing ourselves – it being a remarkable sign of an ill cause when aspersions supply the place of arguments. We bless God that he hath given us time and hearts to bring it to this issue. What further He hath for us to do is yet only known to his wisdom, to whose will and pleasure we shall willingly submit. We have, if we look with the eyes of frailty, enemies like the sons of Anak, but if with the eyes of faith and confidence in a righteous God and a just cause, we see more with us than against us.

From our causeless captivity
in the Tower of London,
John Lilburne
William Walwyn
Thomas Prince
Richard Overton

The Agreement itself then followeth

After the long and tedious prosecution of a most unnatural, cruel, home-bred war, occasioned by divisions and distempers amongst ourselves – and those distempers arising from the uncertainty of our government and the exercise of an unlimited or arbitrary power by such as have been trusted with supreme and subordinate authority – whereby multitudes of grievances and intolerable oppressions have been brought upon us; and finding after eight years' experience and expectation, all endeavours hitherto used or remedies hitherto applied to have increased rather than diminished our distractions, and that if not speedily prevented, our falling again into factions and divisions will not only deprive us of the benefit of all those wonderful victories God hath vouchsafed against such as sought our bondage, but expose us first to poverty and misery, and then to be destroyed by foreign enemies; and being earnestly desirous to make a right use of that opportunity God hath given us to make this nation free and happy; to reconcile our differences and beget a perfect amity and friendship once more amongst us, that we may stand clear in our consciences before Almighty God as unbiased by any corrupt interest or particular advantages, and manifest to all the world that our endeavours have not proceeded from malice to the persons of any, or enmity against opinions, but in reference to the peace and prosperity of the commonwealth and for prevention of like distractions and removal of all grievances: we the free people of England, to whom God hath given hearts, means and opportunity to effect the same, do with submission to His wisdom, in His name, and desiring the equity thereof may be to His praise and glory, agree to ascertain our government, to abolish all arbitrary power and to set bounds and limits both to our supreme and all subordinate authority, and remove all known grievances.

And accordingly do declare and publish to all the world that we are agreed as followeth:

1. That the supreme authority of England and the territories therewith incorporate, shall be and reside henceforward in a Representative of the People consisting of four hundred persons, but no more; in the choice of whom (according to natural right) all men of the age of one-and-twenty years and upwards (not being servants, or receiving alms, or having served the late king in arms or voluntary contributions) shall have their voices, and be capable of being elected to that supreme trust – those who served the king being disabled for ten years only. All things concerning the distribution of the said four hundred members proportionable to the respective parts of the nation, the several places for election, the manner of giving and taking of voices, with all circumstances of like nature tending to the completing with equal proceedings in elections, as also their salary, is referred to be settled by this present parliament in such sort as the next Representative may be in a certain capacity to meet with safety at the time herein expressed. And such circumstances to be made more perfect by future Representatives.

2. That two hundred of the four hundred members, and not less, shall be taken and esteemed for a competent Representative; and the major voices present shall be concluding to this nation. The place of session and choice of a Speaker, with other circumstances of that nature, are referred to the care of this and future Representatives.

3. And to the end all public officers may be certainly accountable and no factions made to maintain corrupt interests, no officer of any salary forces in army or garrison, nor any treasurer or receiver of public monies, shall (while such) be elected a member for any Representative; and if any lawyer shall at any time be chosen, he shall be incapable of practice as a lawyer during the whole time of that trust. And for the same reason, and that all persons may be capable of subjection as well as rule.

4. That no member of the present parliament shall be capable of being elected to the next Representative, nor any member of any future Representative shall be capable of being chosen for the Representative immediately succeeding, but are free to be chosen, one Representative having intervened. Nor shall any Representative be made either receiver, treasurer, or other officer during that employment.

5. That, for avoiding the many dangers and inconveniences apparently arising from the long continuance of the same persons in authority, we agree that this present parliament shall end the first Wednesday in August next (1649), and thenceforth be of no power or authority; and in the meantime shall order and direct the election of a new and equal Representative, according to the true intent of this our Agreement, and so as the next Representative may meet and sit in power and authority as an effectual Representative upon the day following: namely, the first Thursday of the same August, 1649.

6. We agree, if the present parliament shall omit to order such election or meeting of a new Representative or shall by any means be hindered from performance of that trust, that in such case we shall for the next Representative proceed in electing thereof in those places and according to that manner and number formerly accustomed in the choice of knights and burgesses, observing only the exceptions of such persons from being electors or elected as are mentioned before in the first, third, and fourth heads of this Agreement: it being most unreasonable that we should either be kept from new, frequent and successive representatives, or that the supreme authority should fall into the hands of such as have manifested disaffection to our common freedom and endeavoured the bondage of the nation.

7. And for preserving the supreme authority from falling into the hands of any whom the people have not or shall not choose, we are resolved and agreed (God willing) that a new Representative shall be upon the first Thursday in August next aforesaid. The ordering and disposing of themselves as to the choice of a Speaker and the like circumstances is hereby left to their discretion; but they are, in the extent and exercise of power, to follow the direction and rules of this Agreement and are hereby authorised and required – according to their best judgements – to set rules for future equal distribution and election of members as is herein intended and enjoined to be done by the present parliament.

8. And for the preservation of the supreme authority in all times entirely in the hands of such persons only as shall be chosen thereunto, we agree and declare that the next and all future representatives shall continue in full power for the space of one whole year; and that the people shall, of course, choose a parliament once every year, so as all the members thereof may be in a capacity to meet and take the place of the foregoing Representative on the first Thursday in every August for ever (if God so please). Also – for the same reason – that the next or any future Representative, being met, shall continue their session day by day without intermission for four months at the least; and after that shall be at liberty to adjourn from two months to two months[2] as they shall see cause, until their year be expired; but they shall sit no longer than a year upon pain of treason to every member that shall exceed that time; and in times of adjournment shall not erect a Council of State but refer the managing of affairs in the intervals to a committee of their own members, giving such instructions – and publishing them – as shall in no measure contradict this Agreement.

9. And that none henceforth may be ignorant or doubtful concerning the power of the supreme authority and of the affairs about which the same is to be conversant and exercised, we agree and declare that the power of Representatives shall extend without the consent or concurrence of any other person or persons: (1) to the conservation of peace and commerce with foreign nations, (2) to the preservation of those safeguards and securities of our lives, limbs, liberties, properties, and estates contained in the Petition of Right made and enacted in the third year of the late king, (3) to the raising of monies, and generally to all things as shall be evidently

---

[2] I.e. for two months at a time, each adjournment requiring a meeting to authorise it.

conducing to those ends or to the enlargement of our freedom, redress of grievances, and prosperity of the commonwealth.

For security whereof, having by woeful experience found the prevalence of corrupt interests powerfully inclining most men once entrusted with authority to pervert the same to their own domination and to the prejudice of our peace and liberties, we therefore further agree and declare:

10. That we do not empower or entrust our said Representatives to continue in force or to make any laws, oaths or covenants, whereby to compel by penalties or otherwise any person to anything in or about matters of faith, religion, or God's worship; or to restrain any person from the profession of his faith or exercise of religion according to his conscience – nothing having caused more distractions and heart-burnings in all ages than persecution and molestation for matters of conscience in and about religion.

11. We do not empower them to impress or constrain any person to serve in way by sea or land – every man's conscience being to be satisfied in the justness of that cause wherein he hazards his own life, or may destroy another's.

And for the quieting of all differences and abolishing of all enmity and rancour, as much as is now possible for us to effect:

12. We agree that after the end of this present parliament, no person shall be questioned for anything said or done in reference to the late wars or public differences, otherwise than in pursuance of the determinations of the present parliament against such as have adhered to the king against the liberties of the people, and saving that accountants for public monies received shall remain accountable for the same.

13. That all privileges or exemptions of any persons from the laws or from the ordinary course of legal proceedings by virtue of any tenure, grant, charter, patent, degree, or birth, or of any place of residence, or refuge, or privilege of parliament, shall be henceforth void and null; and the like not to be made nor revived again.

14. We do not empower them to give judgement upon anyone's person or estate where no law has been before provided, nor to give power to any other court or jurisdiction so to do, because where there is no law there is no transgression for men or magistrates to take cognisance of; neither do we empower them to intermeddle with the execution of any law whatsoever.

15. And that we may remove all long-settled grievances and thereby as far as we are able take away all cause of complaints and no longer depend upon the uncertain inclination of parliaments to remove them, nor trouble ourselves or them with petitions after petitions (as has been accustomed) without fruit or benefit; and knowing no cause why any should repine at our removal of them except such as make advantage by their continuance or are related to some corrupt interests, which we are not to regard, we agree and declare:

16. That it shall not be in the power of any representative to punish, or cause to be punished, any person or persons for refusing to answer to questions against themselves in criminal cases.

17. That it shall not be in their power, after the end of the next Representative, to continue or constitute any proceedings in law that shall be longer than six months in the final determination of any cause past all appeal; nor to continue the laws or proceedings therein in any other language than English, nor to hinder any person or persons from pleading their own causes or of making use of whom they please to plead for them.

The reducing of these and other the like provisions of this nature in this Agreement provided, and which could not now in all particulars be perfected by us, is intended by us to be the proper works of faithful Representatives.

18. That it shall not be in their power to continue or make any laws to abridge or hinder any person or persons from trading or merchandising into any place beyond the seas where any of this nation are free to trade.

19. That it shall not be in their power to continue excise or customs upon any sort of food or any other goods, wares, or commodities longer than four months after the beginning of the next Representative, being both of them extreme burdensome and oppressive to trade and so expensive in the receipt as the monies expended therein (if collected as subsidies have been)[3] would extend very far towards defraying the public charges. And forasmuch as all monies to be raised are drawn from the people, such burdensome and chargeable ways shall never

---

[3] Subsidies (a combination of land tax and property rate) were collected locally and submitted by local receivers-general direct to the Army treasurers, for which they received a commission. Customs and excise were collected by parliamentary commissioners who were leading financiers working centrally in London and who received a commission on the money they raised.

more be revived, nor shall they raise monies by any other ways (after the aforesaid time) but only by an equal rate in the pound upon every real and personal estate in the nation.

20. That it shall not be in their power to make or continue any law whereby men's real or personal estates, or any part thereof, shall be exempted from payment of their debts; or to imprison any person for debt of any nature – it being both unChristian in itself and no advantage to the creditors, and both a reproach and prejudice to the commonwealth.

21. That it shall not be in their power to make or continue any law for taking away any man's life – except for murder or other the like heinous offences destructive to human society, or for endeavouring by force to destroy this our Agreement – but shall use their uttermost endeavour to appoint punishments equal to offences: that so men's lives, limbs, liberties and estates may not be liable to be taken away upon trivial or slight occasions as they have been; and shall have special care to preserve all sorts of people from wickedness, misery and beggary; nor shall the estate of any capital offender be confiscate but in cases of treason only; and in all other capital offences, recompense shall be made to the parties damnified,[4] as well out of the estate of the malefactor as by loss of life, according to the conscience of his jury.

22. That it shall not be in their power to continue to make any law to deprive any person in case of trials for life, limb, liberty or estate, from the benefit of witnesses on his or their behalf, nor deprive any person of those privileges and liberties, contained in the Petition of Right made in the third year of the late king Charles.

23. That it shall not be in their power to continue the grievance of tithes longer than to the end of the next Representative; in which time, they shall provide to give reasonable satisfaction to all impropriators; neither shall they force, by penalties or otherwise, any person to pay towards the maintenance of any ministers, who out of conscience cannot submit thereunto.

24. That it shall not be in their power to impose ministers upon any the respective parishes, but shall give free liberty to the parishioners of every particular parish to choose such as themselves shall approve, and upon such terms and for such reward as themselves shall be willing to contribute, or shall contract for. Provided none be choosers but such as are capable of electing Representatives.

---

[4] parties damnified = injured parties.

25. That it shall not be in their power to continue or make a law for any other way of judgements, or conviction of life, limb, liberty or estate, but only by twelve sworn men of the neighbourhood to be chosen in some free way by the people, to be directed before the end of the next Representative, and not picked and imposed as hitherto in many places they have been.

26. They shall not disable any person from bearing any office in the commonwealth for any opinion or practice in religion, excepting such as maintain the pope's (or other foreign) supremacy.

27. That it shall not be in their power to impose any public officer upon any counties, hundreds, cities, towns or boroughs; but the people capable by this Agreement to choose Representatives shall choose all their public officers that are in any kind to administer the law for their respective places for one whole year, and no longer, and so from year to year. And this as an especial means to avoid factions and parties.

And that no person may have just cause to complain by reason of taking away the excise and customs, we agree:

28. That the next, and all future representatives shall exactly keep the public faith and give full satisfaction for all securities, debts, arrears or damages (justly chargeable) out of the public treasury; and shall confirm and make good all just public purchases and contracts that have been or shall be made; save that the next Representative may confirm or make null in part or in whole, all gifts of lands, monies, offices, or otherwise made by the present parliament to any member of the House of Commons or to any of the Lords or to any of the attendants of either of them.

And for as much as nothing threatens greater danger to the commonwealth than that the military power should by any means come to be superior to the civil authority:

29. We declare and agree that no forces shall be raised but by the Representatives for the time being; and in raising thereof, that they exactly observe these rules, namely: that they allot to each particular county, city, town and borough, the raising, furnishing, agreeing, and paying of a due proportion according to the whole number to be levied; and shall to the electors of Representatives in each respective place give free liberty to nominate and appoint all officers appertaining to regiments, troops and companies, and to remove them as they shall see cause, reserving to the Representative the nominating

and appointing only of the General and all general-officers, and the ordering, regulating and commanding of them all upon what service shall seem to them necessary for the safety, peace, and freedom of the commonwealth.

And inasmuch as we have found by sad experience that generally men make little or nothing to innovate in government, to exceed their time and power in places of trust, to introduce an arbitrary and tyrannical power, and to overturn all things into anarchy and confusion where there are no penalties imposed for such destructive crimes and offences: 30. We therefore agree and declare that it shall not be in the power of any Representative in any wise to render up or give or take away any part of this Agreement, nor level men's estates, destroy propriety, or make all things common. And if any Representative shall endeavour, as a Representative, to destroy this Agreement, every member present in the House not entering or immediately publishing his dissent shall incur the pain due for high treason and be proceeded against accordingly; and if any person or persons shall by force endeavour or contrive the destruction thereof, each person so doing shall likewise be dealt withal as in cases of treason.

And if any person shall by force of arms disturb elections of Representatives, he shall incur the penalty of a riot; and if any person not capable of being an elector, or elected, shall intrude themselves amongst those that are, or any persons shall behave themselves rudely and disorderly, such persons shall be liable to a presentment by a grand inquest and to an indictment upon misdemeanour, and be fined and otherwise punished according to the discretion and verdict of a jury. And all laws made or that shall be made contrary to any part of this Agreement are hereby made null and void.

Thus, as becomes a free people thankful unto God for this blessed opportunity, and desirous to make use thereof to His glory in taking off every yoke and removing every burden in delivering the captive and setting the oppressed free, we have in all the particular heads aforementioned done as we would be done unto. And as we trust God will abolish all occasion of offence and discord and produce the lasting peace and prosperity of this commonwealth, we accordingly do in the sincerity of our hearts and consciences, as in the presence of Almighty God, give clear testimony of our absolute agreement to all and every part hereof by subscribing our hands thereunto.

Dated the first day of May, in the year of our Lord 1649.
John Lilburne
William Walwyn
Thomas Prince
Richard Overton
30 April 1649

Imprimatur Gilbert Mabbot

FINIS

London. Printed for Giles Calvert at the black spread-eagle at the west end of St Paul's

13
The young men's and the apprentices' outcry.
Or an inquisition after the lost fundamental laws and liberties of England

Directed (29 August 1649) in an epistle to the private soldiery of the Army, especially all those that signed the Solemn Engagement at Newmarket-Heath, 5 June 1647. But more especially to the private soldiers of the General's regiment of horse, that hoped to plunder and destroy the honest and true-hearted Englishmen traitorously defeated at Burford, 15 May 1649 By Charles Collins, Anthony Bristlebolt, William Trabret, Stephen Smith, Edward Waldgrave, Thomas Frisby, Edward Stanley, William White, Nicolas Blowd, John Floyd,[1] in the name and behalf of themselves, and the young men and apprentices of the City of London. Who are cordial approvers of the paper called The agreement of the free people, 1 May 1649, and the defeated Burford-men's late vindication,[2] dated 20 August 1649

Lamentations 2: 11–12 'Mine eyes do faile with tears: my bowells are troubled: my liver is powred upon the earth, for the destruction of the daughter of my people, because the children and the sucklings swoon in the streets of the City.

They say to their mothers, where is corne and wine? when they swooned as the wounded in the streets of the City, when their soule was poured out into their mothers bosome.'

Gentlemen,

We are all of one nation and people; it is the sword only that differs. But how just a title that is over us, your own private thoughts surely are our determiners, however your actions import. For it is not imagin-

---

[1] Nothing is known of these men. Lilburne was almost certainly the author.
[2] The Levellers (falsely so called) vindicated, or the case of the twelve troops . . . truly stated (1649), published in A. L. Morton (London, 1978). *Freedom in arms: a collection of Leveller writings.*

able – except amongst bears, wolves, and lions[3] – that brethren of one cause, one nation and family, can without remorse and secret check of conscience impose such iron yokes of cruelty and oppression upon their fellows as by the awe and force of your sword rampant is imposed upon the people of this nation. You see it. We are at best but your hewers of wood and drawers of water. Our very persons, our lives and properties are all over-awed to the supportation only of the raging, lawless sword, drenched in the precious blood of the people.

The ancient and famous magistracy of this nation, the Petition of Right, the Great Charter of England (above thirty times confirmed in open and free parliament),[4] with all other the fundamental laws, safeties and securities of the people – which our ancestors at an extraordinary dear rate, as with abundance of their blood and treasure, purchased for the inheritance of us and of the generations after us, and for which you pretendedly took up arms against the late king and his party – are now all subverted, broken down and laid waste, the military power being thrust into the very office and seat of the civil authority: the king not only most illegally put to death by a strange, monstrous, illegal, arbitrary court such as England never knew; monarchy not only extirpated – not rectified – without, and besides, the consent of the people (though the actors of that bloody scene have owned and declared them to be the original of all such human authority); but even our parliaments – the very interest, marrow, and soul of all the native rights of the people – put down, and the name and power thereof transmitted to a picked party of your forcible selecting. And such a parliament[5] as your officers (our lords and riders) have often and frequently styled no better than a 'mock parliament', a 'shadow of a parliament', a 'seeming authority' or the like, pretending the continuance thereof but till a new and equal Representative by a mutual agreement of the free people of England could be elected[6] – although now, for subserviency to their

---

[3] *The Levellers . . . vindicated* quotes John Cook, *King Charles his case* (1649) in making the case against the king, as arguing that rule 'enforced and obtruded by conquest' is 'more fit for wolves and bears than amongst men'. Cook was president of the court which tried and condemned the king.

[4] Coke, *The second part of the institutes*, A Proeme, spoke of the Great Charter being confirmed in later statutes 32 times, and typically depicts these acts as 'declaratory of the principal grounds of the fundamental laws of England', the idea being that the later acts added nothing to the law of England, merely confirmed it.

[5] 'a parliament' added.

[6] Lilburne made this charge against Ireton in his *Legall fundamental liberties* (8 June 1649).

exaltation and kingship, they prorogue and perpetrate the same in the name and under colour thereof, introducing a Privy Council, or as they call it a Council of State, of superintendency and suppression to all future successive parliaments for ever, erecting a martial government by blood and violence impulsed[7] upon us, making soldiers to be executioners of orders and warrants, pretending to the civil authority; and in every particular – notwithstanding all your famous and glorious declarations of freedom and liberty – dealing with us as an absolute conquered and enslaved people: the law being nothing but a mock protection to our lives, liberties and properties; the judges set aside for the executors of it, a mere delusion; our Sheriffs, Mayors, Justices of Peace, Constables, etc. being laid by or made no better than ciphers – the choice of them, by will without right appropriated to a few factious men, while the right owners (the people) are robbed of their free and popular elections of them – as not daring to execute justice upon the rudest or meanest soldier in England although the law sufficiently warrants them thereunto; but contrariwise, commoners are forcibly convented[8] and tried before a Council of War, and some sentenced even unto death, others by a private verbal order made to run the gantlop[9] and whipped most barbarously for refusing to take false and illegal oaths; and the blood of war – expressly against the Petition of Right, and for which amongst other crimes the earl of Strafford lost his head as a traitor – shed in times of peace: as the blood of Mr Richard Arnell upon 15 November 1647 near Ware;[10] of Mr Robert Lockyer upon 27 April 1649 (so much bewailed and lamented at London);[11] of Colonel

---

[7] impulsed = movement brought about by application of force.

[8] convented = summoned to.

[9] run the gantlop = run naked from the waist up between rows of men who thrash one with cords and sticks.

[10] A Leveller demonstration in favour of the 1647 *Agreement of the people* by Colonel Robert Lilburne's (John's brother's) regiment together with Colonel Thomas Harrison's, was treated as a mutiny by Cromwell and Fairfax, and was crushed at a rendezvous at Corkbush Field near Ware. Three men were sentenced to death; two were reprieved, but one, Richard Arnell or Arnold, was shot on the field before the assembled regiments. Lilburne, who was waiting in Ware for the Army to reform itself and declare for the *Agreement*, slunk back to London.

[11] On Lockyer, see p. 207. He was court-martialled and shot as the leading mutineer in Captain John Savage's troop of Whalley's regiment. The troop, on being ordered to move to the outskirts of London where they would be less accessible to Leveller influence, had seized the regimental colours and holed up in the Bull Inn, Bishopsgate, enunciating demands for pay and arrears. They were easily overcome. Lockyer died bravely, and his funeral was attended by perhaps 4,000 Londoners wearing the sea-green

Poyer;[12] of Cornet Thompson, Mr Perkins and Mr Church upon 16 May 1649 at Burford[13] – contrary to promises, and solemn engagements at the taking of them (as their friends lately defeated with them, in their *Vindication* of the 20 of August, 1649, fully declare (pp. 6–7) and others yet fresh in our memory doth witness.

Parties of horse and foot (contrary and in direct defiance of the due course and process of law) are sent at unreasonable hours to hale and pull people out of their beds and houses, from their wives and children, without so much as ever summoning of them and without any crime or accusation shown or accuser appearing or the least pretence or shadow of law produced – some sent into remote garrisons, where they have been most barbarously used and endeavoured to be starved and tossed from garrison to garrison, others locked up close prisoners with sentinels night and day upon their doors, and all due trials and help at law stopped and denied, and no remedy to be obtained. Yea, free men are most barbarously put out of their legal possessions by force of arms without any manner of trial at law; yea, the law damned and stopped up against them for recovering of their legal rights, and they threatened severely to be punished if they desist not their suits at law; yea, and free men's estates – never pretended to be within the compass of the ordinances of sequestrations – are seized on to a great value (by some great men's wills, protected by their swords, to do even what they list,

Leveller colours – more than the impressive number who had attended Thomas Rainborough's funeral in November 1648.

[12] Colonel John Poyer, who in 1642 was Mayor of Pembroke and became a zealous parliamentarian captain. A firm Presbyterian, in February 1648 he declared for Charles and seized Pembroke castle and town, where he was joined by parliamentary deserters and resisted Cromwell's siege in June and July. As an apostate and central figure in the Welsh resistance to parliament during the second civil war, he was court-martialled, and was executed by shooting in the Piazza at Covent Garden on 24 April 1649.

[13] These three were executed after a court martial for their part in the mutiny of most of Colonel Scrope's regiment, together with elements of Ireton's and Harrison's. These horse regiments complained of material grievances as to the Irish service to which they had been selected by lot, and, joined by a few soldiers and citizen volunteers from London and encouraged by civilian Levellers, insisted also on the revival of General Councils of the Army (which had been discontinued in mid-November 1647) and on the freeing of the Leveller leaders from the Tower; they complained also of the neglect of the Agreement of 1 May 1649. The mutiny began in Salisbury about 1 May, continued in a process of marches and declarations, and ended with a surprise night attack, defeat and capture of 340 men at Burford near Oxford, engineered by Fairfax, on 14–15 May. About 540 men escaped. Four ringleaders were sentenced to be shot. One, Cornet Henry Denne, showed such penitence that he was pardoned, and lived to write against the Levellers.

without control) without any manner of trial or conviction or any shadow of legal pretence, or ever so much as laying any pretended crime to the party's charge: all which are the very (if not higher) crimes than the earl of Strafford principally lost his head for as a traitor – as clearly appears by his Act of Attainder, and by his large printed additional impeachment, 1641, both in English and Irish cases, as clearly appears in the preamble thereof and in Articles 2–8.[14]

But that which is worst of all, the best and most faithful maintainers of the English freedoms are most maligned, abused, and vilified, that it is now become a crime of the greatest peril and penalty to be faithful to the declared interest of parliaments or rights of the people therein – a thing so dreadfully complained of by the parliament in the beginning of their first Remonstrance of December 1641.[15] New acts of high treason[16] to that end [are] devised to ensnare and entrap the most conscientious, so that we cannot talk or discourse of our lost freedoms or open our mouths of our oppressions, but we are in as bad a condition as our fore-fathers were in the days of William the Conqueror (that thought any fact crime enough to entitle him to their estates), if not worse by being treason-struck. And besides all this, multitudes of pick-pocket, murdering taxes are heaped and continued upon the old, and in default of payment soldiers are put upon straining,[17] seizing and plundering of our masters' goods and houses, for which violence and villainy they must be largely paid or else they will plunder over again for that. Yea and the late large Act about excise[18] – so transcendent and ensnaring in its penalties that no man well knows how to behave himself in his trading for fear of being undone – yea, so numberless are our most insufferable cruelties, overspreading and wounding the whole land and people, that our borders are even filled with the lamentations, mourn-

---

[14] Articles of impeachment, 28 January 1641; Act of Attainder 10 May 1641.

[15] *A remonstrance of the state of the kingdom*, 15 December 1641. In *Exact collection*, pp. 3–21.

[16] Acts of 14 May and 7 July 1649 made it treason if 'any person shall maliciously or advisedly publish by writing, printing, or openly declaring that the . . . government is tyrannical, usurped and unlawful; or that the commons in parliament . . . are not the supreme authority of the nation; or shall plot, contrive or endeavour to stir up and raise force against the present government, or for the subversion or alteration of the same'. It was also mutiny to subvert the Council of State or (if a civilian) to stir up mutiny in armies.

[17] I.e. distraining.

[18] An ordinance of August 1649 extending the powers of excise officials to enforce its levy.

ings, tears, sighs and doleful groans of the oppressed and enslaved ruinated people. Trade decayed and fled, misery, poverty, calamity, confusion, yea and beggary grown so sore and so extreme upon the people, as the like never was in England under the most tyrannical of all our kings that were before these in present power, since the days of the Conqueror himself: no captivity, no bondage, no oppression like unto this, no sorrow or misery like unto ours (of being enslaved, undone and destroyed by our late pretended friends, for whose preservation we could have even pulled out our very eyes); the people become desolate and forsaken, wandering, pining, and mourning (like those in Jeremiah's *Lamentations* unto whose sorrows they said none was like) after their lost fundamental laws, their native, and just freedoms and rights; and there is none to comfort, none to pity, none to relieve, none to help or save. Alas, alas for pity.

For your hearts seem to us as obdurate as the flinty rock, as savage and inhuman as if the flesh and blood, the bones and marrow of the people were become your meat – as already it is in effect – and instead of encouragement and support to our true friends and real relievers (at least in faithful desire and endeavour) as shall stand in the gap betwixt our destroyers and us, all ways and means are used to impoverish, destroy, and suppress them, and in them to break and vassalage the spirits of all the English – which in all ages have had the pre-eminency of other nations – that there may not be so much of gallantry or courage left amongst the people that one amongst them shall dare to assert or maintain their freedoms (which Act is not a little aggravated by Mr John Pym, in his remarkable speech against the earl of Strafford, as the highest of treasons against any nation or commonwealth).[19] For if any do but murmur and complain or seek for remedy, though by way of petition or address to the House, presently their House, as with furies, are beset with armed mercenary janissaries, guards and sentinels set upon their doors and passages, no consideration had of the terror or affrightment of our masters, their wives, children or servants, or of reason or law, and their persons as traitors therefore imprisoned for weeks and months; yea, and close imprisonment from the society of all their friends without ever so much as ever seeing either informer, accuser, prosecutor, or witness; yea, or ever seeing indictment,

---

[19] *The speech or declaration of John Pym, esquire: after the recapitulation or summing up of the charge of high treason against Thomas, earl of Strafford, 21 April 1641* (1641). See below n. 34.

impeachment or charge; yea, or face to face, or in their *mittimuss*[20] or any other formal or legal way ever so much as having any crime or pretence of a crime laid unto their charge by those very men before whom they are brought, and who by the rules of their mere will commit them.

Therefore, although the parliament in several declarations have declared that they have received petitions for the removal of things established by law – and we must say, and all that know what belongeth to the course or practice of parliament will say, that we ought so to do and that both our predecessors and his majesty's ancestors have constantly done it, there being no other place wherein laws that by experience may be found grievous and burdensome can be altered or repealed, and there being no other due and legal way wherein they which are aggrieved by them can seek redress, and that it is no tumult to deliver petitions by popular multitudes (*1 part Book of parliament's declarations*,[21] pp. 23, 201–2, 209, 532[22]–35, 548, 691, 720) – yea, and your very selves and your juggling officers quarrelled with and took up arms against the parliament (your creators and original lords and masters) for prohibiting you to petition and make known your grievances to them, and sufficiently envy and exclaim against them for so doing and impeach some of them as traitors therefore (as clearly appears in your own *Book of declarations*,[23] pp.10–11, 17, 23, 33, 35, 44, 60–2, 83, 85, 118); and yet nothing but the boundless wills and humours of those fore-mentioned men of blood, rages and rules over us.

And is this all the return and fruit that people are to expect at your hands? Doth your Solemn Engagement at Newmarket (and Triploe Heath) with your declarations, remonstrances, vows and protestations unto us all, centre in this bed-roll of cruelties? We pray you give us leave to make enquiry amongst you after those things, and give losers leave to complain. Remember you not with what cheerfulness and alacrity our fellow-apprentices – the glory and flower of the youth of this nation – and multitudes of ourselves yet surviving, ran in to your assistance out of a conscientious intent to uphold and maintain the

---

[20] A warrant committing a person to prison.

[21] *An exact collection.* The preceding words are a paraphrase of *A remonstrance of the Lords and Commons* (26 May 1642), p. 720. (The reference to p. 23 is not clear.)

[22] P. 533 in original.

[23] 'your own *Book*' (often called *The Army's book of declarations*) was *A declaration of the engagements, remonstrances . . . from his excellency Sir Thomas Fairfax and the general command of the army*, 27 September 1647.

fundamental constitution of this commonwealth, viz. the interest and right of the people in their parliaments (it being most rational and unquestionably just that the people should not be bound but by their own consent given to their deputies in parliament, which by the laws and customs of England ought, wholly new, to be annual, to deliver and clear the land from its heavy pressures and bonds) not engaging in the least against the person of the king, as king, or with any thoughts of pretence of destroying, but regulating, kingship, and merely for the removal of all those cruelties and oppressions he had laid upon the people by his will, contrary to law?

This you know to be true. Your own papers extant to the world are our record and witnesses, as might plentifully be recited, but they are known to all men that know your affairs. You cannot deny it. But where is the fulfilment of all your glorious words, registered in your *Book of declarations* in which (p. 14) you say you shall 'through the grace of God' discharge your duties to the parliament, etc. and also demonstrate that 'the good and quiet of the kingdom' is much dearer to you than any 'particular concernment' of your own? And on p. 23, the General to both Houses in his letter of 6 June 1647 assures the parliament it is his study and care to avoid a new war, and further thus saith: 'so I find it to be the unanimous desire and study of the Army that a firm peace in this kingdom may be settled, and the liberties of the people cleared and secured accordingly to the many declarations by which we were invited and induced to engage in the late war', most seriously there promising them they will not meddle 'to the advancement of any particular party or interest whatsoever'. And in your *Solemn engagement* of the 5 June 1647, p. 26, you promise and engage to God, the kingdom, and to each other that you 'will not disband, divide, nor suffer yourselves to be disbanded nor divided' (either for Ireland, or any other place else) until 'we' have 'first such satisfaction' (as you say) 'to the Army in relation to our grievances and desires heretofore presented, and such security that we of ourselves (when disbanded and in the condition of private men) or other the freeborn people of England (to whom the consequence of our case about petitioning[24] doth equally extend) shall not remain subject to the like oppression, injury or abuse as in the premises hath been attempted and put upon us while an Army'.

---

[24] The authors add 'about petitioning' to the original *Solemn engagement*.

Oh that there had been an heart in you to have made this good before your gross apostasy from all your engagements and promises, that has already occasioned so much misery, war and bloodshed. Or oh that yet there were hearts within you vigorously and effectually to go about the accomplishment and fulfilment thereof – and thereby prevent all the miseries, bloodshed and desolations that for want thereof undoubtedly must and will ensue – which you are bound and tied unto both before God and man, as is (in our judgements) unanswerably proved in the foresaid treacherously defeated Burford men's *Vindication*, pp. 8–10. But to return: in your said *Engagement*, on the fore-recited p. 26, you positively there disown and disclaim all purposes or designs in our late or present proceedings to advance or inflict upon a particular interest, to the overthrow of magistracy, etc. 'Neither' (say you) 'would we (if we might or could) advance or set up any . . . particular party or interest in the kingdom (though imagined never so much our own) but shall much rather (as far as may be within our sphere or power) study to promote such an establishment of common equal right and freedom to the whole, as all might equally partake of.'

And in that most choice and best of declarations made by the whole army of soldiers as well as officers, 14 June 1647, tendered to the parliament, concerning their just and fundamental rights and liberties of themselves and the kingdom (*A declaration of the engagements*, pp. 36–7) you say: 'That we may no longer be the dissatisfaction of our friends, the subject of our enemies' malice to work jealousies and misrepresentations upon, and the suspicion (if not astonishment) of many in the kingdom in our late or present transactions and conduct of business, we shall in all faithfulness and clearness profess and declare unto you these things which have of late protracted and hindered our disbanding: the present grievances which possess our army and are yet unremedied, with our desires as to the complete settlement of the liberties and peace of the kingdom – which is that blessing of God than which of all worldly things nothing is more dear unto us or more precious in our thoughts, we having hitherto thought all our enjoyments (whether of life or livelihood or nearest relations) a price but sufficient to the purchase of so rich a blessing, that we, and all the free-born people of this nation may sit down in quiet under our vines, and under the glorious administration of justice and righteousness, and in full possession of those fundamental rights and liberties without which we can have little hopes, as to human consideration, to enjoy either any comforts of life or so much as life itself, but at the pleasures of some men ruling merely according to will and power.'

And in the same declaration (pp. 38–9) you further say thus: 'Nor will it now (we hope) seem strange or unreasonable to rational and honest men who consider the consequence of our present case to their own and the kingdom's (as well as our) future concernments in point of right, freedom, peace and safety, if, from a deep sense of the high consequence of our present case both to ourselves in future and all other people, we shall, before disbanding, proceed in our own and the kingdom's behalf to propound and plead for some provision for our and the kingdom's satisfaction and future security in relation to those things; especially considering that we were not a mere mercenary army, hired to serve an[25] arbitrary power of a state, but called forth and conjured by the several declarations of parliament to the defence of our own and the people's just rights and liberties; and so we took up arms in judgement and conscience to those ends, and so have so continued them, and are resolved, according to your first just desires in your declarations and such principles as we have received from your frequent informations and our own common sense concerning those our fundamental rights and liberties, to assert and vindicate the just power and rights of this kingdom in parliament for those common ends premised against all arbitrary power, violence and oppression, and[26] against all particular parties and interests whatsoever; the said declarations still directing us to the equitable sense of all laws and constitutions, as dispensing with the very letter of the same, and being supreme to it when the safety and preservation of all is concerned, and assuring us that all authority is fundamentally seated in the office and but ministerially in the persons.'

And on p. 41, speaking in general of purging some evil members out of the parliament, you declare your carriage towards them shall be such 'as that the world shall see we aim at nothing of private revenge and animosities, but that justice may have a free course, and the kingdom be eased and secured by disenabling such men at least from place of judicature, who, desiring to advantage and set up themselves and their party in a general confusion have endeavoured to put the kingdom into a new flame of war, than which nothing is more abhorrent to us'. And

[25] 'any' in the original.
[26] The authors add the 'and'.

in the same declaration, spending the 42nd and 43rd pages in most excellent expressions of the excellency and benefit of frequent and successive parliaments (totally new) and the mischief, bondage and vassalage of the long continuance of any parliament, on p. 44, you say: 'And thus a firm foundation being laid in the authority and constitution of parliaments for the hopes at least of common and equitable[27] right and freedom to ourselves and all the freeborn people of this land, we shall for our parts freely and cheerfully commit our stock or share of interest in the kingdom into this common bottom of parliaments, and though it may (for our particulars) go ill with us in one voyage, yet we shall thus hope (if right be with us) to fare better in another.'

And in the last end of that transcendent declaration (p. 46), you conclude thus: 'We have thus freely and clearly declared the depth and bottom of our hearts and desires in order to the rights, liberties and peace of the kingdom; wherein we appeal to all men whether we seek anything of advantage to ourselves or any particular party whatever, or to the prejudice of the whole; and whether the things we wish and seek for do not equally concern and conduce to the good of others in common with ourselves according to the sincerity of our desires and intentions (wherein, as we have already found the concurrent sense of the people in divers counties by their petitions to the General expressing their deep resentment of these things and pressing us to stand for the interest of the kingdom therein, so we shall wish and expect the unanimous concurrence of all others who are equally concerned with us in these things and wish well to the public)'.

And on pp. 52–3, being written to the Lord Mayor, Aldermen, and Commons of the City of London in Common Council assembled, it is thus said:[28] 'To conclude, we say from our hearts that as our especial ends are the glory of God and the good of this whole land, so our endeavours shall be to prosecute the same without prejudice to the being or well-being of parliaments in general, the maintenance whereof we value above our own lives or (as we have formerly said) of this parliament in particular, but altogether in order to the good and peace of this nation, and with a most tender regard to your city.'

And on pp. 57–8, it's said that: 'In our last representation it may appear what our desires are as members of the commonwealth in behalf

---

[27] 'equal', not 'equitable' in the *Declaration or representation*.
[28] Fairfax to the right honourable the Lord Mayor, Aldermen and Commons of the City of London, 21 June 1647.

of ourselves and all others for the clearing, settling and securing of the rights, liberties and peace of the kingdoms; for the justness, reasonableness, necessity and common concernment whereof unto all, we dare appeal to the whole kingdom and to the world.' And on p. 76 to the Lord Mayor of London, etc.,[29] it is said that: 'It is a sudden and substantial settlement of the whole we desire, in a general, safe, and well-grounded peace and the establishment of such good laws as may duly and readily render to every man their just rights and liberties; and for the obtaining of these, not only our intentions had led us to, but we think that all the blood, treasure and labour spent in this war was to the accomplishing those very things, which are of that concernment both to ourselves and posterities that neither we nor they can live comfortably without them.' And therefore their help is much preferred for to bring things to a 'happy conclusion, to the satisfaction of all honest men's expectation, and that in all our undertakings we shall be found men of truth, fully and singly answering the things we have held forth to the kingdom in our several declarations and papers without bias or base respects to any private end or interest whatsoever.

And on p. 97 is recorded a notable proposal to the parliament from Reading, 18 July 1647, which doth sufficiently condemn your late tyrannical dealing with some of the very parties therein mentioned. The proposal thus follows. 'We do earnestly desire that all persons imprisoned in England or the Dominion of Wales, not for delinquency in relation to the late war but for other pretended misdemeanours, and whose imprisonment is not by the regulated course of law but by order from either House of parliament or of committees flowing from them, may be put into a speedy, regular and equitable way of trial; or if the necessity of settling the general affairs of the kingdom admit not their present trial, then they may have present liberty (upon reasonable security) for their appearance at a certain day to answer what shall be charged against them in a legal way; and that when they should be tried, if they appear wrongfully or unduly imprisoned, they may have reparation according to their sufferings.

In particular we desire this may be done in behalf of Lieutenant-Colonel John Lilburne, Master John Musgrave,[30] Master Overton and

---

[29] Fairfax to the Mayor, etc., 8 July 1647.
[30] John Musgrave had been imprisoned by the JPs and Commissioners of Array in Cumberland in 1645 for a too-vigorous prosecution of the war and his too great familiarity with the Scots; on his release he had carried a petition from Cumberland against the

others in their condition: imprisoned in and about London.' Read also more fully to this purpose, pp. 101, 105, 110, 112, 118, 128, 132, 137[31] – as also the large remonstrance from Saint Albans of the 16 of November 1648,[32] pp. 6, 8–9, 12, 14–15, 22–3, 29, 43, 45, 47, 48, 57, 62. (But especially pp. 65–9.)

But after this large (but yet profitable and necessary) digression, let us seriously expostulate with you and put you in mind of your most wicked and gross apostasy – such as the world never saw nor read of before, from men that profess God and godliness in a strict manner and would be reputed the choicest saints in England – and cry out unto you with astonishment and admiration, and thus interrogate your very consciences (where God alone ought to sit king). Oh hear you not the blood of our dear fellow-apprentices and of the rest of the good people of England split for the redemption of this enthralled nation (especially since your first contest with the parliament) cry aloud in your ears and hearts wherever you go for vengeance upon you, the people's perfidious abusers, betrayers and destroyers? Oh do not you hear them cry out unto your very consciences:

Oh give our fathers, our mothers, our brothers, our sisters, and others of our near and dear relations the full and speedy accomplishment of all your fore-mentioned enravishing promises and engagements, by virtue of the power and efficacy of which you stole away their hearts and spirits from all their relations, and made them with willingness and cheerfulness become sacrifices for your assistance, for that end principally (if not only): that they that survived might enjoy the full and ample fruition of all your glorious promises and engagements for common freedom, distributive justice and righteousness upon the earth. Oh do you hear their blood cry unto you? Oh mock not nor dally with God any longer, but without delay give our friends and countrymen the promised price of all our blood by the full and speedy paying of all your vows and engagements made unto God for that end – lest for all your perjury, apostasy and perfidiousness He create a mighty and unresistable spirit of revenge amongst the people, and knit together

county committee and a county MP; he was imprisoned in March 1646 by the parliamentary Committee for Examinations. He remained in the Fleet, an example of parliamentary justice.

[31] It is not clear what these references from the Army's *Book of declarations* are supposed to show: perhaps their public-spiritedness and desire for a safe and lasting peace.

[32] *A remonstrance of the Army* (20 November 1648).

their otherwise divided hearts in one, as one man to rise up in one day to destroy you with a more fatal scouring[33] destruction than you have already destroyed others (yea the highest in the nation) pretendedly for oppressions, breach of oaths, faith and covenants; yea to sweep you away from the land of the living with an overflowing deluge of destruction, as the enslaved women about six or seven hundred years ago did the Danes in one night throughout England.

Oh do not your hearts at all relent? Can you consider this your forecited unparalleled and horrible defection and apostasy, and not tremble and be amazed and even confounded? Is there less remorse of conscience in you than was in Belshazzar, who at his seeing the hand writing upon the wall, changed his countenance, and his thoughts troubled him so that the joints of his loins were loosed and his knees smote one against another – though otherwise in as great jollity and prosperity as any of yourselves or officers.[34] Or have you less apprehension of the majesty of God than was in the heathen Roman governor, Felix, who when he heard Paul reason or preach of righteousness, temperance and judgement to come, trembled and feared and durst not proceed in fury against him, although much thereunto provoked by his adversaries (Acts 24). Sure all sense and compunction of conscience is not totally departed from you? Hear us therefore in the yearning bowels of love and kindness. We entreat and beseech you with patience – and do not abuse us for complaining and crying out – for the knife has been very long at the very throats of our liberties and freedoms, and our burdens are too great and too many for us. We are not able to bear them and contain ourselves. Our oppressions are even ready to make us despair – or forthwith to fly to the prime laws of nature, viz. the next violent remedy at hand: light it where it will or upon whom it will. They are become as devouring fire in our bones ready to burn us up, rendering us desperate and careless of our lives, prizing those that are already dead above those that are yet living – who are rid of that pain and torment that we do and must endure by sensibly seeing and beholding, not only the dying, but the daily burial of our native liberties and freedoms, that we care not what becomes of us, seeing that we are put into that original state or chaos of confusion wherein lust is become a law; envy and malice are become laws, and the strongest sword rules

---

[33] The printing is unclear: 'scouring' is a guess.
[34] Daniel 5: 5–6.

and governs all by will and pleasure.[35] All our ancient boundaries and landmarks[36] are pulled up by the roots and all the ties and bonds of human society in our English horizon totally destroyed and extirpated. Alas for pity.

We had rather die than live this life of languishing death in which our masters possess nothing – to buy themselves or us bread to keep us alive – that they can call their own. Therefore it's no boot for us to serve out our times and continue at our drudging and toiling trades while these oppressions, cruelties and inhumanities are upon us and the rest of the people, exposing thereby the nation not only to domestic broils, wars and bloodsheds (wherein we are sure our bodies must be the principal butts[37]) but to foreign invasions by France, Spain, Denmark, Sweden, etc. – as was well observed by our endeared and faithful friends of the fore-mentioned late treacherously defeated party at Burford in their book of the 20 of August, 1649, entitled *The Levellers (falsely so-called) vindicated, or the case of their 12 troops truly stated*, pp. 11–12, which we cannot but seriously recommend (with them) to your serious perusal and judgement.

And we desire to know of you (but especially the private soldiery of the General's regiment of horse, who we understand had a hand in seizing upon and plundering our true friends at Burford) whether you do own the abominable and palpable treacherous dealings of your General and Lieutenant-General Cromwell and their perfidious officers with them, or not?[38] (That so we may not condemn the innocent with the guilty and may know our friends from our foes.) As also we desire you to tell us whether you do approve of the total defection of your army under which it now lies, from their faith and *Solemn engagement* made at Newmarket Heath, 5 June 1647 – not one of those righteous

---

[35] John Pym against Strafford, *The speech or declaration*, April 1641: 'The law is that which puts a difference betwixt good and evil, betwixt just and unjust. If you take away that law all things will fall into confusion; every man will become a law unto himself . . . Lust will become a law, and envy will become a law; covetousness and ambition will become laws . . . .The law is the safeguard of all private interest. Your honours, your lives, your liberties and estates are all in the keeping of the law. Without this, every man hath a like right to anything.' Pym was echoed by Charles I, in May 1642, *Exact collection*, p. 163.

[36] 'Remove not the ancient landmark, which thy fathers have set' (Proverbs 22: 28).

[37] butts = targets.

[38] Fairfax's and Cromwell's horse had been used, together with Fairfax's, Ewer's and Hewson's foot, to dog the mutineers in their progress from Salisbury to Burford. Cromwell led a forlorn hope of horse into the town while the mutineers slept.

ends in behalf of the parliament and people on which your vow was made being yet fulfilled or obtained, but on the contrary (as we have before rehearsed) a whole flood-gate of tyrannies are let in upon us, and even overwhelm us; and whether you justify all those actions done in the name of the Army upon your account, and under pretext of that engagement since the *Engagement* itself was broken, and your Council of Agitators dissolved?[39] And whether you will hold up your swords to maintain the total abolition of the people's choicest interest of freedom, viz. frequent and successive parliaments by an Agreement of the People, or obstruct the annual succession? Whether you do allow of the late shedding of the blood of war in time of peace, to the subversion of all our laws and liberties? And whether you do countenance the extirpation of the fundamental freedoms of this commonwealth (as their revocation or nullity of the Great Charter of England, The Petition of Right, etc.)? And whether you do assent to the erection of arbitrary prerogative courts, that have or shall over-rule or make void our ancient ways of trials in criminal cases by a jury of twelve men of the neighbourhood? And whether you will assist or join in the forcible obtrusion of this martial and tyrannical rule over us? Also whether you will fight against and destroy those of our friends that shall endeavour the composure of our differences, together with the pronouncement of our freedoms and settlement of our peace (your plenty and prosperity) accordingly as it was offered by the four gentlemen prisoners in the Tower of London upon 1 May 1649 (as a peace-offering to this nation) by the Agreement of the People?[40]

Lastly, we earnestly beseech you to acquaint us whether from your hands – from your power – we may expect any help or assistance in this our miserable distressed condition, to the removal of those iron bands and yokes of oppression that have thus enforced us to complain and address ourselves thus to your serious consideration?

For we cannot choose but acquaint you that we are seriously resolved, through the strength and assistance of God (with all the interest we have in the world) to adhere to the righteous things contained in our treacherously-defeated friends' forementioned late *Vindication* –

---

[39] I.e. General Council of the Army. On 8 November 1647, Cromwell moved a successful motion in the General Council that the agitators should be sent back to their quarters. After the next day no agitators met in the General Council which was now in effect the old Council of War, composed of officers advising Fairfax.

[40] Text 12 above.

very much approving of that unparalleled expedient of an Agreement
of the Free People they propose in the latter end thereof for the firm
settling of the peace, liberties and freedoms of this distracted nation,
which has so much justice, righteousness and safety in it that we hope
it will in a very short time level all self-interests before it and make it
clearly appear to him that claims the greatest personal share[41] in the
government of this nation that there is no way to obtain the true love
of the understanding English people (without which he will never
obtain his desired crown) but by a cheerful, hearty and real promotion
of such principles therein contained as do sufficiently tie his hands from
cutting the people's throats at his will and pleasure, the endeavouring of
which exposed his father to that fatal end that befell him (which may
be a seasonable caveat to all princes etc. to take heed of that desperate
rock, viz., the attempting to govern the people by will and not by law,
by force and not by love – the only and alone durable and permanent
tie or bond amongst the sons of men).

We say that expedient of an Agreement of the Free People appears
to us to have so much equity, righteousness and common safety in it
that we are resolved to bury all by-past distastes at the greatest of
Englishmen that shall heartily and cordially sign and put forth their
power and interest to promote the establishment of the principles
therein contained; and in the adhering to and standing by all such as
shall be in any danger for walking in such paths, we shall through the
strength of the Lord God omnipotent (to the uttermost of our power
and abilities) resolvedly hazard our lives and all that is dear to us.

For the effectual promotion of which said Agreement we are necessi-
tously compelled to resolve in close union to join ourselves – or our
commissioners chosen for that end – in council with our foresaid Burford friends or their commissioners; and to resolve to run all hazards
to methodise[42] all our honest fellow prentices in all the wards of
London and the out-parishes to choose out their agents to join with us
or ours; to write exhortative epistles to all the honest-hearted freemen
of England in all the particular counties[43] thereof to erect several councils amongst themselves, out of which we shall desire and exhort them

[41] I.e. Charles I's son, Charles Prince of Wales, who was in 1660 to be Charles II. During
late 1648 and 1649, Lilburne had shown distinct sympathy with the royal cause, believ-
ing a king would at least balance the tyranny of parliament.
[42] methodise = organise.
[43] 'Countries' in original.

to choose agents or commissioners, empowered and entrusted by them, speedily to meet us and the agents of all ours, and the Agreement of the People adherents, at London, resolvedly to consider of a speedy and effectual method and way how to promote the election of a new and equal Representative or parliament by the Agreement of the Free People – seeing those men that now sit at Westminster and pretendedly style themselves the parliament of England, and who are (as they say, although most falsely) in the *Declaration for a Free State*, dated 17 March 1649, p. 27, 'entrusted and authorised by the consent of all the people of England whose representatives they are', make it their chiefest and principalest work continually to part and share amongst themselves all the great, rich, and profitablest places of the nation, as also the nation's public treasure and lands, and will not ease our intolerable oppressions, no nor so much as of late receive our popular petitions, having upon Thursday last, 23 August 1649, rejected that most excellent of petitions ready at their door to be presented to them by divers honest men (our true-hearted neighbours of Surrey) the true copy of which for the worth of it although it be at large already printed in Friday's *Occurrences* and the Tuesday *Moderate*),[44] we desire here to insert.

> *To the supreme authority of this nation, the Commons of England assembled in parliament: the humble petition of the oppressed of the County of Surrey, which have cast in their mite into the treasury of this commonwealth*

Shows,

That, as the oppressions of this nation in time foregoing this parliament were so numerous and burdensome as will never be forgotten, so were the hopes of our deliverance by this parliament exceeding great and full of confidence, which, as they were strengthened by many acts of yours in the beginning, especially towards conscientious people without respect unto their judgements or opinions, so did the gratitude of the well-minded people exceed all precedents or example, sparing neither estate, limb, liberty or life to make good the authority of this honourable House as the foundation and root of all just freedom. Although we many times observed (to our grief) some proceedings holding resemblance rather with our former bondage, yet did we impute the same

[44] *The Moderate*, no. 59 (21–28 August), and probably *Perfect Occurrences* (17–24 August).

to the troublesomeness of the times of war, patiently and silently passing them over as undoubtedly hoping a perfect remedy so soon as the wars were ended. But perceiving our expectations in some particulars frustrated, and considering some late dealings with some of our friends, etc., the consideration of which lies so heavy on our spirits, that for prevention thereof we conceive ourselves bound in conscience and duty to God to set before you once more the general grievances of the commonwealth and the earnest desires of the ingenuous and well-minded people.

First, that the *Petition of 11 September* last, and the *Agreement of the people*[45] may be reassumed, and the particulars thereof speedily established.

Secondly we most earnestly beg, with many other of your faithful friends in all the counties of England, that that most irksome and intolerable oppression of tithes, which is retained in no reformed church but is neverthless more firmly established than ever by your ordinance for treble damages made in the parliament's corruption, and yet no Act against it, which causes our hearts to be discouraged and brought into much fear and doubt of the removal of these and other bondages by this Representative – wherefore we cannot pass it by, but again entreat that the ordinances for tithes may be speedily revoked and that a more equal way of maintenance be provided for the public ministry.

Thirdly, that all proceedings in law may be in English; that a short time may be inserted for the trial of all causes (and that by twelve men of the neighbourhood); and that none may be debarred of freedom to plead his own or his neighbour's cause (as by law any man may and ought to do, as clearly appears by the Statute of 28 Ed. I cap. 11) before any court of justice, although no lawyer. And that no member of your House be suffered to plead as a lawyer, whilst a member thereof.

Fourthly, that some course may be taken for the future to pay the Army, not laying such intolerable burdens and taxes on the people which we are not able to bear; and so we shall for ever stand by you and all representatives for the freedom of this nation, as formerly, desiring that we may obtain speedily a new and equal Representative.

We say: considering what is before premised we are necessitated and compelled to do the utmost we can for our own preservation and for

---

[45] The Agreement had been republished on 21 August and the Surrey petition was presented on the 23rd. Some kind of organisation of which the *Outcry* is a part, is obvious.

the preservation of the land of our nativity, and never – by popular petitions – address ourselves to the men sitting at Westminster any more or to take any notice of them than as of so many tyrants and usurpers, and for time to come to hinder (as much and as far as our poor despised interest will extend to) all others whatsoever from subscribing or presenting any more popular petitions to them – and only now as our last paper-refuge mightily cry out to each other of our intolerable oppressions in letters and remonstrances, signed on the behalf and by the appointment of all the rest by some of the strongest and fittest amongst us (that we hope will never apostatise, but be able through the strength of God to lay down their very lives for the maintaining of that which they set their hands to).

You our fellow-countrymen, the private soldiers of the Army, alone are the instrumental authors of your own slavery and ours. Therefore as there is any bowels of men in you, any love to your native country, kindred, friends or relations, any sparks of conscience in you, any hopes of glory or immortality in you, or any pity, mercy, or compassion to an enslaved, undone, perishing, dying people: oh help! help! Save and redeem us from total vassalage and slavery; and be no more like brute beasts, to fight against us or our friends, your loving and dear brethren after the flesh – to your own vassalage as well as ours. And as an assured pledge of your future cordialness to us and the true and real liberties of the land of your nativity, we beseech and beg of you (but especially those amongst you that subscribed the *Solemn engagement* at Newmarket Heath, 5 June 1647) speedily to choose out from amongst yourselves two of the ablest and constantest faithful men amongst you in each troop and company, now at last (by corresponding each with other and with your honest friends in the nation to consider of some effectual course beyond all pretences and cheats) to accomplish the real end of all your engagements and fightings, viz. the settling of the liberties and freedoms of the *people* – which can never permanently be done but upon the sure foundation of a popular agreement – who (viz. the people) in justice, gratitude, and common equity cannot choose but to voluntarily and largely make better provisions for your future subsistence by the payment of your arrears than ever your officers or this pretended parliament intends, or you can rationally expect from them: witness their cutting off three parts of your arrears in four for freequarter and then necessitating abundance of your fellow-soldiers, now cashiered, etc., to fill their debentures at two shillings and six pence, three shillings, and at most four shillings per pound, by means of which you that keep your debentures are necessitated to vie with the greatest bidder in the purchase of the late king's lands, whilst they are able to give about thirty years' purchase for that you cannot give eight year's purchase for; and if you will not give with the most you must have no land – so that the most of your debentures are likely to prove waste papers; and those that purchase will have but a slippery security of their possessions by reason of general discontents amongst all sorts of people, and particularly by so extraordinarily disengaging and cheating so many soldiers (as they have done) of their just expected recompense of reward.[46]

And also, as a further demonstration of the cordialness of your hearts to us, our Burford friends, and your own and our liberties: we desire you to take some speedy course for the faithful restoring to the right owners all such houses, money, clothes, etc. as you, or any of you, plundered or stole from our true friends (cheated and defeated) at Burford; and publish some kind of demonstration of your or any of your remorse of conscience for your being instrumental in destroying of them there, that stood for *your* good, freedom, and arrears as much (and as well) as their own – especially considering they have by their foresaid *Vindication* made it evident and apparent (and we understand they are ready face to face to prove) that both your General and Lieutenant-General Cromwell broke their solemn faith with them and treacherously surprised them, and so dealt worse and more vilely with them than ever they did with the worst of cavaliers, with whom in that kind they never broke faith with in their lives. But more especially we desire the last fore-mentioned thing at your hands; because – upon that traitorous and wicked defeat of those our true friends (and wilfully murdering of three of them) that really stood for the nation's interest, liberties, and freedoms – your General, and Cromwell, with the rest of their faction, made a most transcendent feast to insult[47] over the liberties and freedoms of the servants of the most high God, as though by that most vile act they had subdued and buried all the liberties of the nation in eternal oblivion and foiled the Lord of life and glory himself

---

[46] Debentures were treasury orders payable as and when funds were able to meet them, issued to soldiers as security for their arrears of pay. Payment was slow: they were forged, traded in by soldiers with their officers for advances of pay, and used as negotiable instruments.

[47] to insult = to manifest arrogant or scornful delight.

from distilling any more spirit of courage and resolution into any to stand for them.

And in that wickedest of feasts, not only in a great measure imitated Belshazzar (Daniel 5) that made a great feast to a thousand of his lords, and fetched out the vessels that by the spoil of the people of God his father Nebuchadnezzar had got out of the Temple of the Lord, and drank wine in them, and praised the gods of gold and of silver, of brass, of iron, of wood and of stone, but also imitated the greatest of the enemies of Christ, who at the slaying of the two witnesses (Revelation 11) rejoiced over them and made merry and sent gifts one to another (as in gold and silver plate, etc. was most largely done to your General Fairfax and Lieutenant-General Cromwell) – the reason of which is there tendered, which is: 'because the two prophets' (of Truth and Justice) 'tormented them that dwelt on the earth'. But with comfort and joy we cannot but observe the next words to them, which is, that within a little season after, the spirit of life from God 'entered into them' (as we hope and doubt not, but it will abundantly now do upon the true standers for justice and righteousness amongst men): 'and they stood upon their feet, and great fear fell upon them that saw them', and great earthquakes followed, in the nick[48] of which is proclamation made, that 'the kingdoms of this world are become the kingdoms of our Lord, and of his Christ: and he shall reign for ever and ever'. Unto which we heartily say, Amen, Amen.

So with our hearty and true love remembered to you all, expecting your, or some of your speedy answer, we commit you to God, and rest.

London this 29 August, 1649[49]   *Your faithful though abused*
                                          countrymen

---

[48] in the nick of which = at the precise moment.

[49] Captain Jones of Dean's Court in St Martin's Westminster organised the printing of this tract. He took copies to Colonel Ingoldsby's regiment of foot at Oxford, where it was distributed by Sergeant John Radman, a Leveller, and in 1647 an official agitator. The men of the regiment, joined by some from Colonel Tomlinson's horse to the number of perhaps 800 to 900, demonstrated against deductions from their arrears for quarter and against the payment of arrears by debentures. They then mutinied, capturing some of their officers and fortifying themselves in New College. They demanded the reconstitution of the General Council of the Army and the implementation of the Agreement of the People published by 'our four friends in the Tower'. They hoped for, but did not obtain, help from the Bristol garrison, and they were overpowered by others of their officers before the reinforcements arrived from London. The leaders were court-martialled, and two of them (Biggs and Piggen) were shot. The Leveller leadership renounced these acts of mutiny and violence, but Lilburne had clearly by

Signed in the behalf of ourselves
and the unanimous consent of
the agents of the young men
and apprentices of the City of
London, that love and approve
of the Agreement of the People,
dated 1 May 1649, and the
vindication of the late defeated
men at Burford, entitled *The
Levellers vindicated.*

Charles Collins   Anthony Bristlebolt
William Trabret   Steven Smith
Ed. Waldegrove   Thomas Frisby
Ed. Stanley   William White
Nicholas Blowd   John Floyd

FINIS

September rejected the idea of peaceful approaches to either the officers or to parliament, and – he probably had a large hand in the Burford men's *Vindication* as well as in the *Outcry* – was advocating settlement by means of a constitutional convention backed by the arms of the soldiers. Royalists insisted that Levellers planned the mutinies but just could not co-ordinate them. The question as to central leadership remains an open one. In the event, this was the last serious army mutiny and the last episode in which there is any trace of Leveller organisation in the Army. After a brief period of negotiation between the independents and Levellers, the *Outcry* was condemned on 11 September as seditious and its authors declared traitors. The Levellers' last major pamphlet was *The remonstrance of many thousands of free people* (21 September 1649). It proposed an armed rebellion which never occurred. Future demonstrations, large as they were, and successful as they may have been in intimidating the judges, were confined to London and connected with three unsuccessful trials of Lilburne for treason in 1649 and 1653.

Select biographies

The best place to find biographies of, and further reading on, anyone even slightly 'radical' is Richard L. Greaves and Robert Zaller (eds.), *Biographical dictionary of British radicals in the seventeenth century* (3 vols., Brighton, 1982–4).

Allen, William (*fl.* 1642–67) A Particular Baptist and Southwark feltmaker who served with distinction in parliament's armies as a private soldier. In 1645 he joined the New Model as a trooper in Cromwell's regiment of horse, was chosen as an agitator and frequently spoke at General Councils. Lilburne thought him a 'creature' of Cromwell's and he was replaced as an agitator in October 1647, but he continued in the Councils. He was more of a sectarian and army man than a Leveller. He was present at the meeting at Windsor Castle, in April 1648, when it was determined to bring Charles to justice. During the interregnum he served with Cromwell in Ireland where he became a lieutenant-colonel and adjutant-general. With other Baptists, he did not approve the Protectorate. He was a committed republican, and when Sexby put Allen's name to *Killing no murder* (1657) he found himself in trouble; but the restored Rump made gave him command of a regiment in Ireland from whence he wrote republican and millenarian pamphlets. He was accordingly briefly imprisoned by the restored monarchy.

Arnold, Richard (d. 1647) A private trooper in Col. Robert Lilburne's (John's brother's) regiment of foot, which regiment, together with elements of Thomas Harrison's, mutinied at Corkbush Field near Ware on 15 November 1647. After the mutiny was suppressed, Arnold was shot at the head of his regiment.

Cromwell, Oliver (1559–1658) He was to be Lord Protector of England from 1654–1658. As an obscure country gentleman from Huntingdonshire and MP for Cambridge in 1640, he defended Lilburne against religious persecution. He rose to prominence because of his position as both an MP and an army officer. By 1644 he was a Lieutenant-Colonel and embroiled (with Lilburne as his ally and client) with the earl of Manchester as to whether the war should be pursued with vigour, and as to whether inefficient officers should be replaced. His military leadership was decisive at Marston Moor in 1644 (as it was to be at Naseby in 1646) and he soon took a lead in forming the New Model Army, of which he was Lieutenant-General under Fairfax until August 1649 when he sailed to Ireland as Commander-in-Chief. He secured Ireland, and returned briefly to England in 1650 before replacing the reluctant Fairfax in July as Commander-in-Chief against Scotland, which he conquered by September 1651. On his return he became the leading politician in England, and ultimately Lord Protector. He knew Lilburne well and clearly liked, as well as was exasperated by him. He was, like Lilburne, one who loved religious liberty. But he would not stomach mutiny, could not agree to changes in forms of government unless the providence of God showed him they were necessary, and cannot much have liked the Levellers' rigid, moralistic, legalistic and highly public modes of thought and action. His role in deciding that the king should be taken by the Army in 1647 and should be brought to a second war and a trial; his role in the decision to purge the parliament in 1648; the nature of his own ambition to rise – all were, probably purposely, unclear. A revolutionary, he was not a systematic one, and was no Leveller.

Erle, Sir Walter (1586–1665) A Presbyterian opponent of religious toleration and thus of the Levellers. In the Long Parliament he was a supporter of war in 1642, was prominent in charging the earl of Strafford with treason, was a Colonel in the parliamentary army, and from 1643 to 1649 was Lieutenant of the Ordinance. He sat on a large number of parliamentary committees (260) until he fell victim to Pride's Purge in September 1648. A religious as well as political Presbyterian, he served as teller in 1645 and 1646 against both Independents and Erastians. He reconciled himself to the Protectorate and survived to sit in the Convention Parliament of 1660 which restored kingship.

Everard, Robert (*fl.* 1647–64) A Leveller and General Baptist, who served as a trooper in Cromwell's regiment of horse, which he represented in the General Council of the Army as an agitator. He was one of the 10 signatories of the *Case of the army*, and signed the *Agreement of the people*. He was present at the Putney debates, and, the day they began (28 October 1647), he and eleven other agents signed letters to the soldiers defending their freedoms and calling for a biennial parliament. He left the Army in 1651.

Fairfax, Sir Thomas, later Third Baron (1612–71) Parliamentary General and Cromwell's superior in the New Model Army. He had a distinguished military career in the Low Countries and in the parliamentary armies, and was made Captain-General of the New Model in January 1645, and then Commander-in-Chief of all parliament's forces in July 1647. He led the New Model against London that August, and against parliament in December 1648, but was generally unhappy at political developments and concentrated on maintaining the discipline of the Army. He did not intervene to oppose the trial and execution of the king, though his wife famously did. He was an inactive member of the Council of State during 1649, except in the matter of suppressing the Levellers. But his only important political activity thereafter was his support of restoration.

Holles, Denzil (1598–1680) A leading MP in opposition to the king, he was one of the five MPs Charles attempted to arrest in January 1642. His regiment was destroyed at Brentford, one of the battles Lilburne thought showed the incompetence of parliamentary military leaders. He always sought for a peaceful and accommodating solution to the civil wars and was suspected of secret dealings with the king in 1645. An ally of the Scots, he rallied support in parliament in 1647 to attempt a Presbyterian and conservative settlement with the king, and led an attempt to disband the New Model. The Army impeached him and ten other Presbyterian leaders, and they were forced by the approaching Army to withdraw from the Commons in June. Over the next two months he tried but failed to rally support from the City, disbanded royalist soldiers and the Scots. When the Army entered London in August, that phase of his career was over and he fled to France.

Ireton, Henry (1611–51) A leading New Model political theorist, politician and General. By 1645, with an education in Arts and law, he was Commissary-General of the New Model and an MP, thanks to the patronage of Cromwell (whose son-in-law he became in 1646) and to his own courage and intelligence. He drafted the *Solemn engagement* and other manifestos of the New Model in 1647, and worked with leading independent politicians and army leaders on the *Heads of the proposals*, debated at Putney, which would have removed the veto power of the king and Lords. In the autumn and winter of 1648–9 he took the lead in the New Model's moves against the king and worked to try to reconcile the Levellers' views of a settlement with those of leading city and parliamentary radicals and with both more moderate and more radical elements in the Army. He failed to be elected (as too dangerous) to the first Commonwealth Council of State. In 1651 he succeeded Cromwell as Commander-in-Chief in Ireland, where he died. The Levellers, Lilburne in particular, were suspicious of him; his ideals for a form of government were not much different from theirs (he was largely responsible for the officers' Agreement of January 1649); but he had a more complex political agenda. He acceded to a purge of parliament rather than an Agreement of the People, and he did not mind limits to religious toleration.

Lambe, Thomas (*fl.* 1638–48). In 1647 he was called a 'soap-boiler' but more likely he derived a living from his London General Baptist congregation which met successively at Whitechapel (*c.* 1638–44), Coleman Street (1644–5) and Spitalfields (late 1645). He was a prisoner of the Court of High Commission in 1639, probably because of his religious heterodoxy, and had a history of General Baptist political activity dating back to 1640, when he participated in riots against the Court. In early 1645 he was named in the Lords as responsible for distributing an attack on the earls of Essex's and Manchester's prosecution of the war, published by Overton and Tew's press in Coleman Street. Later in the year he was imprisoned for a short time for unlicensed preaching. A great publicist, by 1642 he was energetically evangelising throughout southern England. His church was notoriously the site of open and heated debate on religious and political matters. From 1645 it featured women preachers; in 1646 Overton debated the mortalist heresy there. It was at his church that the Large Petition of March 1647 was read out, corrected by Lambe during the reading, subscribed by the congregation, and reported to parliament by an informer. Lambe was the author of *The fountain of free grace opened* (1645, reprinted 1648).

Larner William (*fl.* 1636–49) Originally from Gloucestershire, he was a London separatist printer and bookseller, and member of the Merchant Taylors' Company. He was a friend of Lilburne from at least 1636. He printed a second edition of Lilburne's *Christian mans trial* (1641), fought for parliament but was invalided home, and was distributing independent literature in Kent in 1643. Constantly at odds with the Stationer's Company for illegal printing, he was accused by Prynne in 1645 of printing Lilburne's pamphlets. From March to October 1646 he was imprisoned by the Lords for illegal printing, and his and Lilburne's cases were the subject of much Leveller and other radical literature. He was accused in 1649 by the New Model's newspaper of being one who would 'divide the soldiers' by insisting on a Leveller programme.

Lilburne, John (1615–57) Leveller leader, he was born the second son of a Durham gentry family. He was author of over eighty pamphlets, broadsheets and petitions, and about seven times a political prisoner. He was apprenticed in 1630 to a wholesale clothier in London and soon became involved in the practices and beliefs of Calvinist Separatist congregations. In 1637–8 he was flogged, pilloried and imprisoned by the Star Chamber for having an attack on bishops printed in the Low Countries and distributing it. Released by the Long Parliament in 1642, he joined a parliamentarian regiment; he was a prisoner of the royalists at Oxford November 1642 to May 1643; he fought again under the earls of Essex and Manchester, rising to be a Lieutenant-Colonel; but he was the only commissioned officer to refuse to take the Solemn League and Covenant, and so returned to civilian life in 1644, by now a leader in London sectarian political circles. His embroilment with Manchester set off a chain of imprisonments and deepening financial problems, and added to his commitment to religious liberty a distrust (and often more) of all the governing institutions, professions, factions and persons. He was even (in 1653) to attack his long-suffering and courageous wife, Elizabeth Dewell. Never consistent as to his preferred institutional arrangements – he was a royalist at times – he nevertheless developed a democratic and individualist formula of the legitimacy and limits of government together with doctrines of armed resistance, and he consistently stood for religious liberty. As the Leveller movement was dissolving in 1649, he was tried for treason but acquitted; in early 1652 he was exiled for libel; he returned without permission in 1653 and was tried for treason a second time; he was again acquitted, again amidst public rejoicing; but he was imprisoned by Cromwell on the island of Jersey and, in 1655, in Dover Castle. There he became a Quaker – around 1647 he had already abandoned the Calvinist belief in salvation only being for the elect – and embraced the quiet life of non-resistance to magistrates, and the cultivation of the light within. But his last pamphlet contains a virulent attack on a writer who advocated infant baptism.

Lilburne, Robert (1613–65) John Lilburne's elder brother. An army officer from 1643 to 1660 (with Essex, Manchester and the New Model); signed Charles I's death warrant; sat in the second protectoral parliament; was a deputy Major-General in the north of England from 1655 to 1657; governor of York from 1658 to 1660; was sentenced to death as a regicide, but the sentence was commuted to life imprisonment. A Baptist. A professional soldier who accepted changes of régime without demur. He supported John at his trial in 1649, but otherwise disassociated himself from his brother's activities, especially at Corkbush field and during his second treason trial.

Lockyer, Robert (*c.* 1626–1649) A General Baptist known for his piety. He was a trooper in and agitator for Col. Edward Whalley's regiment, and a Leveller. He was involved in the mutiny at Ware in November 1647, where the attempt was to persuade Cromwell and Fairfax to accept the *Agreement of the people*. He was executed for his part in a mutiny in April 1649. Lilburne and Overton pleaded for him. Leveller, sea-green colours were worn at his funeral.

Marten, Henry (1602–80) An anti-monarchical MP. Before the war he was singled out by royalist propaganda as holding views derogatory to monarchy. He criticised inefficient aristocratic leadership of parliamentary armies, upheld religious toleration (as a pagan rather than a puritan) and was sent to the Tower 1643 for supporting the deposition of the king. He was eventually allowed back to parliament in 1646 where he became an extreme political independent, much opposed to the Scots, a Presbyterian settlement and negotiations with the king. He led radical independent attempts to co-operate with the Levellers in

opposing settlements proposed by parliamentarians and the army officers in 1647, and though associated by his enemies with the Levellers,
had problems in dealing with them. Nevertheless, he may have had a
hand in the second Leveller *Agreement of the people* in 1648, which the
army officers transformed, to Lilburne's disgust. He supported Pride's
Purge and was a member of the High Court which tried the king. He
was a republican of a Commonwealth stamp from 1649 onwards,
opposed all other interregnum régimes, and was nearly executed as a
regicide, for complicity in which act he was instead imprisoned until
his death.

Overton, Richard (*fl.* 1631–64) After obscure beginnings – perhaps
the son of a midlands clergyman, a refugee with a General Baptist
congregation in the Netherlands (1615–16), a matriculand at Queen's
Hall Cambridge (1631), a professional actor and occasional playwright
in Southwark – he began writing, mostly anonymously, attacking Cath-
olicism, the Anglican establishment, monopolists and king's counsellors
in 1640 to 1642. He maybe wrote 50 tracts during this period. He was
silent from April 1642 until January 1644 – he may have been imprisoned for debt; he certainly married; he may have tried to join a Men-
nonite congregation in Amsterdam, but he was back in London by late
1643. In January 1644 he published *Mans mortality,* arguing against the
separation of soul and body, and thus (like Milton and Hobbes) for the
death of the soul with the body. Late that year he had a secret printing
press in Colemen Street with Nicholas Tew and was engaged in General Baptist politics. Between April 1645 and January 1646 he wrote six
anti-Presbyterian tracts under the name of 'Young Martin Marpriest'.
His career as a Leveller was marked by two periods of imprisonment
(August 1646 to September 1647, and March to November 1649), and
a hand in perhaps forty tracts, together with articles in the Leveller
paper, *The Moderate.* He seems to have been not much trusted as an
organiser by the other Levellers. His last Leveller tracts appeared in
July 1649. In September 1654 he tried to become a secret service agent
working for the Protectorate; at about the same time he seems to have
joined Sexby and Wildman in an attempt to forge an alliance between
Levellers, republican army officers and royalists against the regime; he
fled with Sexby to France and then Flanders in February 1655; he
settled in Delft where he prepared another edition of *Mans mortality.*
He returned to London, still plotting against the régime, around

December 1655. The failure of Sexby's designs in 1656 and Sexby's trial in 1657 silenced him until 1659, when after the collapse of Richard Cromwell's Protectorate he wrote two more tracts, neither noticeably Leveller ones. He was arrested briefly in December 1659, and emerges as the subject of arrest for republican plotting in 1663. Nothing is known of his later life.

Parker, Henry (1604–52) A parliamentary propagandist (and professional writer and parliamentary secretary) who argued from 1642 for the sovereignty of a bicameral parliament (with occasional hints as to the necessity of the Commons ruling alone) on the grounds that such a parliament represented the people and was the best institution for ensuring the safety of the people. Author of *A question answered*, and the *Observations upon some of his majesties late answers and expresses* in 1642, and of many other pamphlets which influenced the Levellers, he never remained a parliamentarian, and attacked them in 1649.

Peter (or Peters), Hugh (1598–1660) An Independent minister before the civil wars at Rotterdam and Salem, Mass., he returned to England in 1641. Became a parliamentary army chaplain in 1642 and became famous as a militant preacher to the New Model. Supported Pride's Purge, the execution of the king, and the republican regime. He was a chaplain and confidant of Cromwell, and remained close to him until Cromwell died. Executed as a regicide.

Petty (or Pettus), Maximilian (1617–after 1660) A Leveller. Of an Oxfordshire gentry family, he met Sexby when they were both apprenticed to the Grocers' Company of London. Perhaps he was one of the group of radical apprentices who supported Lilburne in his troubles with the bishops and Star Chamber in 1637–9. A prominent figure in the Leveller movement, he helped write the *Agreement of the people* and was chosen with Wildman as a civilian speaker at the Putney debates. He helped write the second Leveller *Agreement* of 1648 which the army offices remodelled. Obscure after 1649, he was a member of the republican club, the Rota, in 1659 to 1660.

Prince, Thomas (*fl.* 1640–53) A well-to-do London cheese merchant, who fought, was wounded for (and supplied cheese to) parliament. A Leveller organiser from 1647 to 1649, co-treasurer with Samuel Chidley from January 1648. He was imprisoned briefly in November 1647 for presenting *The humble petition of many freeborn people* which urged parliament to debate the *Agreement of the people* and to 'make inquisition for the blood' of Richard Arnold. He was charged with high treason in March 1649, together with Lilburne, Overton and Walwyn, for the publication of *The second part of England's new chains discovered.* He joined them while they were in the Tower in publishing *A picture of the Council of State, A manifestation,* and *An agreement of the free people.* He published his own *The silken Independents' snare* in June, arguing for religious toleration and that the people are the fountain of all power. He was released with the other Levellers in November and probably took the engagement to be faithful to the Commonwealth. He contacted Lilburne in a friendly way when Lilburne returned from the Netherlands in 1653, but had probably settled down as a merchant after his release.

Prynne, William (1600–69) A Presbyterian MP. A Puritan martyr-hero (he had had his ears clipped twice) at the calling of the Long Parliament, and the author of the *Sovereign power of parliaments,* a notably non-traditionalist defence of the Commons, he was at first a mentor of Lilburne's. But his Presbyterianism (in 1644) and growing ancient-constitutionalism (from 1646) set him against Lilburne, and against all who would not restore the king. A victim of Pride's Purge, he lived to be Keeper of the Records of the Tower of London.

Pym, John (1584–1643) The effective leader of the Long Parliament against the king.

Rainborough (or Rainsborough or Rain borowe), Thomas (d. 1648) A Leveller fellow-traveller. A seaman and son of a naval officer in the king's service, he fought both on sea and land against the king, and was a Colonel under Fairfax in October 1643. He gained fame in arms and became in 1645 a Colonel in a newly formed infantry regiment of the New Model. Again he fought with distinction and became an MP in 1646. He allied himself with the Levellers, following the refusal of his regiment in May 1647 to proceed to Jersey, leaving the main bulk of the Army. He was the one key officer to support them, notably at the Putney debates This affected his career in parliament and Army, but by December 1647 he was reconciled with Cromwell and Ireton; and in January 1648 the Commons reversed a previous order that he not take up the position as Vice-Admiral of the fleet to which he had been appointed in September. He was not liked by the

Navy because of his radicalism and returned to the Army, where he was a leader in the reduction of Colchester during the second civil war. He was assassinated in October 1648 and his funeral provided an occasion for large Leveller demonstrations.

Sexby, Edward (*c.* 1616–58) A soldier, Leveller, and later secret agent and conspirator. He emerged from obscurity as a private soldier in April 1647 as an agitator and as the main link between the City and New Model Levellers. He was called before the Commons for petitioning but aided by Independents there, and was influential in setting up an 'army of able pen-men' in Oxford to express Army demands as to political as well as military grievances. He may in September have instigated the election of the 'new agents' in the five regiments who devised the *Case of the army*. He spoke at Putney, but left the Army after the collapse of the mutiny at Ware. He kept contact with both Lilburne and Cromwell however, and from mid-1648 seems to have been instrumental in producing a *rapprochement* between the Cromwellian and Leveller groups. He worked for the Commonwealth, and in 1651 was working at La Rochelle and Bordeaux for the Council of State, with an eye to annexation. At Bordeaux he produced a 1653 translation of the 1649 *Agreement of the people* in an attempt to stir up the Ormée, a republican brotherhood which had grown up in the town. He was discovered plotting with Wildman against the Protectorate in 1655, and fled to make contact with royalists at Amsterdam. He spent the rest of his life opposing Cromwell, plotted his assassination, and was author of *Killing no murder* (1657). He died in the Tower for his pains.

Nicholas Tew (or Tue) (*fl.* 1644–7) A member of Lambe's General Baptist congregation, deeply implicated in the Levellers' March 1647 petition. By late 1644 he had an illegal printing press in his house in Coleman Street, where Overton collaborated with him, and probably lived. This led to Tew's association with William Larner, and, in early 1645, to his arrest for illegal printing.

Tulidah, Major Alexander (*fl.* 1647) He was a friend of Lilburne's, and active in City politics in 1647. His imprisonment for prosecuting the March 1647 Leveller petition attracted the notice of Army radicals in *A new-found stratagem* (4 April), and marked their realisation that they had interests in common with the city-based petitioners. In June, with General Baptist contacts, he was working for a personal Treaty with the king which would undercut parliament and the Scots. A link between city and Army Levellers, he was in the New Model for only a few months as Adjutant-General of the horse from July 1647. He was prominent on the General Council in mid-July but then dropped from sight. His military title was a continental one, gained in earlier service.

Walwyn, William (1600–80) The second son of a Worcestershire gentleman, he was apprenticed in 1630 to a London silk merchant and became a moderately prosperous member of the Merchant Adventurers' Company. Before 1641 he had become a convinced believer in free grace (holding that justification and salvation were potentially available to all, and not restricted to a pre-ordained elect), of the necessity of each man and woman to find the Christian truth for themselves, and of practical christianity (holding that Christian love bound men and women together in mutual duties of good works and succour). He remained a communicant in his parish near the Moorfields where he lived, under both its Anglican and Presbyterian dispensations; but from 1641 onwards he wrote of the need for toleration (even of Catholics and infidels) and for good works, and he always demonstrated a great interest in others' beliefs, keenly attending their lectures, meetings and sermons. In 1643 he began working through Salters' Hall, the meeting place of London and parliamentary radicals, and was active in ward politics and petitioning. After meeting Lilburne in mid-1645, he supported the younger man in his trouble with a Commons committee and then with the Lords in 1646, though admonishing him for his too great dependence on Magna Carta and the common law, and himself appealing to more abstract principles of reason and equity. In 1646 and until mid-1647 he continued to urge religious toleration in a series of pamplets; in 1647, his basically religious inspiration led him to urge political reform. He produced the 'Large Petition' of March, was prominent in the composition of the *Agreement of the people* of October, and was active in promoting linkages between the London Levellers and the New Model. He may even have worked with Ireton on the *Heads of Proposals* to the king. Generally more peaceable and moderate than the other Leveller leaders, he was nevertheless imprisoned with them in March 1649. There his hand was very evident in the *Manifestation* and in the *Agreement of the free people*. While in the Tower, he found himself attacked by an Independent pamphleteer as an atheist, blasphemer, antiscripturalist and seducer of the innocent. He replied, concentrating on his religion more than his politics. After his release he wrote *Juries justified* in 1651, after which his interests – and profession – turned definitively in the direction of medicine. He practised as an apothecary and published *A touchstone for physick* in 1667.

Wildman, John (1623–93) A Leveller. Of obscure origins, he was a soldier by 1647, was to become an officer in 1649 and a Major in 1653. In the autumn of 1647 he was a new agent of the Army, contributed to the *Case of the army* and the *Agreement of the people*, and debated at Putney. When Cromwell purged Levellers from the New Model after the mutiny at Ware he produced *Putney projects*, a vitriolic attack on him. He was imprisoned from January to August 1648, and refused the other Levellers' attempts to persuade him to join with them in producing a new *Agreement of the people* in conjunction with army officers and other radical groups, but was prominent on the Leveller side at debates (Lilburne and Overton were there too) with army officers at Whitehall in December 1648 on the question of liberty of conscience. After the execution of the king he successfully set about assembling a landed estate, and he continued to be politically active. He was elected as an MP in 1654. But he usually acted against Cromwell (though he spied for his government against royalists in France 1656), and was imprisoned twice (1655–6, and 1657) for pamphleteering against him and plotting his assassination. Nor was he allowed to sit in parliament. He became a Harringtonian republican in 1657 and held a Commonwealth Club in his local pub. The remainder of his career was marked by republican plotting and increasing riches so that he was knighted in 1692, though he lost his lucrative position as Post-Master General in 1691.

Index

Index

Index

Vane, Sir Henry the younger, 126n
Vote of no Addresses, xxvii, 131n

Waldgrave, Edward, 179, 201
Wales, viii, xxiv, xxvii, 7, 36, 190
Walker, George, 29
Walwyn, William, viii, xiii, xviii, xix, xxiii, 7, 10n, 18n, 38n, 40n, 131n, 141n, 144n, 165n, 167, 168–9, 178, 210
Agreement of the people, 92–101
Gold tried in the fire, 73–91
Juries justified, xxx, 213
A manifestation, 158–66, 168, 210, 212
Petition of 11 September 1648, 131n
Putney projects, xxvii
Toleration justified, viii, xxv (modernisation of *Tolleration*), 9–30

A touchstone for physick, 213
A remonstrance of many thousand citizens, ix, xxv, 33–53
Ware, mutiny at, xvii, xxvii, 181n, 203–4, 207, 211, 213
watermen, 99n, 144n
Weale or Whealey, Matthew, 98, 101
Weaver's Hall, 49n
Westminster Assembly of Divines, xx, xxv, 9, 11, 14n, 15, 30, 43
Whalley, Robert, 181n
Wharton, Lord, 126n
White, William, 179, 201
Wildman, John, xiii, xvi, xxxiii, 92n, 103n, 115–16, 137n, 141n, 144n, 208, 211, 213
Putney projects, 213
women and females, in general terms, 31, 78, 83, 205
Wootton, David, xii

Cambridge Texts in the History of Political Thought

Titles published in the series thus far

Aristotle *The Politics* and *The Constitution of Athens* (edited by Stephen Everson)

Arnold *Culture and Anarchy and Other Writings* (edited by Stefan Collini)

Astell *Political Writings* (edited by Patricia Springborg)

Austin *The Province of Jurisprudence Determined* (edited by Wilfrid E. Rumble)

Bacon *The History of the Reign of King Henry VII* (edited by Brian Vickers)

Bakunin *Statism and Anarchy* (edited by Marshall Shatz)

Baxter *A Holy Commonwealth* (edited by William Lamont)

Beccaria *On Crimes and Punishments and Other Writings* (edited by Richard Bellamy)

Bentham *A Fragment on Government* (introduction by Ross Harrison)

Bernstein *The Preconditions of Socialism* (edited by Henry Tudor)

Bodin *On Sovereignty* (edited by Julian H. Franklin)

Bolingbroke *Political Writings* (edited by David Armitage)

Bossuet *Politics Drawn from the Very Words of Holy Scripture* (edited by Patrick Riley)

The British Idealists (edited by David Boucher)

Burke *Pre-Revolutionary Writings* (edited by Ian Harris)

Christine de Pizan *The Book of the Body Politic* (edited by Kate Langdon Forhan)

Cicero *On Duties* (edited by M. T. Griffin and E. M. Atkins)

Conciliarism and Papalism (edited by J. H. Burns and Thomas M. Izbicki)

Constant *Political Writings* (edited by Biancamaria Fontana)

Dante *Monarchy* (edited by Prue Shaw)

Diderot *Political Writings* (edited by John Hope Mason and Robert Wokler)

The Dutch Revolt (edited by Martin van Gelderen)

Early Greek Political Thought from Homer to the Sophists (edited by Michael Gagarin and Paul Woodruff)

The Early Political Writings of the German Romantics (edited by Frederick C. Beiser)

The English Levellers (edited by Andrew Sharp)

Erasmus *The Education of a Christian Prince* (edited by Lisa Jardine)

Ferguson *An Essay on the History of Civil Society* (edited by Fania Oz-Salzberger)

Filmer *Patriarcha and Other Writings* (edited by Johann P. Sommerville)